Penguin Education

Penguin Science of Behaviour
General Editor: B. M. Foss

Cognitive Psychology
Editors: P. C. Dodwell and Anne Treisman

Perception and Cognition
A Cross-Cultural Perspective
Barbara B. Lloyd

Barbara B. Lloyd

Perception and Cognition

A Cross-Cultural Perspective

Penguin Books

Penguin Books Ltd, Harmondsworth,
Middlesex, England
Penguin Books Inc., 7110 Ambassador Road,
Baltimore, Md 21207, U S A
Penguin Books Australia Ltd,
Ringwood, Victoria, Australia

First published 1972

Made and printed in Great Britain by
Cox & Wyman Ltd, London, Reading and Fakenham
Set in Monotype Times

To my Mother and Father

Penguin Science of Behaviour

This book is one of an ambitious project, the Penguin Science of Behaviour, which covers a very wide range of psychological inquiry. Many of the short 'unit' texts are on central teaching topics, while others deal with present theoretical and empirical work which the Editors consider to be important new contributions to psychology. We have kept in mind both the teaching divisions of psychology and also the needs of psychologists at work. For readers working with children, for example, some of the units in the field of Developmental Psychology will deal with psychological techniques in testing children, other units will deal with work on cognitive growth. For academic psychologists, there will be units in well-established areas such as Cognitive Psychology, but also units which do not fall neatly under any one heading, or which are thought of as 'applied', but which nevertheless are highly relevant to psychology as a whole.

The project is published in short units for two main reasons. Firstly, a large range of short texts at inexpensive prices gives the teacher a flexibility in planning his course and recommending texts for it. Secondly, the pace at which important new work is published requires the project to be adaptable. Our plan allows a unit to be revised or a fresh unit to be added with maximum speed and minimal cost to the reader.

Above all, for students, the different viewpoints of many authors, sometimes overlapping, sometimes in contradiction, and the range of topics Editors have selected will reveal the complexity and diversity which exist beyond the necessarily conventional headings of an introductory course.

B.M.F.

Contents

Editorial Foreword

People in different parts of the world look different and behave differently, and, according to most psychologists who have made such studies, they think and even perceive differently. Will these 'cross-cultural' differences eventually be ironed out through education, travel and the mass media? Already there is a tendency for preferences in food, dress and music to cut across national boundaries. Will this happen too for the very psychology of individuals? Dr Lloyd starts with this kind of question, but by the end of the book she concludes that such questions are not as simple as they seem. She arrives at this after a most carefully documented account of the now large number of cross-cultural studies and the several theories. Methodologically there are considerable problems involved in obtaining data. Dr Lloyd considers for instance the consequences of the fact that most studies have been carried out by white Westerners, and that there may be insuperable difficulties involved in translating tests from one language to another.

Despite such problems, cross-cultural investigators are in surprisingly high agreement on many points of fact, though not always in such agreement over the explanation of those facts. Dr Lloyd seems able to steer an unbiased course between these explanations. She is particularly thorough on the effects of language on thinking; on the rather surprising relevance of some of Piaget's theorizing (Dr Lloyd herself has practical experience of giving Piaget's tests to non-Europeans); and on the relations between culture, race and ability. Theoretically she makes a valuable contribution by considering psychological processes according to their macro or micro depth of analysis.

There are several strategies available to anyone wanting to get comparative data on human psychology. He can look at the evolution of behaviour from 'lower' animals to primates and man; he can study the development of the psychology of the individual from infancy to maturity; he can compare the psychology of the normal with various kinds of deviancy and abnormality; and he can compare the psychology of various cultures. Cross-cultural study can thus be seen to be complementary to a variety of related comparative techniques. It is a branch of psychology which is in rapid growth. This book provides a scholarly up-to-date account of the subject.

B.M.F.

Acknowledgements

At first glance the cross-cultural study of perception and cognition appears to be a well-defined area within a larger and more diffuse field. In fact, the range of psychological processes covered takes one into a great many fields and requires diverse expertise. The limitations of my own training in psychology have been in part overcome by the kind and willing assistance of many people. I should like to thank the following colleagues who have read one or more chapters and offered many constructive criticisms: Tony Agathangelou, Pierre Dasen, Ronald Dore, Brian Foss, Jacqueline Goodnow, Roger Goodwin, Marie Jahoda, Gustav Jahoda, Alison Jolly, Kenneth Lovell, Tony Marcel, Harvey Sarles, Robert Serpell, Maggie Stroebe, Neil Warren. Responsibility for the shortcomings which remain is mine alone.

Special thanks are offered to my husband, Peter, for his constant encouragement and help. Jennie Laishley sought out obscure references. I have been fortunate in having considerable institutional support which has allowed me to study the literature on cross-cultural perception and cognition. During a year's Fellowship (1970/71) at the Institute of Development Studies at the University of Sussex I was given ample time for my own research. Both at the University and at the Institute I have been fortunate in having cheerful and generous secretarial assistance.

Thanks are also due to the following for granting permission to reproduce illustrations: Figure 1, Bobbs-Merrill; Figure 2, Addison-Wesley; Figure 3, *Journal of Comparative and Physiological Psychology*; Figure 4, *International Journal of Psychology*; Figure 5, *Perception and Psychophysics*; Figure 6, *Psychological Review*; Figure 7, Methuen.

1 Issues: Methodological and Theoretical

A weary traveller, with London now 3000 miles behind him, emerges from a jet at Kano Airport in the chilly morning and casually wonders whether the black men in their flowing robes are a tourist attraction specially arranged for his benefit. This scepticism about the exotic – the feeling that cultural differences in today's world are often contrived – is nurtured by a belief that, with universal education, jet travel, communication satellites and the other marvels of an advanced technological age, men are becoming the same in their thoughts, just as in their food and dress. Cultural differences are expected to vanish as soon as science is taught in schools, as television becomes universal and as literacy replaces illiteracy. The knowledge and rational thought processes of Western man are expected to become universal and any barriers to the diffusion of Western knowledge are expected to be questions of time and attitude rather than questions of basic differences in perception, thinking and learning.

The opposite view, that non-Western men think in modes qualitatively different from our own, has also had its protagonists (Lévy-Bruhl, 1922). Studies starting from an interest in language have suggested that we are each ensnared in the thought system of our mother tongue (cf. pages 36 to 44). Between these extremes which hold on the one hand that all men are essentially the same and on the other that thought is powerfully constrained by the cultural conditioning of language lie a multitude of issues for cognitive psychology. These issues underlie the recurring question asked in this book: what impact do cultural variables have on the processes of thought and perception?

In asking and answering this question it is necessary to remember that in the last decade psychologists' ideas of how Western men think have altered radically. No longer is man regarded, as he was in the hey-day of S–R behaviourism, as a passive receiver vulnerable to the vagaries of his environment. The success of the Chomskian revolution in linguistics and the attractiveness of the transformational approach has brought renewed vigour to the study of internal, central processes. Typical of this new approach are the writings of Neisser who proclaimed in *Cognitive Psychology* (1967, p. 10), '. . . the central assertion that seeing, hearing and remembering are all acts of construction, which may make more or less of stimulus information depending on circumstances'.

We may ask how cultural factors, but one set of 'circumstances', are held to modify the acts of construction. Almost all the data presented in Neisser's monograph are based upon studies with American college students. Even comparative material on the behaviour of American children is lacking, in part, the author suggests, because so little is known about the development of cognitive processes. The cross-cultural material is not of sufficient weight to allow its serious consideration in Neisser's context.

A modicum of success in the search for the impact of cultural variables on the understanding of cognitive processes is encountered in Eleanor Gibson's (1969) monograph on perceptual development, but generally they were not considered. Starting from the position that perception is an active search of an ordered world, Gibson sought to explain how learning and development modify the processes which initiate and direct the search. She quoted data from a cross-cultural study of visual illusions (Segall, Campbell and Herskovits, 1966) which were congruent with her formulation and showed how visual inference tendencies were related to characteristics of the visual environment. By and large, cross-cultural data have not been brought to bear on elaborating the new active view of intellectual processing.

My own belief is that individuals growing up in different cultures may well learn different rules for processing information from the world around them. Similarly, the world in which they are socialized may in itself be different from that of Western man. Thus cross-cultural studies have an important comparative function and should, when they are adequately carried out, contribute to our understanding of cognitive processes. But before this contribution can be realized cross-cultural psychologists must present reliable and meaningful data on cognitive processes. The cross-cultural enterprise would be much easier if a well-known experiment such as the Bruner Concept Formation Task with its eighty-one cards could be employed with little modification with non-Western subjects (Bruner, Goodnow and Austin, 1956). Unfortunately, the more usual outcome is low levels of response or total failure which do not allow the diagnosis of cultural difference. Results of the latter sort fail to yield new information and suggest a breakdown in communication between the researcher and his subjects.

What is the cross-cultural psychology of perception and cognition?

A cognitive psychologist turning to consideration of cross-cultural variables must limit his problem area. A great deal of material purporting to describe psychological processes in non-Western peoples is available not only in the psychological literature but in that of philosophy, anthropology and religion. A generation ago anthropological research of this type was labelled the study of 'personality and culture'. These interdisciplinary studies which owed intellectual debts to psychoanalysis and functional anthropology were initially concerned with motivational questions but later focused on socialization and learning. By the mid-1960s two sub-areas could be identified: 'psycho-cultural analysis' or 'psychological anthropology', and 'cross-cultural psychology'. In a recent review, Honigmann, an anthropologist by training, has suggested that the term 'psychological anthropology' has come to denote the psychological analysis of cultural terms while 'cross-cultural psychology' indicates work in which psychological concepts are developed 'through employing the vantage point afforded by data from other cultures' (Honigmann, 1969, p. 145).

The definition of culture and the usefulness of psychological explanations of cultural terms are issues of debate within anthropology (Gluckman, 1967; Kroeber and Kluckhohn, 1952). The discussion is only marginally relevant to attempts to define the cross-cultural psychology of cognition. Even in this restricted effort there are risks of disputation. Admittedly a definition is a logical proposition and thus not subject to empirical verification, but it is useful to consider how the term 'cross-cultural psychology' is used.

The *Journal of Cross-Cultural Psychology* was first published in March 1970. A sociologist concerned with the development and institutionalization of academic disciplines might have predicted its appearance by extrapolation. The *Journal of Social Psychology* began to offer cross-cultural research priority publication in 1958 and the *International Journal of Psychology* founded in 1966 has a strong cross-cultural bias.

It is clear from examination of these journals that the term 'psychology' in the cross-cultural context has not been the special preserve of professional psychologists. The new journal, whose full title contains the words 'international and interdisciplinary', includes among its consulting editors researchers who claim disciplinary affiliation with anthropology, criminology, criminal law, management, political science, psychiatry, pharmacology, sociology and social relations. Whatever cross-cultural psychology is, everybody is interested in doing it! Publication constraints may have guided the editorial policy of the new *Journal of Cross-Cultural Psychology* but it leaves the field in some confusion.

Price-Williams (1969), in his introduction to a book of readings, wrestled with the same issues. He decided that while a distinction 'could be made between cultural studies which are aimed at finding out information concerning theories in experimental psychology and those which are concerned with the relationship of the individual to his culture' (p. 12), many interesting investigations fall at neither pole but somewhere in between. Wishing to include the entire range he entitled his collection *Cross-Cultural Studies*. The pole which Price-Williams characterized as concerned with the relationship of the individual to his culture seems closer to Honigmann's notion of 'psychological anthropology' than to the definition of 'cross-cultural psychology' employed in this monograph.

In an analysis of the contribution of cross-cultural research to psychology, Jahoda (1970) has found a fruitful way to deal with the issue and it is this which is adopted here. Repeatedly the question will be asked, what does the addition of results from other cultures add to our understanding of the psychological process? Cross-cultural psychology is thus defined as any field of psychological research in which cultural variables are considered in order to clarify our understanding of a psychological process.

Specification of the term 'cross-cultural' is easier. Conventionally, it is employed to designate the comparison of Euro-American and non-Euro-American or non-Western behaviour, as in Goodnow's (1962) studies of cognitive skills with Chinese and American children. Comparisons among Western groups are usually termed 'cross-national' but this is not a hard and fast rule. Some investigators working within a Western society may study group differences and write about the 'culture of poverty' or 'working-class culture'. These comparisons may well make a contribution to our understanding of psychological processes whatever we choose to label them. Often a combination of comparisons between and within societies is most conducive to fuller understanding of psychological processes (cf. Cole, Gay, Glick and Sharp, 1971).

The examination of perception and cognition cross-culturally will, however, be limited primarily to those studies in which psychological theories and paradigms developed by European and American psychologists are investigated in settings which allow comparisons of the behaviour of individuals from Western and non-Western societies. Sometimes, as in Vernon's (1967 a and b) study on intelligence in East Africa, the comparison is not immediate but with his own earlier published material on Europeans. The point is that comparisons with Western subjects' behaviour are at least implicitly the aim of cross-cultural research. The cultural differences of prime importance here are those between Western and non-Western societies, or among non-Western societies, and not the extensive cross-national and social class data on intellectual functioning.

Evidence produced by psychologists to answer questions of cultural differences in thinking is reported under the headings 'perception' and 'cognition' in chapters 3, 4, 5 and 6. A brief examination of certain linguistic topics is presented in chapter 2 because language is at the same time an obvious example of cultural variability and also the source of much confusion in the formulation of theories about the impact of cultural milieux on thought processes.

The decision to employ a perception–cognition dichotomy is one of strategy and its usefulness can be determined in so far as order is brought to the variety of studies examined under these headings. The categories are not mutually exclusive and from a reductionist perspective can be considered cumulative. Thus studies based on Witkin's theory of cognitive style are reviewed in chapter 6 on macro models of cognition, while consideration of some of the perceptual measures used in research on cognitive style is contained in chapter 3 which surveys perceptual processes reliant on environmental information. The topics considered include colour perception, the perception of orientation, depth and visual illusions. Chapter 4 deals with perception at a remove from the topics of the preceding chapter, that is, with time, space and emotion. Micro models of cognition, i.e. learning and memory, are considered in chapter 5.

A starting point in mapping the areas of perception and cognition are the definitions which French offered to aid anthropological research in these fields. French suggested that (1963, p. 402)

> perception can be defined as the process of immediate experience in organisms. This links perception with sensation; such primitive terms as 'seeing', 'tasting' and 'feeling' are refinable into perceptual processes. As experience becomes less immediate and the amount of inference by the organism increases, processes of cognition have become involved. Among the primitive terms are 'knowing' and 'thinking'.

Tajfel adopted the notion of immediacy in defining perception in his chapter on social and cultural determinants of perception in *The Handbook of Social Psychology* (Lindzey and Aronson, 1969) but specified four necessary qualifications. These required that the stimulus material allow the possibility of only one correct response, that responses must occur at the time the sensory material is received, and must not be based on complex and abstract inference, nor on an awareness by the perceiver of alternatives. In the sense that Tajfel outlined, the topics dealt with in chapter 3 are more immediate than those of the following chapter.

The boundaries used for ordering the cross-cultural data are consonant with definitions of perception and cognition used generally in psychology. This must be the case if variables reflecting cultural factors are to be included in existing psychological models of intellectual functioning. However, a casual examination of the cross-cultural literature, or of the topics covered in chapters 3 to 6, indicates that the focal concerns of cross-cultural research do not mirror the major interests in the experimental study of perception and cognition. The search for evidence of cultural differences and the need to modify designs to fit different cultural settings have produced a cross-cultural literature unrepresentative of the areas in psychology from which they have developed.

There is also a Western bias in the cross-cultural study of cognitive processes. In part this reflects the state of knowledge but also reveals Western ignorance of non-Western efforts to develop systematic theories of psychological functioning. Although books such as the Murphys' (1968) on Asian psychology and the Chins' (1969) on Chinese research are available, I have encountered no reports in which a theory of psychological processes developed outside the Western scientific tradition was tested comparatively. Non-Western psychologists are generally trained in the Euro-American traditions of academic psychology. In the past even these people have been few in number but the most thriving group, that in Japan, now has the largest entry in the current *International Directory of Psychologists* (International Union of Psychological Science, 1966) with almost 1000 professional psychologists.

In Africa there have been few indigenous psychologists. Most of the cross-cultural research has been undertaken by strangers, i.e. Euro-American psychologists with little knowledge of the cultures whose dimensions they wish to assess and usually only limited linguistic skills with which to communicate with those they hope to study. These shortcomings pose special problems which will be considered below; but they may be overcome most successfully when enough indigenous psychologists have been trained.

The research strategy of many of the investigators whose studies are reported in this book can be characterized as that of the 'explorer'. The term 'explorer' is used to denote the predicament in which many psychologists have found themselves in non-Western settings. Often with little anthropological or sociological training, psychologists have lived in developing countries for a few years, teaching or taking part in large research programmes. Enthusiasm to get on with their investigations, time limitations and perhaps lack of sensitivity have led to various forms of cultural blindness. One is that carefully annotated by Doob in a review of psychological research carried out in Africa (1965). He marked with one asterisk, for mild opprobrium, studies in which the investigator mentioned the cultural affiliation of the Africans he examined but lumped all together without furnishing evidence of having tested for cultural differences. Studies lacking any cultural identification were marked with two asterisks. Clearly studies which fail to identify subjects' societal affiliation can add little to our understanding of how psychological processes are modified by cultural variables.

To avoid ambiguous shortcuts, more sustained research effort is needed. It is worth noting that Gay, one of the authors of an important series of studies on cross-cultural cognition, spent over ten years teaching at Cuttington College in Liberia (Cole, Gay, Glick and Sharp, 1971; Gay and Cole, 1967). If the impact of cultural factors on psychological processes is to be assessed, more 'settlers' are required. Whether these long-term researchers should be expatriates, who come to know another culture thoroughly, or indigenous psychologists may be debated. It is clear, however, that major contributions will only come when there are more psychologists trained in field techniques who have a deep knowledge of the non-Western culture which they study.

The remaining sections of this chapter are organized around answering some of the questions which are encountered in undertaking cross-cultural research on cognitive processes. The first takes up methodological problems while theoretical issues are subsequently examined. Although the sections have clear physical boundaries, the issues they raise do not. Theory and method interact, improvements in one leading to refinements in the other. Ideally, as the role of cultural variables is demonstrated, more researchers will take up the problems of cross-cultural investigation.

Methods

The researcher investigating cognitive processes in a non-Western setting must satisfy the usual criteria of good design in a psychological study as well as solving particular problems which arise from ensuring adequate communication and sampling. This discussion will begin with questions about communicating with non-Western peoples and then look at certain aspects of sampling.

Communication

One of the major constraints in taking a procedure to another culture lies in the need to ensure that the investigation will produce data in the new setting which can be compared with that collected in the original Euro-American situation. Any differences which are recorded should not be due to translation failures of a linguistic, material or situational nature (Frijda and Jahoda, 1966). The testing situation has recently come under the scrutiny of American psychologists (Rosenthal, 1966) but cross-cultural settings have received only informal attention from psychologists. Careful thought has been given to the general problem of communication with people from different cultures, while the actual mechanics of linguistic translation have prompted experimental investigation. This section begins with an examination of the broad question of communication, moves on to a discussion of testing and closes with a review of some research on translation.

Campbell (1964) has argued that it is only possible to diagnose cultural differences when considerable areas of agreement have been established; only against a background of consensus do discrepant items have signal significance. He proposed that rather than showing an absence of cognitive ability, total failure on a test might instead represent a breakdown in communication about the nature of the task between the experimenter and his non-Western subjects. If cultural factors were such as to produce people whose cognitive capacities were radically different from our own we would be unable to measure these differences, for we would lack the critical feature of measurement, a common measuring device. This view implies a partial answer to the question raised at the beginning of the chapter. It argues that men the world over have certain common cognitive capacities.

Drawing examples from a study of optical illusions in which almost 2000 people from twenty societies participated (Segall, Campbell and Herskovits, 1966), Campbell demonstrated methods for ensuring adequate communication and for detecting failure. Four extremely simple pretest items were employed in his study and these allowed him to determine whether individuals understood the questions and could discriminate red and black and the longer or the shorter line. Responses to illusion items in which true differences are small would be worthless from subjects who were unable to make the gross discriminations required in the pretest items and communicate these to the investigators.

An analysis of the consistency of responses was undertaken for those individuals whose pretest performance qualified them for testing on illusion items. The logic of the consistency analysis can be demonstrated by reference to the twelve items of the Müller–Lyer illusion set. Drawings, rather than adjustable apparatus, were employed in this study. In the twelve Müller–Lyer drawings the critical line segments were objectively equal in one drawing (see Figure 1a), were lengthened in the direction of the illusion-produced distortion in a graded series of ten steps (Figure 1b) and were suggestive of a counter illusion effect in one drawing (Figure 1c). The

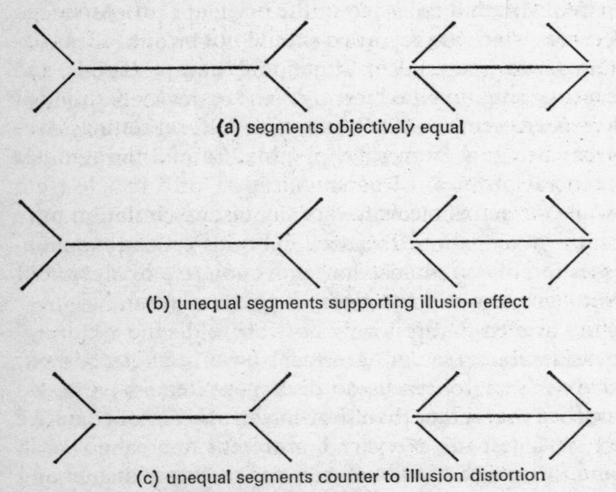

Figure 1 The Müller–Lyer illusion
adapted from Segall, Campbell and Herskovits, 1966, p. 87)

drawings were graded in 5 per cent steps from −5 per cent or the counter illusion suggestion, through 0 illusion or equality of line segments to a 50 per cent suggestion of illusion. They were presented to subjects however, in a fixed, ungraded sequence. A perfectly consistent individual who produced an illusion response at 15 per cent also gave illusion responses at 10 per cent, 5 per cent, 0 per cent and −5 per cent. The major findings of the study were based upon results from those individuals who produced either perfectly consistent responses or responses with only one error, i.e. in the example above perhaps a non-illusion response at 10 per cent, thus breaking the consistency once. An analysis was also undertaken on the non-scale or inconsistent responses which were discarded. Although the proportion of inconsistent cases which were discarded differed across cultures, there was no significant relationship between number of discards and magnitude of illusion reported for a culture. Campbell argued that the discards may well have been communication failures whose inclusion in further analysis would have led to an increased level of illusion especially in low illusion cultures.

In the illusion study reported by Campbell, the same stimulus material was used in all societies and the same consistency criteria applied to all subjects' responses. Two positions have emerged informally regarding the issue of test modification. One view holds that it is worth utilizing a standard instrument, e.g. a Rorschach or ink-blot test, without modification even though the colours are known to have different cultural meanings. The other position advocates adapting instruments such as the pictures of the Thematic Apperception Test (TAT) according to the culture of the people being studied. Thus TAT cards have been redrawn to show Africans in tropical settings attired in national dress. An extreme strategy of test adaptation may soothe the liberal conscience disturbed by comparisons which usually appear to highlight Western superiority, but the lack of genuine comparability and differences when grossly modified material is used can reduce questions and results to triviality (cf. Bernardoni, 1964).

The text situation too, poses problems for indigenous psychologist and expatriate alike. In most non-Western societies, the experimenter, who is probably perceived as a 'doctor' or 'educated person', is viewed as powerful and prestigious. In my own studies in Nigeria I found that the educated Yoruba mothers, who carried out my interviews with illiterate mothers, evoked even greater deference than I had experienced when I interviewed them. Not only is the role of researcher a source of influence but testing itself a great novelty. Research undertaken in an office or laboratory may provoke fear and even refusal; but a visit to peoples' homes often occasions considerable excitement and difficulties in ensuring privacy and quiet are common. Although it is useful to work in conjunction with a clinic or a community development programme, there are added risks of response bias.

Controls for experimenter bias have to be strengthened as the move to non-Western settings adds extra sources of systematic error.

Faulty translation can be a source of bias as well as of communication failure. Cross-cultural researchers have recently begun to examine translation in a systematic fashion and experimental studies focused upon the technical dimensions of translation have been undertaken (Brislin, 1970; Werner and Campbell, 1970). Assessment of the quality of a translation remains a problem but research on the method of back translation offers promise of some solution (Brislin, 1970). The back translation procedure requires at least two people who are bi-lingual in the source language and the language of the planned research, the target language. One translates the source material, e.g. a questionnaire, intelligence test or simple instructions, into the target language, then the other translates the target version of the instrument back into the source language without access to the original. There are, then, two source versions of the material available for comparison, the original and the back translation.

The method of back translation does not in itself guarantee total success. Werner and Campbell (1970) have suggested many rules to apply in preparing the source material. When English is the source language, these include: (a) use of simple sentences, (b) repetition of nouns rather than their replacement by pronouns, (c) elimination of metaphors and colloquial expressions, (d) use of the active rather than passive tense and (e) avoidance of the subjunctive and of hypothetical phrasing. These rules, while facilitating translation accuracy, limit the complexity of the material available for use in cross-cultural research.

Brislin (1970) showed that translation accuracy varied with the subject matter of essays, their linguistic complexity and the choice of target language and also that a combined effect of target language and subject matter could influence accuracy. He demonstrated that when bilinguals were given instructions or a questionnaire in either a target or source language judged to be an accurate back translation, their behaviour, i.e. performance or scores, was equivalent in either language. Translation accuracy was assessed by three linguistic criteria one of which required monolingual raters while the other two depended on the availability of bi-lingual judges. Monolingual judges were asked to rate the number of errors of meaning in a comparison of the original and the back translations of a set of essays. Bilinguals were required to assess errors between the source and the target version or the target version and the back translation. Bilinguals were also tested for comprehension after reading essays in either the source or target language. Estimates of error thus direct improvement in the target material and also, if necessary, suggest changes in the source material.

Back translation is only one method of dealing with translation problems.

Others which have been used include testing bilinguals on both versions of an instrument and then modifying items which yield discrepant replies (Prince and Mombour, 1967), employing a committee of bilinguals to construct, after discussion, the target version of an instrument, or simply testing the instrument before use on an additional or pilot sample and correcting any detectable difficulties in comprehension. These procedures have varying probabilities of success. Ervin (1964) has shown differences in the behaviour of bilinguals which depend on the language of instruction and response.

Non-verbal strategies have also been used in order to avoid problems of adequate translation. In industrial situations in the Republic of South Africa instruction by motion pictures has been used successfully to break down communication barriers which interfered with the technical training of unskilled labourers. Non-verbal tests are popular in assessment batteries. Heron and Simonsson (1969) used a non-verbal test first developed in the United States with deaf children to measure cognitive behaviour in Zambian children. While these non-verbal approaches are inventive and avoid problems of linguistic translation it is necessary to remember that the meaning of non-verbal behaviour may be as culture-bound as that of linguistic behaviour. Not only are problems of communication still present but in so far as non-verbal behaviour is also rule-regulated there are still questions about translation accuracy. Furthermore, there is no basis for the assumption, sometimes implicit, that scores are equivalent when a trait, e.g. intelligence, is measured non-verbally and by traditional verbal measures.

Sampling

Generally psychologists have not been concerned with the representativeness of their samples and the procedures employed by 'explorers' in cross-cultural psychology reflect this lack of attention. Thus a standard instrument, e.g. the Maudsley Personality Inventory (Eysenck, 1959), might be administered to any subjects who fulfilled the high literacy demands of the instrument, but the results would then be representative only of the most educated and Westernized members of that society. Even when illiterates are assessed they are often domestic servants and their families who live in proximity to Europeans. If studies are concerned with measuring the effects of Westernization, such sampling strategies are necessary but when the aim is the isolation of cultural factors they make the analysis complex.

Sampling has traditionally received attention from survey researchers and opinion pollsters. Within the cross-cultural field, sampling has received the most careful consideration from the research group at Yale University which developed the Human Relations Area Files. They used ethnographies for testing hypotheses about human behaviour. Whiting (1954, 1968) has described the procedure which he called 'the cross-cultural method' in successive editions of the *Handbook of Social Psychology*. Naroll (1970) who works within the same paradigm now describes these studies as 'cross-cultural surveys'.

Concern with problems of sampling are clarified by an understanding of the basic strategy of 'the cross-cultural method'. In correlational studies psychologists measure individuals on a number of variables and employ statistical techniques to estimate the degree of relationship between these variables. Whiting and Naroll are interested in assessing the strength of relationships between traits but they sample societies rather than human individuals. The psychologist might correlate university students' performance on final examinations with level of anxiety; Whiting relates explanations of disease in a sample of world cultures with their socialization practices. The population from which the psychologist samples would be all finalists while that of the cross-cultural methodologists would be all societies from which there are accounts of socialization and theories of disease.

Two sampling problems are crucial in successful use of 'the cross-cultural method'; one concerns the definition of the societal unit and the other the criteria to be employed in drawing a sample of these units. Both questions have received extensive attention and have been reviewed by Whiting (1968). On the first issue he concluded (p. 702) that 'the homogeneous community is the most appropriate organized culture-bearing unit and that a sufficient number of these have been described to provide an adequate sample'. Furthermore, he suggested four criteria to define cultural homogeneity: community members should (a) have frequent face to face social contact, (b) speak a common dialect, (c) share some decision-making authority concerning significant aspects of group welfare and (d) have a common name. The third criterion is useful in differentiating, for example, between an old village which has been enveloped by a growing metropolis and the anomic community of a primary school catchment area. Although the criteria ensure that the units will be homogeneous along specified dimensions, they are no guarantee of homogeneity on every variable of interest to the researcher.

The identification and enumeration of the population from which to sample homogeneous communities raises difficult questions concerned both with sampling theory and with particular issues such as the ranges of social complexity and lack of independence resulting from shared cultural experience. Particular sampling solutions are available. Whiting, for instance, proposes the use of criteria of linguistic independence and geographical separation; but the problems are not unique to this variety of cross-cultural research. In their textbook on sampling, Stephan and

McCarthy (1958, p. 351) state that 'scientific laws and hypotheses ordinarily imply that if a set of factors is present, then a certain set of results will follow, except for the effects of any additional factors that may be present to modify these results'. Sampling homogeneous communities to minimize the effects of 'any additional factors', i.e. to choose samples which allow the elimination of rival plausible hypotheses, demands considerable knowledge of potentially relevant variables. Ethnographic, demographic, ecological and historical knowledge of this nature is often beyond a psychologist's range of competence. 'The cross-cultural method' or survey, unless an interdisciplinary venture, is fraught with methodological hazards.

Consideration of 'the cross-cultural' method has taken us a long way from the sampling questions raised by studies examining the effects of cultural variables on cognitive processes. However, just as research on societal differences must ensure that sampling procedures take account of potential sources of explanation, so too must studies assessing individual variability. Examples of hypothesis-directed sampling are Greenfield's (1966) comparisons of conservation in rural and urban, school attending and unschooled Wolof children and Cole and Gay's (1972) investigation of free recall in Kpelle and American adults and children. In both these studies the choice of groups was determined not only by a wish to show differences in behaviour, but also by specific hypotheses concerning the psychological and cultural determinants of these differences.

Theoretical issues

If cognitive psychologists are to be lured from the security of their own culture, which they understand intuitively, to work in a strange environment, it is necessary to consider the costs and benefits for theory building. An adequate cross-cultural test of a psychological hypothesis offers the theorist an opportunity to discover the inherent bias in his own intuitions – for instance, the assumption that a particular cognitive skill is the result of formal tuition or of maturation – can be put to test in a milieu where schooling is unknown or radically different from our own. However, once the researcher, employing the most carefully translated and pretested paradigm, embarks on cross-cultural comparisons his efforts become interpretable in terms of anthropological and sociological models of behaviour and the natural sciences can no longer serve as an exclusive standard. Campbell (1967) has made this point clearly in saying 'that cross-cultural data sets will never be comparable or interpretable at the level of experimental comparability which psychologists are trained to accept as necessary'. There are, none the less, at least two clear benefits from exploring cultural variation. Psychologists may extend parameters in directions which normal experimental considerations prohibit, for example, fostering arrangements resulting in nonparental socialization, and they may find new dimensions to add to their models which are unknown in Euro-American settings, such as the head moulding and limb stretching of African infants.

The data of Sears and Whiting, two vigorous proponents of cross-cultural research, have been presented together to make these points (cf. Whiting, 1954, 1968). In a study which Sears and Wise (1950) carried out in Kansas City, a highly significant positive relationship was found between age at weaning and emotional disturbance displayed by infants. Only five infants in the sample of eighty were weaned after seven months but older infants showed greater upset. Whiting, utilizing ethnographers' reports on

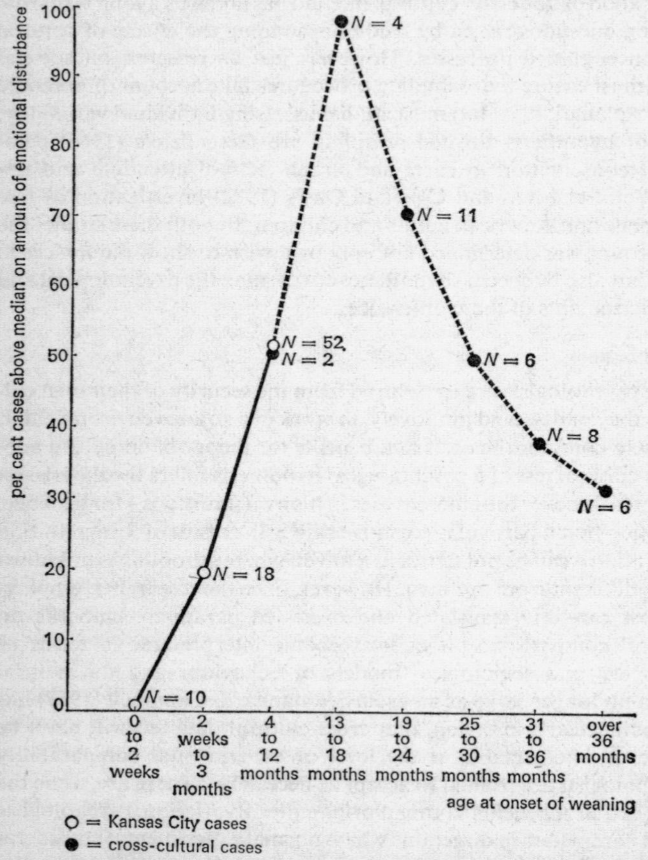

Figure 2 Relationship between age at weaning and emotional disturbance (from Whiting, 1968, p. 695)

age at weaning and emotional disturbance in a sample of thirty-seven societies (that is, using 'the cross-cultural method'), found only two societies in which infants were normally weaned before twelve months. When he divided the sample into those weaned early, i.e. before eighteen months, and those weaned late or after eighteen months, he found a negative relationship between age and disturbance. Greater disturbance was reported for infants from societies in which weaning occurred before eighteen months. Rather than viewing his data as contradictory to that of Sears, Whiting suggested that in fact the two sets of data were complementary and he presented the material in graphic form to support his argument. Examination of the figures from both sets of data reveals a function which reaches a peak at thirteen to eighteen months and then declines sharply.

These data show how a cross-cultural perspective can offer new information on the range of values which variables can take – thus, weaning may normally occur as late as three years – and how such a perspective furnishes knowledge which cannot be obtained by direct experimentation. Even if it were possible in the name of science to persuade some mothers to wean their American children at twenty-four or thirty-six months, their behaviour would be extremely deviant by American standards. Conversely, it would be difficult and non-representative to induce weaning at six months in infants from societies in which the norm is twenty-four months. A point to which we will return shortly is that the cross-cultural comparison is based upon reports of normal behaviour in each of the thirty-seven societies.

Other examples of cultural variation available for observational exploitation are provided by schooled and unschooled children in societies where primary education is not universal, or by comparisons of children raised by their own parents or by others in those cultures in which there is strong social pressure to foster children (Goody, 1970; Greenfield and Bruner, 1966). The ability to capitalize on such natural experiments depends on knowledge and on sensitivity to opportunity. An American researcher interested in the effects of formal instruction on the development of cognitive structures compared black children from a northern industrial city with black children from Prince Edward County, Virginia, who had lost four years' schooling in the battle over desegregation (Mermelstein and Shulman, 1967).

The strategies proposed here to utilize natural variations involve comparisons of individuals who have been assigned to different groups by natural circumstances rather than at random as most statistical models require. Thus the cost of information which cannot be experimentally induced is the necessity to forsake the design requirements of random assignment to treatment groups.

The combined weaning studies also serve as an example of extension in the range of scores which data from other cultures can furnish. Not only was it possible cross-culturally to find infants weaned later than one year, but the intensity of the emotional reaction to weaning was also found to be greater than that recorded in Kansas City alone. Again, in the study of cognitive development, cross-cultural data have led to revision in ages at which Piagetian stages are expected (Peluffo, 1967). In some societies, the concrete operations only begin to appear at ten to eleven years and in certain hunting and gathering societies they may not appear at all. Particular cultural conditions may be required for the development of operational thinking, but as they are always present in Western societies their necessity may pass unnoticed.

The argument that 'the cross-cultural' method allows us to test the pan-human applicability of theories of behaviour has been deliberately neglected until this point. In the example presented by Whiting (1954, 1968) it was only by combining the American and cross-cultural material that the general law stating that emotional disturbance is an increasing function of age until eighteen months but then declines with age, could be expressed. Implicit in his formulation of a general law is an assumption that it is valid to combine information based on individual behaviour and behaviour representative of socially agreed or normative action. Whiting (1968, p. 696) makes this point explicitly when he states:

> Furthermore, the cross-cultural method, by studying cultural norms, holds individual variation constant. Psychological studies of individuals in a single society do just the opposite, in that cultural norms are held constant and individual variations are studied. A combination of these two methods should supplement and correct each other in the development of a general theory of human behavior.

Granted that the use of naturally occurring variations in other societies may allow us to free our psychological theories from ethnocentric bias, it is necessary to examine more closely the general theory of behaviour which Whiting proposes. In order to state the general law it was necessary to neglect the information that half the data represented individual differences while the other described 'typical reactions' of groups of individuals. The further assumption that whatever processes were involved in individuals' reactions to weaning were also operative at the normative level is implied by the willingness to group both sets of data. This reduction of anthropological categories to those of psychological analysis has provoked criticism from traditional psychologists (Frijda and Jahoda, 1966) sociologists (Dore, 1961), and anthropologists (Wallace, 1961). Before attacking 'the cross-cultural method' it is necessary to understand the paradigm fully.

The aims of 'the cross-cultural method' as it was applied to psychological hypotheses were clearly stated in the first major publication utilizing this approach. Whiting and Child (1953, p. 15) described the broad characteristics of their work as follows:

> First, it is concerned with the problem of how culture is integrated through the medium of personality processes. This concern leads us inevitably to be interested in the influence both of culture upon personality and of personality upon culture.
>
> Second, it is oriented toward testing general hypotheses about human behavior in any and all societies rather than toward achieving a detailed understanding of any one society.
>
> Third, it uses the correlational method for testing hypotheses. The particular form this takes in our study is the cross-cultural method, in which each culture is considered as a unit.
>
> Fourth, while it draws upon psychoanalytic theory as an important source of hypotheses, the concepts of general behavior theory are used in formulating hypotheses.

These statements, and the implication that problems of cultural integration can be approached through general behaviour theory (i.e. a version of Hullian drive reduction learning theory, and psychoanalytic theory), evidence the early bias towards psychological reductionism.

In a recent series of papers, Whiting has investigated the relationship between stimulation in infancy and adult stature (Landauer and Whiting, 1964; Whiting, Landauer and Jones, 1968). In the first paper he used 'the cross-cultural method' to show that stress experienced in infancy was related to greater adult height. In the second study he turned to longitudinal data from American investigations of physical growth and health to analyse the relationship between early stress, i.e. inoculation before two years of age, and adult stature. Having controlled for parental stature, a relationship between early stress and greater height was substantiated, but an explanation was not forthcoming. Whiting examined a considerable body of research which allowed him to rule out the effects of diet, race, geography, parental stature, illness and selective mortality, benign treatment effects and self-selection of treatment by parents, but he was forced to conclude that as yet there was no clear understanding of the growth mechanism. Whiting's belief in explanation at the physiological level was evident when he stated (Whiting, Landauer and Jones, 1968, p. 67):

> What is needed is direct evidence of a common physiological effect of such growth-enhancing infant-care practices as mother separation, hospital birth, immunization and birth anoxia, etc., and a real understanding of how such a physiological effect, if it exists, leads to acceleration of growth.

In this series of studies, Whiting abandoned his earlier aim of verifying hypotheses from general behaviour theory and has taken instead a somewhat atheoretical, functional stance. In fact, his concluding sentences stated his belief that the relationship he demonstrated, between infantile stimulation and growth, might prove useful to those investigators who eventually explained the processes of growth. This functional position is less vulnerable to attack than that of his earlier cross-cultural studies tied to general behaviour theory and cultural integration. The charge of psychological reductionism was only valid in so far as the explanatory mechanisms invoked were derived from psychoanalytic or general behaviour theory.

The 'cross-cultural method' tied to general behaviour theory is vulnerable to attack from psychologists, sociologists and anthropologists alike. Frijda and Jahoda (1966), speaking as psychologists, raised three major objections to the explanatory model which Whiting (1963) had invoked to explain the integration of culture through the medium of personality processes. Firstly, they attacked the notion that the child-rearing practices of a society (assuming a certain uniformity) can and in fact need to produce a narrow range of variation in adult personality. Secondly, they questioned the idea that child-rearing practices directly reflect the maintenance systems of the society without feedback mediated by adult personality change. Finally they doubted that, even with the necessary feedback specified, a society can legitimately be viewed as a system functioning in isolation. They held the isolation premise to be unrealistic in the face of rapid social change throughout the world. Considering the possibilities of empirical research they concluded that methods are not yet powerful enough to begin to cope with the gigantic, multivariate task this formulation involves. Frijda and Jahoda suggested instead that studies should be undertaken to specify limited relationships between child-rearing practices and specific adult characteristics such as achievement motivation or field dependence.

Criticisms of Whiting's explanation of cultural integration were made by Wallace, an anthropologist, in his general attack on personality and culture studies. He pointed out that these theories led to a position in which the terms, personality and culture, both dealt with cognitive and affective variables and were analysed at both group and individual levels. Whiting's notion that child-rearing practices mediate between culture (or maintenance systems) and personality perpetuates this confusion. Wallace (1961, p. 131) proposed instead the concept of 'mazeway' which he defines as:

> A mazeway ... the organized totality of learned meanings maintained by an individual organism at a given time ... is the cognitive map of the individual's private world regularly evoked by perceived or remembered stimuli. Mazeway includes motivation but also includes much cognitive content that is not motivationally weighted.

Culture, Wallace suggested, can only be appropriately considered in social groups in which members are able to develop and maintain principles of mazeway equivalence or mutually predictive cognitions. According to his view and distinct from the older personality and culture formulation, there is no necessity for shared motivational content. The equivalence is based upon cognitions which reflect shared inferences based on observed stimulus–response sequences. Culture thus defined can only be considered at the level of group behaviour. The term 'personality' Wallace reserved for higher level abstractions from mazeway but at the individual level only. While Wallace's theory invokes psychological phenomena to explain culture, these phenomena are cognitive processes which allow the sharing of inferences of stimulus–response sequences which make organized social life possible.

A concern with appropriate levels of analysis and reductionism has exercised sociologists for some time. In a discussion of social facts and reductionism, Dore (1961) has suggested that the individualist thesis has virtue over the holist approach because it has greater explanatory power. While endorsing explanation at an individual level, this would not imply blanket endorsement of Whiting's laws of general behaviour theory, especially when they involve the lumping of individual and group data. When the sociological lens is trained on these data, two different processes can be seen at work. In the cross-cultural material based on thirty-seven societies we have measures of normative behaviour; in fact the measured emotional disturbance and estimated ages are based upon ethnographers' accounts of normative behaviour. The Kansas City data are different in just this respect. First of all, there is no indication in the Kansas City data of what the norms are concerning weaning; secondly, there is no attempt to separate the behaviour of the eighty infants into those whose responses were made to normal weaning practice and those whose disturbances resulted from abnormal weaning conditions. Dore (personal communication) has suggested that the relevant causal relationship may be that weaning at an abnormal age, societally defined, leads to upset. To test such an hypothesis, information on the variance as well as the modal behaviour of a society would be necessary. Unfortunately, ethnographic accounts rarely present material on the range of behaviour within a society.

It is reasonable to ask whether it was necessary to submit Whiting's theories to so much critical analysis or whether this discussion is simply the manifestation of a narrowly trade unionist approach from traditional social scientists faced with an ambitious interdisciplinary effort. Certainly there are differences in research style and anthropologists seem happier and more able to borrow theories and concepts from psychology than the reverse. Psychologists have traditionally looked to the natural sciences for their paradigms but the complexity of cross-cultural research can be seen to require an understanding of anthropological and sociological models as well. Once the psychologist, employing the most carefully adapted procedures, embarks on cross-cultural comparisons his efforts become interpretable at new levels of theoretical integration. The lesson of this analysis is the need to carry on theory building appropriate to the level at which the variables are measured. Thus with this final conclusion to the discussion of levels of analysis and reductionism we return to that point made when the separate analysis of method and theory was begun, that the divisions may be more apparent than real. Researchers' ranges of interest, theory and method all require refinement if cultural variables are to clarify our understanding of psychological processes involved in perception and cognition.

Conclusions

By now it is clear that a gain in our understanding of the psychologically defined processes of perception and cognition may be expected from adequate investigations of these functions in non-Western settings. The usefulness of these studies in increasing our awareness of the range of independent variables to study and to include in theories will vary with the skill with which the problems general to psychological investigation and particular to cross-cultural research are met.

Psychological research employing subjects from non-Western societies must resolve many methodological questions which overlap those of conventional investigations. These include problems of sampling, of response bias and experimenter effects, and of validity. There is, however, a prior issue confronting the psychologist newly concerned with cultural variables. He must determine which aspects of an extensive literature will be useful in sharpening his understanding of the effects of cultural factors on behaviour as these functions are conceptualized by psychologists. The position adopted here is that the cross-cultural perspective is, like the developmental approach, a dimension along which any problem area within psychology can be studied. Just as one asks how intelligence changes over time, i.e. with age, so one can ask how different cultural milieux affect intelligence. Of course, the developmental/cross-cultural question – how do different cultural experiences affect intelligence over time? – is also valid. The core issues then are: how do the additional dimensions increase our understanding of cognitive behaviour as conceptualized by psychologists and how do research designs deal with the problems raised by the addition of these dimensions?

The journey through the cross-cultural literature on perception and cognition will indicate considerable methodological failure and may explain the lack of impact of cultural variables on recent theories in cognitive psychology. The need for more sustained effort by researchers who view themselves as 'settlers' in particular cultures to investigate psychological theories whose Western bias is acknowledged is great. Much of the research which we shall consider suffers from defects springing from its exploratory nature. It is debatable whether the researchers who will undertake the sustained effort necessary to add coherently to our understanding of the cultural dimension should be indigenous psychologists or expatriates.

Unease about cross-cultural comparisons springs in part from failure to compare the appropriate groups. Often, in fact, the comparison has only been implicit, with a researcher comparing non-Western behaviour not with data which he has collected but with Euro-American norms. One solution is for the same investigator to study the processes both in a Western setting and in another culture using equivalent techniques. Bilingual researchers who are 'at home' in two cultures would be ideal but joint research programmes and new translation procedures may enable all psychologists interested in the cross-cultural perspective to undertake useful studies.

While it is clear that the goals of ideal research have yet to be achieved, the cross-cultural literature on intellectual functioning relevant to psychology is sufficient in breadth to merit attention. Examination of this material is useful for the research cautions it contains as well as for the prospects for future study which may be gleaned from it.

2 Issues: Linguistic

The reliance psychologists place on linguistic procedures in their research on intellectual processes and the everyday experience of language barriers in communication combine to highlight the need to examine the role of language before considering cross-cultural studies of perception and cognition. To the layman, language is one of the obvious sources of cultural difference. Formalized as linguistic relativism, the question of the effect of language on thinking has stimulated much lively debate and is the starting point of the discussion of problems of a linguistic nature which are relevant to cross-cultural research in psychology.

Linguistic relativism

The German philosopher, von Humboldt (1796–1835), is often credited with being the first writer to state that 'the character and structure of a language expresses the inner life and knowledge of its speakers and that languages differ from one another as their speakers differ' (cf. Salus, 1969, p. 17). Sapir (1907–8), an American linguist who also espoused linguistic relativism, has traced the ideas of von Humboldt to a prize-winning essay of 1772 by Herder on the origins of language, in which Herder proposed that language and cognition had developed together and that all languages had derived from a common source. However, with the development of diverse languages and the presumed impossibility of complete translation, he argued that access to the culture and literature of a particular society lay only through its own language.

The interest of psychologists was awakened by formulations of linguistic relativism sometimes referred to as the Whorf–Sapir hypothesis. Whorf (1897–1941), a gifted and influential linguist, was trained as an engineer and employed as an insurance adjustor. He studied with Sapir at Yale University and his sympathy and respect for his mentor are evidenced in this excerpt from Sapir's writings which appeared at the beginning of Whorf's memorial essay to his teacher (see Whorf, 1956, p. 134):

Human beings do not live in the objective world alone, nor in the world of social activity as ordinarily understood, but are very much at the mercy of the particular language which has become the medium of expression for their society. It is quite an illusion to imagine that one adjusts to reality essentially without the use of language. . . . We see and hear and otherwise experience very largely as we do because the language habits of our community predispose certain choices of interpretation.

Whorf shared Sapir's views on the interconnectedness of language, culture and cognition. Whorf drew on his own experiences as a fire inspector for evidence of the linguistic conditioning of behaviour (see Whorf, 1956). He noted that great care was exercised in storing 'gasoline drums' but when the drums no longer contained gasoline and hence might be described as 'empty gasoline drums' they were disposed of in a haphazard fashion. Whorf viewed the lack of concern with fire precautions when dealing with 'empty' drums as linguistically determined carelessness and interpreted the adjective 'empty' as a negation which denied the need for caution.

Whorf also drew upon his knowledge of American-Indian languages for evidence of linguistic relativism. He invented SAE, Standard Average European, against which to compare exotic languages. SAE was based on the premise that English, French, German and other Western European languages were semantically and syntactically similar when contrasted with non-European languages. The relation of SAE and non-Western languages was examined in order to answer two questions about the nature of language and thought. The first issue concerned the concepts used to organize experience while the second pertained to the nature of the relationships between the structure of language and cultural and behavioural norms. Whorf's comparative analysis of concepts is illustrated in the discussion which follows by his examination of time and space in terms of Hopi and SAE forms of the plural; consideration of the role of the Crier Chief illumines Whorf's view of the interrelations of language, thought and behaviour.

In the Hopi language only physical objects which can be grouped in space may take the plural form, i.e. 'ten' men. In SAE, however, 'ten' days is also an acceptable construction; but according to a Hopi world-view the grouping of days violates the nature of time. Whorf suggested that SAE speakers were able to employ the plural of day by marking phases in the cyclic sequence and that that was how they quantified the passage of time. Thus, SAE allows the objectification of sequence by encouraging quantification; days are laid out in a string just as inch units are counted on a yardstick. Rules of Hopi grammar allow objects to take the plural only if they can be aggregated in space, but it should be noted that this stricture would not interfere with a Hopi informant attending a meeting in ten days' time. The Hopi speaker could describe the arrangement by employing the ordinal, tenth, and the singular day, thus avoiding use of the metaphorical plural. Whorf argued that these different modes of expressing a time relationship indicated different concepts of time and space and reflected differential experience of time and space. Whorf's appeal is largely to intuition and we are encouraged to sense differences in the worlds of Hopi and SAE speakers.

The Whorfian analysis of concepts and cognition may have appeared tenuous, but the evidence and conclusions on the interrelation between cultural norms and linguistic patterns is more intricate as illustrated by the analysis of the Crier Chief's role in Hopi society. Since the Hopi language failed to mark tense and prevented objectification of time, the Hopi could only know the next moment in terms of duration, i.e. only via ongoing actions in the present. Preparations were central in Hopi culture, Whorf contended, because it was only through continuous and repetitious activity that the future could be known. The Crier Chief was important in Hopi society as the official concerned with making known social preparations. Whorf reported various cultural activities concerned with preparation, but despite a detailed analysis of aspects of Hopi preparation Whorf asserted that it would be impossible to predict specific relationships. The need for an existence of Crier Chiefs could not be established from analysis of tense grammar or vice versa. Whorf argued that anthropological and linguistic descriptions alone could not uncover the relationships he sought. He envisaged analyses of 'systems of thought' with structures which reflected the interdependent language and culture of their societies.

Whorf's restatement of linguistic relativism in psychological terms prompted attack from many directions. There have been a number of attempts to systematize the complex interrelationships between language and cognition only hinted at in the original formulations (Fishman, 1960; Heider, 1972a; Miller and McNeill, 1969), while Lenneberg (1953) has queried both the material produced to argue for the inadequacy of translation and to establish links between language and thinking. His contention, that no evidence has been offered which indicates how linguistic differences affect psychological processes directly, is important because it had been claimed that the Whorf–Sapir hypothesis was relevant for cognitive psychology. Psychologists will perforce attempt to interpret vague terms such as 'systems of thought' to imply psychological processes. The hypothesis can offer direction for cross-cultural research only if such specifications are made clear.

Re-examination of Whorf's arguments for the cultural and linguistic moulding of concepts or the interrelations of cultural norms and linguistic patterns highlights the lack of any evidence on the psychological experience of time (cf. chapter 4). The data presented is primarily linguistic; the language of Hopi and SAE was analysed but no non-linguistic evidence was examined.

Lenneberg's (1953) attack on the Whorfian analysis of translation emphasized shortcomings of a technical nature. Lenneberg disputed the premise that good translation was impossible and contended that the English sentence which Whorf offered in translation of the Apache *to-no-ga* was a string of words taking no account of Apache grammar. As an Apache's revenge, with credit to Lenneberg, Miller and McNeill (1969, p. 731) have suggested the following translation of 'It is a dripping spring':

The subject is an object or organism, not an adult human being, the predicate is a generic or indefinite idea of a process in which liquid falls in small natural segments, but which has not ended, and which operates on something not static. How different from our way of thinking.

Fishman (1960) surveyed the intellectual history of the Whorf–Sapir hypothesis from a social psychological perspective and proposed a four-level restatement which facilitated systematic examination of the evidence for and against linguistic relativism (Table 1). One dimension divided

Table 1 **Schematic systematization of the Whorfian hypothesis**

Data of language characteristics	*Data of (cognitive) behaviour*	
	Language data ('cultural themes')	*Non-linguistic data*
Lexical or 'semantic' characteristics	Level 1	Level 2
Grammatical characteristics	Level 3	Level 4

Source: Fishman (1960, p. 336).

features of a particular language into semantic and syntactic characteristics, i.e. aspects of meaning and rules of combination. The second factor splits the resultant 'cognitive' data into verbal behaviour of a group nature which was concerned with 'cultural themes', and non-verbal behaviour which was primarily measured in terms of individual difference. Memory experiments showing that individuals' performance is a function of their ability to code colour chips would be an example of behaviour in the non-verbal domain.

The model allowed Fishman to consider a range of material but is eschewed here for reasons related to his original choice of dimensions. At the time Fishman proposed his semantic/syntactic dichotomy, theoretical linguists dealt confidently with syntactic analysis in the absence of much concern with meaning. Scepticism has greeted such attempts recently and it may prove difficult, in identifying aspects of language which impinge on other cognitive behaviours, to maintain a clear dichotomy between syntax and semantics. A second problem arises from our focus on the effects of cultural differences on psychological processes. Fishman identified anthropological and ethnological data as the prime sources of evidence for the effects of language on levels 1 and 3. Only Fishman's levels 2 and 4 fall squarely within the rubric of cross-cultural psychology adopted here.

The framework proposed by Miller and McNeill (1969) is employed because it stresses the impact of language on particular cognitive processes, i.e. thought, perception and memory and thus makes psychological sense of a proposition fraught with theoretical ambiguity. Their model sets forth the Whorf–Sapir hypothesis in a strong, a weak and a weakest form.

The strong form of the Whorf–Sapir hypothesis asserts that thought derives from language and that this influence can be observed in non-linguistic cognitive behaviour. Thus Hoijer (1951) claimed that Navaho concepts of movement were inexorably bound up with objects because his language required the Navaho speaker expressing movement to specify by verb suffixes the characteristics of the object he manipulated. Hoijer also held that the effects of language were not restricted to situations specifically requiring verbal behaviour but acted diffusely throughout the speaker's thought system.

Language is held to affect perception in the weak form of the hypothesis. Linguistic principles are employed to guide non-verbal behaviour when perceptual difficulties are encountered as the result of ambiguity or arbitrariness. Confronted with the necessity of choosing two like items from among a blue rope, a yellow rope and a blue stick – a choice which would strike English speakers as arbitrary, i.e. one to be based either on colour or shape – a Navaho speaker, used to employing a suffix denoting the nature of objects, would be expected to choose the two pieces of rope. The arbitrariness of the perceptual task would be resolved for a Navaho by the linguistic encoding of shape in the verb suffix.

In the weakest form of the Whorf–Sapir hypothesis, language is believed only to influence cognition by affecting memory. Thus objects which can be easily encoded in a language are more likely to be recalled or recognized than items whose encoding is difficult.

Research based upon Hoijer's speculations about the effects of language on ambiguous perceptual tasks (the weak form of the hypothesis) was carried out by Carroll and Casagrande (1958). Children were presented with ten pairs of objects and asked on each of ten trials to match a third object to one of the original pair. Matching for all ten pairs was deliberately ambiguous in English but four items placed Navaho verb suffix determined choices in competition with choices based on colour, while the remaining six items contrasted shape and size, shape and colour, and colour and size. Statistically significant differences were found between the performance of English-speaking and Navaho-speaking Navaho children on the four Navaho choice items and on two other items. Doubt was cast on this seemingly clear support for the weak form of the Whorf–Sapir hypothesis by results obtained from English-speaking white American children. Their choices were in the same direction as those of Navaho-speaking Navaho children. Carroll and Casagrande explained this unexpected finding in terms of class differences, i.e. upper middle-class children having had toys which socialized attention to form rather than colour.

The *post hoc* explanation for responses based on form which resorted to linguistic experience in one case and play experience in the other, may be clarified by reference to a similar study. Maclay (1958) noted from his own unclear results that real objects are classified in a number of ways and he concluded that the frequency with which the culturally dominant, i.e. language-determined, labels would be employed varied with individual experience. Carroll and Casagrande's upper middle-class American control provided evidence of the shift from a culturally ambiguous choice based on indeterminate linguistic labelling to concern with form as the result of particular experiences. By and large results attempting to show the effect of language on perception have been unclear because insufficient attention has been given to determining the habitual dimensions used within particular subcultural groups.

In examining the results which have supported the weakest form of the hypothesis, i.e. that language affects memory, it is important to note that most paradigms have included pretest measures of subcultural linguistic habits. It is also possible that these measures, i.e. codability and communicability, do come close to reflecting individual labelling patterns. The codability (Brown and Lenneberg, 1954; Lenneberg and Roberts, 1956) and communicability (Lantz and Lenneberg, 1966; Lantz and Stefflre, 1964; Stefflre, Vales and Morley, 1966) of colours has been systematically related to colour recognition memory.

Brown and Lenneberg (1954) assessed the codability of twenty-four colour chips of equal intensity and brightness but differing hues by asking English-speaking subjects to name the chips. Measures were taken of the length of the colour names supplied both in terms of words and syllables, the length of the delay between stimulus presentation and naming, and, also, the degree of agreement with other subjects on the name of a particular colour chip as well as the subject's self-agreement on later testing. The various measures were summed to produce an overall index of codability. The relationship between codability and memory was investigated in a recognition task which required subjects to choose the chips they had been shown earlier, from an array of 120 chips. New samples of subjects from the same population of university undergraduates were tested in four recognition conditions which differed in the number of stimuli used and the length of delay between initial presentation and the memory test. Only when subjects were asked to recognize just one colour chip with a minimal (seven-second) delay, did the relationship between greater codability and easier recognition fail to appear. It is possible that a visual memory mechanism aided recognition with only a seven-second delay. The results suggest that performance on a task involving memory but no overt linguistic response, is determined in part by the language-derived variable, codability. Further support came from a study by Lenneberg and Roberts (1956) with Zuni subjects. The Zuni language places yellow and orange in one category while in English these hues are differentially coded in distinct categories. Zuni speakers' errors in recognizing yellows and oranges were greater than those of English subjects while the performance of bilingual Zuni speakers fell in between.

Operational definitions of codability are clear but the underlying theoretical assumptions are complex. Although codability derives from language as an operational measure, it is a characteristic of the distinctiveness of colours which is realized in a certain manner in particular representational systems, i.e. particular languages. The colours which can be imagined by an English speaker from the names red and yellow have high codability and the labels clearly refer to these hues and not to others. The colour that I label 'blush pink' is only moderately codable and this is reflected in the facts that the same hue might fail to elicit the same label from other English speakers and the colours elicited by the label may fail to replicate the hue which I intended.

A colour name aids communication about colours either with other people or internally, as during rehearsal. Communicability or communication accuracy measures the success with which a colour label conveys a message about the signal inter-individually. Lantz and Stefflre (1964) have assessed the accuracy with which information about a range of colours can be communicated by requiring one group of subjects to produce descriptions of twenty-four colour chips and a second group to use these descriptions to select the original chips from a large array. Communication accuracy or communicability thus reflects the average success of the group in recognizing a colour from its description. Lantz and Stefflre replicated three conditions of the Brown and Lenneberg (1954) study employing measures of codability and communication accuracy and tested the relationships with recognition. Codability was correlated with recognition as in the original study but communication accuracy was even more strongly related to recognition.

In an attempt to disentangle the effects of codability and communication accuracy, Lantz and Stefflre repeated the experiment using 100 colour chips moderately saturated in the blue–green range. Communication accuracy proved a far better predicter than codability. The results were also replicated cross-culturally (Stefflre, Vales and Morley, 1966). Brown (1965) explained the earlier results by suggesting that the effects of linguistic factors were reduced since the low codability of the hues implied that appropriate labels could not be found in the lexicon. Linguistic effects would then only be of a grammatical nature.

Accepting Brown's explanation, Miller and McNeill (1969) added further that conceptual differences underlying the two measures suggested other explanations. In so far as communication accuracy was concerned with the transmission of messages it was susceptible to the influence of non-linguistic situational factors. Thus the embedding of a standard blue hue in a blue–green range changed communication accuracy but not codability, an attribute of the colour realized by language; and since recognition was tested in a particular context, a setting-sensitive measure gave better predictability.

The Whorf–Sapir hypothesis has recently been restated and recognition memory tested again with stimuli drawn from the colour domain (Heider, 1972a; Heider and Olivier, 1972). The starting point of this reformulation was the work of Berlin and Kay (1969). They have argued that there are a limited number of basic colour terms in any language, i.e. eleven, when the achromatic colours, white, grey and black are included, and that the stimuli which speakers of a variety of languages choose as best examples of the basic colour terms form clusters called focal colours in the colour space. Acceptance of this structural interpretation of the colour space led Heider and Olivier to test the relationship between the structure of colour naming and of colours in memory imagery. They also investigated correspondences between the structure of colours in the memory imagery of people whose colour-naming structures differed radically. The complexity of the statistical procedures required to evaluate these structural hypotheses makes it difficult to judge the validity of their results. Heider and Olivier presented evidence which indicated that while the colour-naming structures of English and Dani, a New Guinean language, were very different, speakers of these languages structured the colour space in a similar manner in memory imagery.

The cross-cultural results and Heider's other data provide evidence of cultural universals both in the development of colour naming and of colour memory. If she is correct in her conclusions about the universal characteristics of responses elicited by colour stimuli and that they are constrained by features of primate colour vision, the domain would be an inappropriate one for testing linguistic relativism. Heider did not, however, dismiss the hypothesis that language influences cognition through encoding; rather she pointed out the efficacy of translating a string of digits into binary. While Heider's work offers limited help in resolving the major question of the effect of language on cognition it raises two important points; one is the need to re-examine evidence of cultural differences based upon studies of colour and the other is the possibility that other domains may also include perceptually salient stimuli which support certain 'natural' categories (Heider, 1972b).

The view that we are each intellectually prisoners of the language we speak and the Whorf–Sapir hypothesis in strong and weak forms does not survive systematic psychological investigation. The premise that language affects cognition cannot be dismissed as evidence does indicate that language influences memory in terms of the encoding system it provides for organizing data. Furthermore, the discussion of linguistic relativism highlighted two problems which will be relevant throughout the investigation of the effects of cultural factors on perception and cognition. The first is the need to ensure that the search for cultural differences starts from knowledge of the meaningful, frequent and habitual models which are used in a particular society to organize experience, and second is the possibility that certain characteristics of human physiology ensure that some stimuli are similarly or universally perceived by individuals in all societies. The antithesis of culturally specific factors and universally relevant dimensions is a recurrent theme in cross-cultural comparisons.

Language and representation

It is clear from the review of linguistic relativism that language does not determine thought and that all cultural differences need not be ascribed to linguistic factors. The problem of specifying the role of language in thinking remains. Watson (1924), in the heyday of behaviourism, argued that thinking was subvocal speech but, in this radical form, the view that thinking is language has disappeared. None the less, language remains the mode of representation emphasized in analyses of adult cognitive functioning.

The absence of developed speech until the end of the second year of life has forced developmental theorists to examine alternative modes of knowing and serious considerations of alternative means of representing experience are found in analyses of cognitive development. The genetic theory of Piaget (1962), with its emphasis on the role of action in the growth of concepts and of logical thinking, can be attacked for erring in the opposite direction. Support for Piaget's view that language is but the vehicle for thought comes from studies which indicate that deaf children have a much smaller intellectual handicap than blind children (Furth, 1966).

The model of cognitive development which Bruner *et al.* (1966) has proposed places great emphasis on the role of language but outlines three modes of representation. These are: motoric-based or *enactive* representation, image-dependent *ikonic* representation and various forms of *symbolic* representation. An explanation of the primacy of symbolic representation follows from the specifications of the three modes. Bruner portrayed the symbolic system as actualized in language, tool using, sequential behaviour and the organizing of experience all in accord with properties of categoriality, hierarchy, predication, causation and modification. Compared with enactive representation which is tied to an action sequence which must be run through to realize it, or the ikonic system based upon perception and images which are not easily transformed, the symbolic system is efficient and functions rapidly. The transfer from motoric to symbolic functioning is experienced when a new skill, e.g. operating the gears on a motor car, is first learned as separate acts, but is eventually overlearned and smoothly performed.

Once humans have mastered a skill and represent this achievement symbolically there is little likelihood that the more laborious and slower enactive and ikonic systems will be employed without symbolic representation. The aspect of Bruner's discussion of symbolic representation particularly relevant to this argument is his use of language as the model around which he has fashioned symbolic representation. [This choice reflected the apparent triumph of linguistics in the wake of the Chomskian revolution (cf. Lyons, 1970).] Bruner was careful not to assert that language moulded our view of reality but rather that language and other symbolic activities shared a common, basic root. In giving language a prominent role in cognitive development he suggested that 'for the child to use language as an instrument of thought, he must first bring the world of experience under the control of principles of organization that are in some degree isomorphic with the structural principles of syntax' (Bruner, Olver and Greenfield, 1966, p. 47).

Cultural differences arise because societies differ in the techniques used for bringing the world of experience under the control of syntactical principles. Thus, individuals in different societies vary in the extent to which they are able to invoke symbolic modes of representation. Language *per se* does not lead to the primacy of symbolic representation but the use to which language is put in analysing experience determines growth rates in diverse societies. Thus language leads to a re-ordering of perception only when the child is able to experience contradictions symbolically, as in describing an object which has been transformed as simultaneously 'bigger' and the 'same'. Growth occurs when the child notices the contradiction between his experience and his lingustic description of it by inspection of the logical propositions contained in his statements. Schooling and written language are held to foster the cognitive conflict necessary for development.

Bruner's approach to language places great emphasis on syntax. In his description of the development of logical classes, Bruner borrowed the terms used by Vygotsky (1962) to characterize the progression from heaps, to complexes and then to logical classes but departed from a Vygotskian interpretation in his suggestion that the groupings, at different developmental levels, were based upon syntactically derived symbolic rules. In the primitive heap, for example, Bruner detected an isomorphism with the syntactical rule stating the verb–object relationship.

The Piagetian approach to cognitive development can be placed in opposition to Bruner's formulation in terms of the function of language in growth, but there are also similarities when it is realized that Piaget assigns a role to language but a much smaller one than Bruner. The Genevan researchers have responded to the challenge from Harvard and undertaken an extensive programme to test their formulation of Bruner's position (Inhelder and Sinclair, 1969). They have studied both semantic and syntactic features of children's language at different stages of cognitive development and attempted to train children to use advanced linguistic skills earlier than they would normally be employed. Some evidence that verbal training, especially when combined with appropriate operational exercises, does result in moderate change has emerged. Children have been observed to progress from one substage to another but rarely was it possible to move a child from one major developmental level to another, i.e. from pre-operational to operational thinking. A parallel observed between verbal productions and levels of operational logic was interpreted as evidence 'that an operational component is at work in the acquisition of linguistic structures' (Inhelder and Sinclair, 1969, p. 19). The debate between Geneva and Cambridge is not resolved but in the perspective of this discussion there is agreement that cognitive functioning is modified by language even if the amount of change is debatable.

It is worth examining the Piagetian position, not only because it differs from Bruner's 'instrumental functionalism' but also for the importance it attaches to non-linguistic modes of knowing. In Piaget's (1953, 1954, 1962) descriptions of the first years of life, the human infant is seen to build a world of permanent objects, a system accounting for displacements in space and time and a rudimentary appreciation of causality. These fundamental achievements occur as the result of an active sensorimotor interchange with the environment which allows the child to build and re-build his action-based concepts. Fundamental changes occur at the end of the second year when the child begins to substitute symbols for the objects of his active construction and these eventually become the shared public symbols we call language. In Bruner's terminology enactive-ikonic representation gradually gives way to symbolic representation. An often quoted Piagetian example of the use of sensorimotor schemes or enactive representation is Lucienne's imitation of a matchbox opening accomplished by her opening and closing her mouth with her finger (Piaget, 1962, p. 65). These private signs are the end product of sensorimotor intelligence and the basis upon which language develops. Symbolic representation in both its figurative functions of imitation and imagery and its operative aspects of internalized transformations develops prior to language. Piaget argues that language matures only in so far as the underlying logical operations develop.

For Piaget, then, symbols are at first private but they must become socialized if knowledge is to be shared with others. The statement that symbols are private may be misleading if it is interpreted to mean that they are unique to the individual. The cognitive development which results in private symbols is seen by Piaget to have both a biological and, in part, a universally shared social base. Private symbols develop as the result of the infant's ongoing interaction with his environment and, while their meaning is to some extent socially determined, it is language which makes possible communication of this meaning within a particular society.

A model of cognitive development in which language determines thought can be drawn from the Whorf–Sapir hypothesis with only a little exaggeration. If the Piagetian view is forced to an extreme it can be interpreted as stating that language depends on thought. An interactionist view is probably more realistic, i.e. once language develops it may be used in furthering the growth of problem-solving skills. The position is yet to be spelt out clearly but Bruner's formulations are a beginning. A limitation of 'instrumental functionalism', however, is its emphasis on the culture of Western technological societies for the fullest utilization of symbolic representation.

Although language has primacy in adult thinking it is necessary, in cross-cultural research, to emphasize that the experiential basis of the universal categories of knowledge are first represented in modes other than the symbolic. Whether these modes are labelled enactive and ikonic or sensori-motor, it is well to remember that they are also complex rule-regulated systems. The results of cross-cultural studies of orientation and depth (cf. chapter 3) will be interpreted in terms of such structures.

Without doubt cross-cultural investigations which attack the problem of the role of language in the development of thinking successfully will be interdisciplinary. The contribution of trained linguists will be essential in unravelling the complex interrelations of language and cognition. [Analyses such as that of Gay and Welmers (1971) on Kpelle mathematical terms are starting points for further psychological studies.]

Insiders' and outsiders' views of culture

Language has been considered thus far in terms of the difficulties which it raises in the study of perception and cognition. Linguistics has, however, contributed a paradigm which cross-cultural psychologists are beginning to find useful in formulating research questions.

Certain research problems which have been sensed intuitively are crystallized around the distinction between the *etic* and *emic* approach to other cultures, i.e. the outsiders' and the insiders' views. Berry (1969) has employed the distinction in analysis of cross-cultural methodology in psychological studies. The terms were first taken up by anthropologists re-examining their major assumptions in the late 1950s and early 1960s. Two approaches to the study of culture were identified, that from within and that from outside, and the spirit of the differences caught in the terms 'etic' and 'emic'. The labels were introduced by Kenneth Pike, a linguist, who used them in a unified theory of behaviour which he derived from the linguistic paradigm employed in phonology (Pike, 1954, 1956, 1960). Pike identified the positions thus:

In contrast to the etic approach an emic one is in essence valid for only one language (or one culture) at a time . . . it is an attempt to discover and to describe the pattern of that particular language or culture in reference to the way in which the various elements in that culture are related to each other in the functioning of that particular pattern, rather than an attempt to describe them in reference to a generalized classification derived in advance of the study of that culture (Pike, 1954, p. 8).

An etic analytic standpoint . . . might be called 'external' or 'alien' since for etic purposes the analyst stands 'far enough away' from or 'outside' of a particular culture to see its separate events, primarily in relation to their similarities and their differences, as compared to the events of other cultures, rather than in reference to the sequences of classes of events within that one particular culture. (Pike, 1954, p. 10).

The paradigm which Pike employed was borrowed from phonology. The aim of phonological research is to specify the rules defining significant differences in the sounds used in a particular language. Principles of contrast and combination are employed in order to determine which of the sounds that can be recorded phonetically also serve to mark meaningful differences in a particular language. A miniature experiment can be undertaken with a consonant–vowel–consonant morpheme to illustrate the principles of combination and contrast.

Take the c–v–c morpheme 'lot', keep two elements the same and vary the third to produce – rot, let or lob. English speakers would report that all pairs, lot–rot, lot–let and lot–lob, are different but monolingual Chinese subjects would not distinguish the first pair. In Chinese /1/ and /r/ are not recognized as meaningfully different sounds, that is to say in the same environment these sounds would fail to distinguish different words. Phonemes, then, are defined from the perspective of a particular language and are sounds which in the same environment have the effect of distinguishing meaningfully different sound segments in that language.

Transfer of the phonemic model to other domains raises issues, which, although inherent in phonological analysis are not central. Thus the attempt to apply the model to non-linguist behaviour led Pike (1954) to assert that the seemingly continuous behaviour stream is, like the sound stream, composed of units or experiential particles analogous to the phoneme. Furthermore, he suggested that while meaning functioned as the defining characteristic for contrast in linguistic behaviour, purpose would probably serve to contrast two units of behaviour. In keeping with this assumption an informant would be asked if two behavioural units have the same purpose just as earlier we asked whether lot and rot meant the same thing.

Pike proposed two concepts which together serve as an analytic or methodological tool and which avoid the need to identify minimal behavioural units. The place at which a substitution can occur is labelled a 'spot' and the set of items which can meaningfully be substituted in that 'spot' form the emic 'class'. In the miniature experiment there were three 'spots', i.e. the initial and final consonants and the vowel. The emic 'class' filling the first 'spot' includes in part c, d, g, h, j, etc.

In proposing the 'spot–class' unit, Pike recognized that the 'spot' could occur in larger and in smaller emic units. The distinction may be clarified by first considering the larger emic unit, i.e. the command 'Bring me something to eat!' Its class of meaningful substitutions includes 'Would you like x?', 'Here is some x', and 'There isn't any x.' A 'spot–class' unit at this level Pike has called a 'behavioureme'. A smaller emic unit is the 'spot' x in any of the three replies. The emic 'class' which would satisfy these 'spots' would include anything eaten by the people of a particular culture. Fully aware of the problems of analysing linguistic and non-linguistic behaviour simultaneously, Pike hoped that his paradigm would allow the hierarchical structuring of units within units and afford integration of levels in terms of features, manifestation and distinction.

Cognitive anthropologists and those interested in ethno-science have attempted to use procedures deriving from phonemic analysis in organizing ethnographic data (Tyler, 1970). The aim of their methodological innovation has been to devise public and non-intuitive techniques which would allow classification of the ethnographer's observations, of both spontaneous and provoked behaviour, according to the principles employed by the people he is studying.

Recent re-definitions of culture have supplied the venture with theoretical necessity. In chapter 1, Wallace (1961) was identified with the view that culture is realized in the mutually predictive cognitions of the members of a society. Goodenough (1957) has advocated a related position which equates culture not with objects, behaviour, people or emotions *per se*, but with the structuring of these things in people's minds. The results of adopting such a view of culture are clear. The anthropologist's focal concern becomes the shared cognitive processes of the people he is studying and his descriptions must furnish accounts of culturally meaningful systems of behaviour.

Success, according to the major proponents of this approach, would allow the cognitive anthropologist to comment on the interrelations of language, culture and cognition and to suggest universally meaningful dimensions for genuine cross-cultural comparison and it would involve the working out of generative rules for behaviour similar to those which have been furnished for grammar (Frake, 1962; Goodenough, 1957). A similar position, enunciated by Claude Lévi-Strauss, is known as French structural anthropology. Comment on the specific achievements of these approaches lies outside the scope of this monograph.

It is worth asking how successfully the aim of supplying universally meaningful psychological dimensions for genuine cross-cultural research has been met. Most psychologists (e.g. Triandis, Malpass and Davidson, 1972) view their task as the identification of universals of behaviour and consider the aim of anthropological research as essentially that of the insider. Berry (1969) has proposed that emic analysis should supply an intermediary second step which would transform essentially imposed etic concepts into derived etic concepts and hence ensure culturally meaningful comparisons.

It is clear that the emic approach is attractive to psychologists from the methodological innovations proposed by Berry which would use emic analysis to modify imposed etic concepts, making them derived etic concepts. A more difficult question to answer is how successful the venture will prove: whether it will be more than old wine in new bottles. The concepts of intelligence and field dependence were cited by Berry as examples for the application of the three-stage imposed etic/emic/derived etic analysis. His discussion of field dependence was brief and promissory but intelligence was examined at length.

Berry concluded that neither the concept of intelligence A, which is innate potential, nor the concept of intelligence B, which is the result of innate and environmental factors, could survive emic analysis (see page iii for a fuller discussion of these concepts). The bulk of his argument rested on the assumption that in so far as measures of intelligence B are fragmentary within a given society, i.e. tests only measure a small range of intelligent behaviour, there was little likelihood that overlaps between cultures which would produce the derived etic could include much that would be meaningfully designated intelligent behaviour in any culture. While doubting the value of the derived etic concept of intelligence, Berry recognized the usefulness of intelligence tests for purposes of selection within a particular culture.

The conclusions which Berry reached about intelligence are reasonable but it is worth noting that Vernon's (1969) cross-cultural monograph on intelligence covered much the same ground and yielded much the same evaluation. Rather than employing the emic and etic distinction, Vernon used both his own concept of intelligence C, i.e. that part of intelligent behaviour which tests measure, and Biesheuvel's (1952) intrinsic and extrinsic factors affecting test performance to reach similar conclusions. Thus the novel contribution of etic–emic analysis remains to be demonstrated. Perhaps a question to ask those who stress the emic view is why concepts such as intelligence, which they claim with justification have only limited applicability even within a particular culture, persist in common-sense discussion.

Even if the paradigm can best be described as 'old wine in new bottles', the emic–etic distinction functions as a heuristic which is useful in forcing investigators to be aware of at least two conceptual realities – their own and that of the people they seek to study. Innovations have also been made by using different multi-dimensional scaling techniques. These combine an etic and an emic approach. An example of this research is the cross-cultural use of Osgood's semantic differential. Etic factors, such as evaluation, are differently defined from culture to culture. Triandis, Malpass and Davidson (1972) reported that in one culture the 'good', 'fair', and 'clean' scales were highly correlated while in another 'beautiful', 'honest' and 'nectarlike' scales clustered to form an evaluative factor. Similar methods have been employed in studying role perception (Triandis, Vassilou and Nassiakou, 1968) and person perception (Warr and Haycock, 1970) cross-nationally. Attention to etic–emic differences has thus been followed up with methodological innovations which have yielded more meaningful comparative findings. Language raises many questions for the cross-cultural researcher, but its study has also offered a paradigm which has already proved to be useful.

3 Perception: Stimulus-Defined

Theories of visual perception developed in Europe in the nineteenth century endeavoured to explain how the eye, the optic nerves and the brain functioned to perceive coloured stimuli (Boring, 1942). Initial cross-cultural research, on the other hand, attempted to document the evolution of colour vision by comparing different racial groups. When the question, 'Do non-Europeans perceive colour as we do?' was asked, an assumption was usually made that other races were less advanced and thus their behaviour would offer evidence on the processes of evolution. By the turn of the century there was growing doubt that the races of man evidenced different stages in biological evolution and the methodological point, that colour naming did not mirror the discriminatory capacities of man, had been made (Woodworth, 1910a).

In more sophisticated form, however, the search for cultural universals and differences persists and is the starting point for cross-cultural studies. In a real sense there is only need to take account of cultural variables when they do affect a psychological process in a measurable way; ideally, as more adequate theories about intellectual functioning are developed, hypothesis testing will replace raw empiricism and guide the search for evidence of difference. Provocative advice which offers direction to future research comes from Gibson (1966, p. 321):

The fact is that, although different men do not all use their senses the same way, they *can* all use their senses in the same way. The basis for agreement among men exists in the available stimulus information. Men often disagree but they are not fated to do so by their language or their culture. Disagreement is not caused by inherent differences in their habits of interpreting sensory experience – habits permanently fixed by the words they use. A man can always re-educate his attention. For that matter, a man can invent new words for something he has seen himself.

Evidence examined in chapter 2 buttresses Gibson's position. Only in its weakest form could support be found for the relativist argument.

A comprehensive discussion of the issues raised in these introductory paragraphs is available in Segall, Campbell and Herskovits (1966). Their report on one of the largest cross-cultural studies of perception will be considered on pages 66 to 75 which review studies of optical illusions. In the first section I return briefly to the question of colour perception. Orientation, a problem on which many Euro-American psychologists have worked, but which has only recently been investigated cross-culturally, is considered on pages 61 to 66. The problem examined on pages 55 to 60, depth perception, is related both to orientation and to the fourth and final topic, illusions.

Vision is the primary perceptual process involved in all four discussions. The restriction of attention to the visual system may appear prematurely narrow and even unrepresentative of human perceptual functioning but the decision was determined largely by the nature of the cross-cultural literature. The same emphasis on visual perception is evident in a new book of readings on culture and cognition (Berry and Dasen, 1973). These four topics – colour, orientation, depth and illusions – are the major foci of much cross-cultural research on perception.

Colour perception

Colour can be specified in terms of luminosity, dominant wavelength and purity of admixture, and these measures convey exact stimulus characteristics for use by other researchers. Tempering enthusiasm over accuracy of measurement are Brown and Lenneberg's (1954) observations based upon research in optics. They have noted that while the colour cube has yielded approximately 7,500,000 just noticeable differences in colour discrimination, English speakers record only a small proportion of them. English encodes only 4000 categories with distinct colour names and employs only eight of these frequently. The dimension may be easy to measure physically but the processes which result in behaviour are more difficult to specify.

The discussion of colour perception is shorter than those which follow because aspects of the argument have already been considered. The origins of the cross-cultural investigation of colour perception have been traced to evolutionary theory. While this early research leads to separation of the questions of discriminatory capacity and the linguistic encoding of the colour dimension, these issues are hardly resolved. Discussion of the Whorf–Sapir hypothesis in terms of the codability and communicability of colour and colour names has yielded some clear evidence. For example, Zuni and English differences in the codability of particular wavelengths was shown to affect memory in a colour recognition task (Lenneberg and Roberts, 1956). The linguistic encoding of two different target stimuli in one Zuni colour category inhibited Zuni performance on the memory task. The performance of bilingual Zuni fell between that of monolingual Zuni and English speakers. Evidence here is not of differences in colour discrimination but differences in performance on a memory task. Differences in linguistic encoding of the colour dimension were seen as the sources of differential success.

The question of the encoding in different languages of the colour dimension has intrigued anthropologists. Ray (1953), in a carefully controlled study using colour samples of specified wavelength at nineteen points along the perceivable colour dimension, concluded from a comparative examination of colour naming in ten North American Indian languages that there were no natural divisions of the colour spectrum which might lead to universal category characteristics. In particular, he concluded that there appeared to be no psychological, physiological or anatomical limits to colour systems. As in English, each of the systems investigated utilized only a small range of the discriminable differences. Ray concluded that colour encoding was determined by the need to furnish meaningful verbal responses and to allow communication within a particular culture. A psychologist recalling Miller's (1956) comments on the 'magical number seven' might hesitate to agree that there are no psychological constraints on colour encoding and might note that Ray's analysis showed a range of only three to eight categories which were normally used to code the colour spectrum.

The issue is far from resolution. Berlin and Kay (1969) have argued and documented the case for a universalistic view of colour naming. They have asserted that there are eleven basic colour categories – white, black, red, green, yellow, blue, brown, purple, pink, orange and grey – but if white, black and grey are excluded, only eight chromatic colours. Their evidence included an examination of the twenty-two actually occurring basic colour lexicons from the potential of 2038 possible combinations which their eleven categories might yield. They have argued that it is more meaningful to compare the foci of colour terms, i.e. best examples, rather than the boundaries which are unreliable for individuals across repeated tests and which are non-overlapping in different lexicons. Berlin and Kay have also taken up the evolutionary argument once again and have claimed that their rule of occurrence for basic colour terms can be extended to describe the evolutionary stages which result in increasingly more complex basic colour lexicons.

The issue of the universality or arbitrariness of the lexical coding of colour and of the evolution of basic colour terms is largely the concern of linguists and cognitive anthropologists. The psychological studies of Heider (see page 43) suggest that the colour domain is not particularly suitable for studying the effects of language on cognition because its structure may be universally constrained by the physiology of colour vision. The question – 'What problems concerning the perception of colour might engage the cross-cultural psychologist?' – remains. The hint that attention may be responsible for cultural differences has been offered by Gibson (1966).

Although this hypothesis is little more than a guess in regard to the perception of colour it is an idea worth pursuing.

Examination of the studies of Suchman (1966) and Serpell (1968b, 1969a) on attentional preference for colour or form in African children may help to fill two gaps in the cross-cultural picture. One gap results from a lack of research on developmental aspects of perception and the other from an ignorance of attentional processes.

European and American studies generally show a developmental tendency for children of increasing age to select form over colour in an ambiguous choice situation (Corah, 1964; Descoeudres, 1914; Suchman and Trabasso, 1966). The Carroll and Casagrande (1958) study, reviewed on pages 40 to 41, attempted to link colour/form choice to language but was confounded by the finding that upper middle-class American children were more likely to select form-determined alternatives than were some Navaho children. Suchman (1966) who had noted a lack of increasing form preference in deaf children, measured the preference of 120 Hausa children in Nigeria. She found that they also failed to exhibit a maturational tendency to choose form and furthermore, that colour preference persisted into adolescence. Serpell (1968b, 1969a) replicated Suchman's findings in his rural Zambian samples but from evidence of form preference in urban Zambian samples suggested that educational attainment as well as mental age might be better predictors than chronological age of the shift from colour to form preference. He also concluded, from the lack of differences between Indian and English children in a fee-paying school, that specific aspects of the educational experience might account for the developmental tendency previously observed in European and American studies.

Serpell explained his results, those of Suchman and of Carroll and Casagrande by suggesting that experience educates attention. He pointed out that deaf children are given less instruction about form and that upper middle-class children not only have toys emphasizing form, but their tuition directs attention to the form dimension even though the toys are brightly coloured. Serpell's explanation awaits further support, especially experimental evidence on how attention is trained in childhood, but these investigations should suggest to other workers that there is still much to learn about cross-cultural and developmental factors in preferential attention to colour.

Orientation

Anthropologists have reported the difficulties experienced by informants in recognizing themselves in photographs (Herskovits, 1950). Although this problem involves perception of depth and contour as well as orientation, accounts of difficulty in determining which way round to hold a photograph are relevant here.

Systematic cross-cultural studies of orientation date from the 1930s (Beveridge, 1939; Nissen, Machover, and Kinder, 1935), but until recently these have been few and most reports have been rather speculative. Beveridge tested Ghanaian Training College students' perception of the horizontal using a tilting cupboard. He rotated subjects up to twenty-five degrees off the horizontal in a dimly lighted cupboard and then required them to fix a stick parallel to the ground outside. The mean distortion from the true horizontal was smaller for the all-male sample of African students than for a European sample of men and women which Beveridge also tested. Statistical tests of performances above and below the combined groups' error median showed African performance to be significantly more accurate than that of Europeans. Beveridge explained the greater accuracy of African subjects by suggesting that they depended more on internal cues than Europeans and were less affected by misleading visual cues.

Beveridge's hypothesis has been extended by Wober in studies of field dependence (Witkin *et al.*, 1962; Wober, 1966, 1967). Wober required Nigerian subjects in a darkened room to adjust a luminous rod within a luminous frame so that the rod was horizontal; either the chair on which the subjects sat or the frame, as well as the rod, were tilted. Drawing support from Beveridge's work and his own findings, that Nigerian judgments were more accurate when the chair was tilted than when the frame was tilted, Wober suggested that cultures weight differently sensory information coming from different sense modalities. Europeans are expected to excel in tasks dependent on visual cues while Africans would be superior when dealing with non-visual information. These differences in sensory skill and integration are captured in the concept of differing 'sensotypes'. Unfortunately Wober did not test a European sample using the same procedures (cf. chapter 6 for further considerations). In the absence of comparative data, Wober's claim that Europeans and West Africans represent different 'sensotypes' rests largely on Beveridge's data. There is still need for evidence of European performance on the Rod and Frame Test under the conditions employed by Wober in Nigeria and for systematic study of West African and European performance on other perceptual tasks which rely on non-visual cues. Poortinga (1971) reported no evidence of a black superiority in processing auditory material in a careful comparison of the information transmission capacities of black and white South African students dealing with simple auditory and visual stimuli.

Studies in which Africans have been required to reproduce patterns offer indirect support for the interpretations of Beveridge and Wober, and in particular for the corollary that African performance will suffer on orientation tasks mainly dependent on visual cues (Biesheuvel, 1949; Jahoda, 1956; Maistriaux, 1955; Shapiro, 1960). In comparisons of Ghanaian school children of educated and illiterate parents, Jahoda (1956) found better performance on the Kohs Block Test than on the Goldstein–Scheerer Cube Test and better all-round performance from students with educated parents. Jahoda ascribed very large and numerous rotation errors on the Cube Test to an apparent disregard for the spatial arrangements of the blocks on the table and to a general lack of attention to figure ground relations. He also noted great difficulty with patterns on the diagonal and he ascribed improvement on the Kohs Blocks to the absence of diagonal patterns on this test. Maistriaux (1955) has also attributed African difficulties on a copying test to lack of attention to the orientation of the standard form.

Shapiro (1960) has reported overwhelming failure by illiterate African subjects in a study based on the first eight items of the Drawing Rotation Test. Educated and illiterate Central Africans were compared with Englishmen classified as normal, brain-damaged psychiatric patients and mental defectives, and non-organic mental defectives of two intelligence ranges, the lowest having IQs between 55 and 79. Shapiro measured rotation errors as the difference between the orientation of the standard pattern and the reproduction, expressed in degrees. Illiterates produced rotation errors significantly larger than any other group. Despite the extremely unusual nature of the errors made by the illiterate subjects, Shapiro did not consider Biesheuvel's (1949) hypothesis that Africans may redefine the task and respond in accordance with their own task requirements rather than those set by the experimenter; instead he suggested two other explanatory factors. The first, based on the reasoning of Jahoda and Maistriaux, proposed that aspects of the forms may have led the illiterate subjects to disregard information from the background, i.e. orientation of the standard form. Secondly, he suggested that rotations may have occurred when ambiguous symmetry cues led to confusion in locating the top of the figure.

In contrast to these reports of difficulty with orientation in pattern copying are the studies of Serpell (1968a, 1969b, 1971b) in which he demonstrated that African children can perform as well as European children on visual tasks concerned solely with orientation. Serpell's work stems from a research tradition which is comparative in a wide sense and originally focused on infra-human organisms. Rudel and Teuber (1963) had shown that American children's difficulties in a discrimination learning task were systematically related to the orientation of the forms and decreased with age. These results extended the generality of findings which had been reported for rats (Lashley, 1938), for octopuses (Sutherland 1957) and for goldfish (Mackintosh and Sutherland, 1962). Rudel and Teuber concluded that the similarity across species was a remarkable feature of pattern perception, whether one chose to ascribe it to common aspects of the nervous system or to learning.

Serpell replicated the Rudel and Teuber study as closely as conditions in

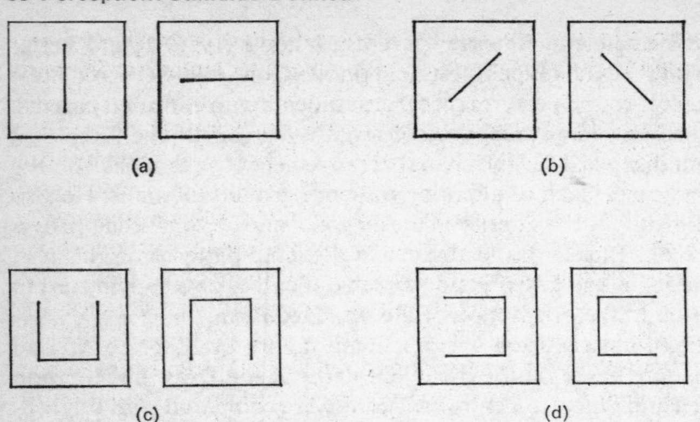

Figure 3 Orientation stimuli (adapted from Rudel and Teuber, 1963, p. 893)

Zambia allowed, adding only a pre-test condition in which the youngest children were trained on a colour discrimination in order to avoid strong position habits. The items used by Rudel and Teuber and shown in Figure 3 can be examined while considering Serpell's results. The only major difference in the performance of Zambian and American children lies in the chronological age at which mastery occurs; Zambian children were two to three years older than American children when they learned a discrimination. Serpell's contention that educational experience, both of a formal and informal nature, would account for these age differences is supported by observations on socialization in the two cultures and by an experimental study in which a training procedure led to improved learning of the usually difficult discrimination (b) by American children (Jeffrey, 1966).

Comparisons of results across the two cultures show similar improvements with age and schooling and similar patterns of item difficulty. The right–left mirror image (d) discrimination was learned more slowly than the top–bottom (c) transformation of the same form. The horizontal–vertical item (a) was much easier to learn than the oblique (b) discrimination. These positive indications that African children respond to the orientation of forms in a manner similar to that of European and American children led Serpell to reconsider the explanations of African failure on pattern-copying tasks. He questioned explanations which held that uneducated Africans attended to the internal shape of the pattern at the expense of information about the orientation of the pattern in relation to its surroundings. Thorough review of the cross-cultural literature and relevant studies on Western children and brain-damaged adults led Serpell (1969b) to propose a response organization hypothesis which could both account for rotation errors in copying and for the finding that Zambian children learn an orientation-based discrimination in a manner similar to Western children.

The response organization hypothesis turns the earlier discussion of the studies by Jahoda (1956), Maistriaux (1955) and Shapiro (1960) on its head in suggesting that uneducated Africans are not unaware of the orientation of the standard form but rather that they have adopted a response strategy organized around a different orientational scheme. Evidence to support this view comes from analysis of errors made in copying which shows their systematic nature and from reports of consistent orientation preferences for a variety of shapes.

Ghent, who holds that form perception in young children is dependent upon orientation cues, has shown that younger children's recognition of familiar and abstract forms is impaired by unfamiliar orientations (Ghent, 1960; Ghent and Bernstein, 1961). Immediately relevant to the response organization hypothesis is Ghent's (1961) study showing that American children aged four to five years are extremely consistent in their preferred orientation of geometric figures; and these results have been replicated in Iran (Antonovsky and Ghent, 1964). Only on the colour card made up of a rectangle of blue and of orange was there a cultural reversal, with Iranian children consistently preferring to have the orange section on top.

Serpell (1969b, 1971a) has furnished similar evidence. He analysed the first trial choices of Zambian children on the Rudel and Teuber items and found a statistically significant preference for the vertical form on item (a) and among urban children for the inverted ⊔ on item (c). It is not surprising that the rural children, who were all at school, showed an initial preference more consistent with alphabet training. Serpell has shown that when children, both naïve and test sophisticated, are asked to draw a pencil, a majority produce vertically oriented drawings of a pencil with over two-thirds showing the point at the top of the paper. Results from tasks which used meaningful drawings of lifelike objects whose normal focal point varies, i.e. a plant with leaves on top, an arrow and a broom, showed in all but the oldest urban groups a preference for the focal point, i.e. leaves, arrowhead or bristles, to be at the top. From the Zambian and Iranian data it may be inferred that uneducated African adults bring strong orientation preferences to pattern-copying tasks.

Serpell has also analysed errors made in copying. For example, when children were required to place a pencil in the same position as a vertical standard, the majority of errors were of a mirror image nature, i.e. reversals. Horizontally or obliquely positioned standards tended to be copied as verticals. Even in pencils correctly positioned, there was a tendency for a correctly copied oblique to be rotated slightly towards the vertical.

Serpell has explored the process implications of the response sequence hypothesis. Urban children from seven to thirteen years old were given a task which required them to copy a pattern composed of three differently shaped, coloured figures displayed in either a horizontally or vertically oriented line. A striking relationship between working systematically in one direction and success was observed. Successful children employed significantly more top to bottom strategies; though not statistically significant, left–right strategies were also in the majority among children who successfully copied horizontal displays. Serpell's theory allows him to make a specific prediction about the direction of the gross rotation errors which Shapiro (1960) reported. The published data do not allow tests of these predictions.

The response sequence hypothesis cannot explain the results which Deregowski (1968a) reported on the orientation copying skills of Zambian subjects in an experiment using as standard stimuli photographs of three-dimensional models taken from different points of orientation. Subjects were required to set three-dimensional models to match the orientations shown in the photographs. A later study by Serpell and Deregowski (1971), using an extended version of the photograph three-dimensional model copying technique, fails to support either Deregowski's suggestion that subjects interpreted the frame of reference of the photograph as though it were the frame of reference provided by the subject's retinal image of the model or Serpell's sequential processing hypothesis. The authors were unable to find any hypotheses in the literature which could explain the pattern of rotation errors. The theoretical issues are unresolved; the experimental task is complex, combining tests of orientation and pictorial depth perception and different factors may determine these processes. The discussion of depth perception which follows indicates the difficulties which have been encountered in trying to explain the failure of African subjects to interpret depth in two-dimensional representations of three dimensions. In addition, Deregowski (1971a) has shown on a simple recognition task that photograph-to-model matching, or vice versa, is more difficult than matching within a single mode of representation, be it pictures or models.

It remains an achievement that Serpell was able to suggest an explanation which is a plausible account of the strategy employed by uneducated Africans in simple tests of orientation. He (Serpell, 1971a) has presented further evidence of Zambians' preference for the vertical over the horizontal in comparisons of simple lines and Bender–Gestalt figures. The ingenuity of the response sequence hypothesis is that it is based on an 'insider's' view of the copying task. This accomplishment reflects a good deal of experience in working with Zambian children as well as considerable theoretical sophistication.

Pictorial depth perception

In our frequent and facile experiences with the pictorial representation of reality, we are unaware of the rules on which it depends and may forget that perspective, in particular, is a recent achievement in Western art. Ancient Egyptians made use of superimposition to represent depth but never employed the fore-shortening that we accept without question. Chinese artists used both superimposition and differences in object size to indicate distance, but their rule system specified line divergence rather than convergence to represent depth. It was only in the Notebooks of Leonardo da Vinci that the system of geometric perspective allowing realistic representation of distance was first formalized. Leonardo da Vinci realized that perspective was but one of the cues which the viewer used when entertaining a hypothesis that the flat drawing before him represented a three-dimensional reality. As might be expected from the preceding discussion, his advice to artists included rules concerning the orientation of objects in space as well as size constancy and superimposition.

Despite ample anecdotal evidence of the difficulties experienced by non-Western peoples in interpreting pictures and photographs and the brief history of perspective in European art, systematic cross-cultural investigations of pictorial depth perception are recent and limited. Current interest can be traced to Hudson (1960, 1962a, 1962b, 1967) who developed a set of pictorial stimuli which have been used to determine whether a variety of peoples of different ages and cultures are two-dimensional or three-dimensional viewers of line drawings.

Both theoretical and applied questions have furnished impetus for this research. Hudson investigated career aspirations using pictorial stimuli with culturally and educationally heterogeneous samples of black South African factory workers. He (Hudson, 1960) concluded that the shaded line drawings of real-life situations used to provoke statements of career aspirations were of equivalent meaning neither for individuals in various tribal subsamples nor for the subjects and the experimenter. Interpretation of projected occupational choice was made inappropriate by the fundamental lack of stimulus equivalence. The problems arising from the use of projective tests in cross-cultural research have provoked considerable discussion (e.g. Lindzey, 1961), but they led Hudson to turn his attention to investigating the cultural determinants of two- and three-dimensional interpretations of pictorial representations of reality.

Object size, superimposition and linear perspective were the cues for depth perception which Hudson studied. In his earlier work he assessed depth perception in horizontal and vertical space with eleven outline drawings and one photograph (Hudson, 1960). The dimension used in Hudson's later work (1962a, 1962b, 1967) and in most replication studies

(Deregowski, 1968b; Kilbride and Robbins, 1968; Kilbride, Robbins and Freeman, 1968; Mundy-Castle, 1966) is horizontal space in which objects may be thought of as aligned from left to right. The objects thus arranged appear to the two-dimensional (2D) viewer to lie in only one plane; but the three-dimensional (3D) viewer, attending to differential size, overlap or linear convergence, sees the objects in a number of planes. Similarly, along the vertical dimension objects may be seen as piled on top of each other, 2D, or projected in a number of planes 3D.

Figure 4 shows four cards selected from the original set depicting depth in horizontal space. Cards 1 and 2 employ depth cues of size and superimposition while cards 3 and 4 make use, in addition, of linear perspective in suggesting depth. Subjects are asked (a) What do you see? (b) What is the man doing? and (c) Which is nearer the man, the elephant or antelope? Mundy-Castle (1966) added questions asking whether the man could see the antelope and vice versa. He also required explanations for the replies. The response, 'the antelope', in reply to question (c) was classified as 3D and all other replies considered 2D.

Originally Hudson (1960) tested eleven samples, six composed of adults of differing educational and occupational background, including black teachers, and five samples of children at different stages in their educational careers. The groups included black and white South Africans as well as black adults from the neighbouring countries which supply mine labour. Over all, the five school samples and black teachers produced a higher proportion of 3D responses than the five other adult samples – which included a white group from an inbred, isolated and culturally restricted rural community. The school samples performed better in response to the photograph than to all the outline drawings of the same scene except that dependent on superimposition (card 2 as shown in Figure 4); white beginners and black children at the end of their primary course were less frequently (72 per cent and 76 per cent) classed as 3D than were white children at the same late stage all of whom gave 3D responses (100 per cent) to the photograph and card 2.

Failure to name items in the drawings was related to 2D perception but the ability to name the objects did not predict 3D responding. Misidentifications occurred more frequently to items associated with depth. The road was frequently seen as an elephant trap or the hill identified as a path. The failure of illiterates to recognize the elephant in card 2, which employs superimposition, can be interpreted as additional evidence of unfamiliarity with the conventions of pictorial representation. The five adult samples were more consistent in their responses than the school samples whose responses were influenced by particular stimulus factors; the photograph and the item based on size plus superimposition produced more 3D responses. The per-

Figure 4 Depth perception. (Note that the sizes of figures in card 2 are slightly larger than in the other three cards, also that the actual distance between the man and antelope is shorter) (from Mundy-Castle, 1966, p. 191)

formance of the white school beginners only resembled that of other school-going groups on these particular items. Intelligence predicted 3D perception for young white children, but most white children gave consistent 3D responses by the end of the primary course.

Hudson concluded that his test was a valid measure of pictorial depth perception, that cultural experience and specific educational experiences were relevant determinants of dimensional perception and that genetic factors could not be ruled out. Socialization in the Western pictorial mode is important although we are as yet unable to specify the precise dimensions of this experience. With this support, individual differences in rates of intellectual maturation (intelligence) affect the ability to entertain a 3D hypothesis; but without it, black adults who have had the ameliorative experience of Western schooling (the sample of teachers) have difficulty in sustaining depth perception. Evidence from a study carried out among Baganda aged four to seventy-five years casts some doubt on Hudson's conclusion (Kilbride and Robbins, 1968). Correct naming of the roads in cards 3 and 4 (see Figure 4) was considered evidence of the employment of linear perceptive cues in depth perception. Linear perspective response levels and amounts of education were positively related and this correlation was sustained in separate analyses for adults and children. Thus, for the Baganda, the education of adults appears to be related to depth perception in so far as it depends on linear perspective cues. The impact of education seems to be less in Ghana; Mundy-Castle (1966) reported far fewer 3D responses for school children five to ten years old than Hudson (1960) found for any South African groups of the same age.

Differences in proportions of 3D responses to various test items in the South African school samples suggest that superimposition may be used as evidence to sustain a 3D hypothesis earlier than linear perspective or size constancy cues. In a study of Baganda children aged four to twenty years, Kilbride, Robbins and Freeman (1968) compared the use of superimposition and size cues with levels of schooling. They found significant evidence that superimposition is acquired as a cue to depth perception earlier than object size and they interpreted this as indicating that the use of superimposition requires less formal education. The hypothesis is reasonable but in our ignorance of educational practices relevant to the utilization of any cues to depth perception this conclusion is still difficult to confirm or refute.

Hudson (1962 a and b) has also extended his research including other measures of depth perception and other samples. Investigations using foreshortened drawings and analyses of drawings freely produced by subjects from different cultural groups yielded results congruent with earlier findings. Hudson found that Indian school children in South Africa gave fewer 3D responses than black children and an analysis of consistency over three pictorial items produced the following proportions of 3D responses: European children 70 per cent, Coloured 48 per cent, Bantu 35 per cent and Indian 30 per cent. Differences in general cultural experience can account for these results especially when attention is given to the particular conventions upon which Indian pictorial representation depends. Indians react differently to test situations as well (Lloyd and Pidgeon, 1961).

Research by Dawson (1963), Deregowski (1968a, 1968b, 1969) and Mundy-Castle (1966) has extended Hudson's work in a number of directions. Dawson (1963) in an extensive study of perceptual and cognitive skills assessed Mende and Temne recruits for work in mines in Sierra Leone using a variety of instruments, including an adaptation of Hudson's Depth Perception Test. He reported a correlation not only between 3D responses and years of schooling but also between Kohs Block and form board scores, presumably measuring intelligence, field dependence and depth perception (see pages 140 to 142). In addition, results from a controlled study, in which one group received six months' training in three-dimensional perception, showed significantly greater improvement in the trained group and a correlation of 0·89 between improvement and initial Kohs Block performance. Interpreted in terms of the response organization hypothesis of Serpell (1969b), poor performance on the Kohs Block Test is a consequence of an inappropriate processing schema, while a good performance would be indicative either of less rigid adherence to an inappropriate schema or of processing sequences more like those of the experimenter. Viewed from this perspective, individuals with good Kohs Block performances might be expected to benefit more readily from training in Western perceptual conventions.

Deregowski (1968a, 1968b, 1968c, 1969), has undertaken a number of studies in an effort to understand pictorial perception in Zambian adults and children. In a study replicating Hudson's work, Deregowski (1968b) used an additional and new measure of depth perception, i.e. a task in which subjects were required to build in three-dimensional space an object shown in a line drawing. He tested Zambian schoolboys and male domestic servants who had an educational background similar to South African mine workers but who were exposed to the visual world of Europeans in their work situation. In comparisons on Hudson's test schoolboys produced more 3D responses than domestic servants but both Zambian groups produced significantly fewer 3D responses than comparable South African groups. Deregowski concluded that passive exposure to a rich pictorial environment in the absence of instruction about the system of representation had little impact on pictorial understanding.

Questions about the generality of Hudson's test as a measure of pictorial perception are raised by the finding that subjects whose responses were classed as 2D on Hudson's test could produce models from drawings. One of the sources of conceptual difficulty may lie in Deregowski's use of a generous scoring system in identifying perceivers on his new task; he stated that many of the constructions scored 3D were inaccurate, containing odd members, bizarre orientations and omissions. Another curious result is the failure of some 3D responders to be able to identify the items in Hudson's drawings. Deregowski's work is interesting for the questions it raises as well as those which he attempts to answer. In his reply to Du Toit's (1966) attack upon Hudson's work in terms of linguistic relativity, Deregowski suggested that the discrepancy between the two measures indicated that linguistic structure could not be the sole determinant of pictorial depth perception. Similarly, the discrepancy between 3D responding and item identification would suggest that semantic knowledge is not sufficient to ensure depth perception.

Systematic knowledge of the effects of cultural experience on pictorial perception is generally restricted to Africa. The literature indicates that depth perception is to some extent task specific (Deregowski, 1968a) and further evidence suggests that it is also stimulus specific. Deregowski (1968c) has shown that familiar animals are recognized from photographs by adults from a pictureless environment but that the use of unfamiliar models leads to failure. Superimposition is the first cue used in depth perception while the use of linear perspective is related to formal education. Cultural experience and formal education together influence the generality of pictorial depth perception but special training is also effective (Dawson, 1963; Hudson, 1967). Furthermore, Deregowski (1971b) has claimed that while depth perception is improved with education it is uninfluenced by the orientation of the stimulus for Zambian students but orientation-sensitive in Scottish subjects.

Information is sufficient to suggest caution in the use of pictorial representation in communicating information be it about health, agricultural change or other aspects of community development in a non-Western cultural setting. Applied research has also shown the dependence of pictorial recognition on formal education and stimulus factors related to familiarity, realism, size and detail (Fonseca and Kearl, 1960; Holmes, 1963; MacLean, 1960). Knowledge about the processes which allow Westerners to translate 2D representations into hypotheses about 3D space is incomplete. Precise understanding of the impact of cultural variables on pictorial depth perception may have to await completion of a formal model of picture interpretation (cf. Clowes, 1971) which describes the rules used in making 3D interpretations of 2D representations.

Visual illusions

Perceptual behaviour which goes wrong has fascinated mankind for centuries. The Bible is replete with tales of dreams and hallucinations and these states have occasioned considerable anthropological inquiry (cf. D'Andrade, 1961; Eggan, 1961). Responses to illusion figures, unlike dreams and hallucinations, are examples of faulty perceptual behaviour which meet Tajfel's (1969) criterion that stimulus material for social psychological investigation of perception must allow the possibility of only one correct answer.

The finding that when the two lines of the Müller–Lyer illusion are metrically equal they appear unequal to most subjects has intrigued researchers for a century. Gregory (1966) has argued that the systematic study of these non-veridical responses was influential in the early development of experimental psychology. Although a hundred years have elapsed since they were first studied, psychologists are only beginning to understand the phenomena (Over, 1968) but our knowledge may be extended if we can identify the variables which lead to faulty perception.

Cross-cultural investigation of visual illusions began about the turn of the century when W. H. R. Rivers (1901), one of the psychologists accompanying the Cambridge Expedition to the Torres Straits, collected responses to the Müller–Lyer and Horizontal–Vertical illusions (Figure 5, items a, b, and c) and other figures. In the Torres Straits studies, Rivers presented a standard horizontal line and asked subjects to draw a vertical line of equal length to form a T, an L or a +. Later while working among the Todas in South India he developed a mechanical testing device which required subjects to set an adjustable vertical rod to match the horizontal standard (Rivers, 1905). The apparatus for Müller–Lyer testing was improved but, despite these changes in instrumentation, the European samples (including children), which Rivers tested, evidenced as great or greater susceptibility to overestimation on the Müller–Lyer as any of the non-Western groups. Conversely, on the Horizontal–Vertical items, non-Western peoples tended to make grosser overestimates of length whatever the method of administration.

Rivers suggested, in explaining his findings, that the two illusions came from different classes. The nature–nurture issue was raised by his argument that the Horizontal–Vertical illusion came from a class which had a primarily physiological basis but was modified by Western experience, while the Müller–Lyer illusion came from a class which was dependent upon psychological factors. Different methods of measuring illusion responses were not used but Rivers's study, in pointing to systematic differences in responses across cultures, in considering the classification of illusions and in offering theoretical interpretations of the underlying perceptual process, did, in fact, explore most of the issues which have been taken up by later researchers. Discussion of the studies which have been concerned with the effects of cultural experience on illusion responses will revolve around these issues, i.e. methods of assessment, the classes of illusions, the nature of cultural differences and their theoretical explanation.

Current interest in cross-cultural research on visual illusions can be traced to an extensive study organized by Segall, Campbell and Herskovits (1963, 1966) and their publication of a field manual providing fifty standard

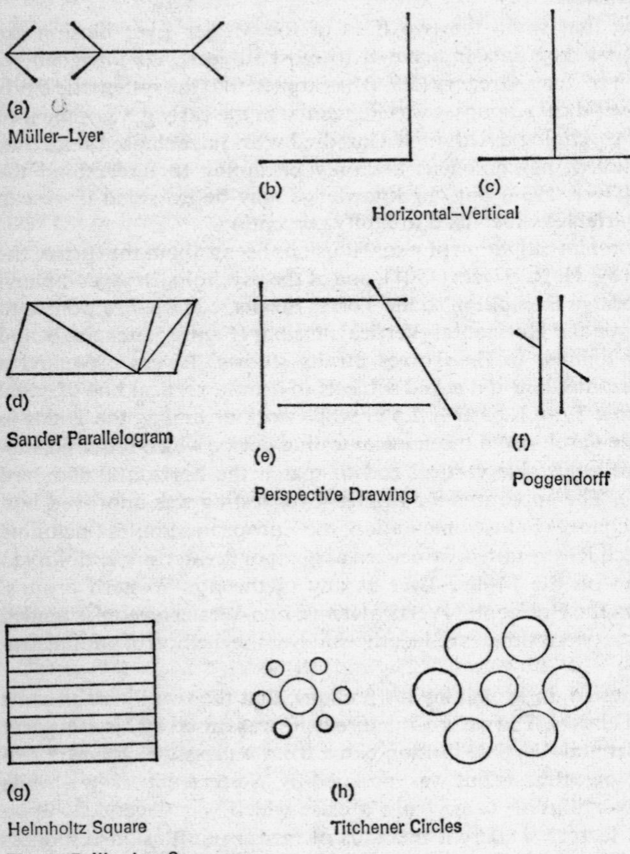

Figure 5 Illusion figures
(adapted from Jahoda and Stacey, 1970, p. 180)

stimuli for testing responses to the first six items shown in Figure 5, as well as the comprehension checks discussed in chapter 1 (Herskovits, Campbell and Segall, 1956). In order to facilitate communication across cultures the crucial segments of figures were drawn in red ink, while the rest of the figure was presented in black; the line segments composing each figure were separated from each other by a millimeter space, except in the case of the Sander Parallelogram (Figure 5, item d).

Researchers, primarily in Africa, but also in the Philippines and the United States, collected data, and their twenty-eight samples included adults and children from the same society, adults only from some societies and one sample where only children were tested. Before any cross-cultural comparisons were undertaken individual replies were checked for consistency (see pages 22 to 23) and points of subjective equality were calculated for each sample using mean number of illusion responses.

Rivers's results were replicated in large measure. Euro-American groups showed the highest susceptibility on the Müller–Lyer and Sander Parallelogram, but on the Horizontal–Vertical illusions non-Western subjects were generally more susceptible. No meaningful differences emerged on the Perspective Drawing and results on the Poggendorff illusion were uninterpretable (Figure 5, items e and f). Data from southern Senegal, Australia and additional information on American children, gathered later, were also congruent with the major findings and with Rivers's reports.

Although Euro-American and non-Western susceptibility patterns were similar to those reported by Rivers, the method of assessment and the theoretical explanations offered by Segall, Campbell and Herskovits differed considerably. Rivers used variants of the method of average error, requiring his subjects to match or reproduce the standard stimulus by manipulating or drawing another variable stimulus. In the method of constant stimuli employed by Segall, Campbell and Herskovits, subjects were required to judge which of a set of two stimuli was longer.

In seeking to explain cultural differences, Segall, Campbell and Herskovits re-examined the nature–nurture issue. They took exception to Rivers's suggestion of a physiological basis to cultural differences of the Horizontal–Vertical illusions and argued that an explanation of perceptual processes relying on hereditary factors was less plausible than one based upon learning. Evidence cited to support their argument ranged from studies of humans who regained sight in adulthood but who had to learn to see (Gregory and Wallace, 1963), to studies of animals deprived of vision from birth (Riesen, 1947, 1958). The particular learning hypotheses which they proposed derived from ideas about probabilistic functionalism developed by Brunswik (1956) implying that visual habits are acquired in respect of their ecological cue validity. Thus, different visual environments, ecologies, give rise to different visual habits or sets. The errors which occur in the atypical settings provided by illusion figures result from the application of normal and useful processes of perception to ambiguous stimuli. Tajfel (1969) has attempted to 'unpack' the concept of ecological cue validity and to delineate effects of functional salience and familiarity.

The 'carpentered world' and 'foreshortening' hypotheses which derive from assumptions of ecological cue validity were used to account for the cultural differences on the Müller–Lyer and Horizontal–Vertical illusions. The carpentered world hypothesis stated that individuals who lived in a rectangularized environment were more likely to interpret oblique and acute angles as right angles and hence to view two dimensional drawings in terms of depth. Gregory's (1966) size-constancy theory of illusions, relating depth perception to inappropriate compensations deriving from constancy scaling, would predict greater susceptibility for individuals who make depth interpretations of drawings. Segall, Campbell and Herskovits accepted Gregory's interpretation which also leads to the prediction that Europeans will be more prone to overestimation on the Müller–Lyer illusion.

The foreshortening hypothesis approached the question of pictorial representation differently by suggesting that compensations made by individuals living in open and spacious environments were transferred directly to the stimuli of Horizontal–Vertical illusions. An ecological inventory completed for each society was used to predict the order of cultural differences, but results were somewhat disappointing.

The differential success of the ecological hypotheses in predicting illusion susceptibility is hardly surprising. Analyses of perceptual processes thus far have revealed lacunae in our understanding of the inferences which Africans make when processing pictorial material intended to assess orientation or depth. Factors such as age, education and Westernization, already considered, are again relevant. The remaining discussion of cross-cultural studies of illusions is organized around three topics – methods of assessing illusion responses, the classification of illusions, and the nature of cultural differences and their explanation.

Methods of assessing illusion responses

Segall, Campbell and Herskovits (1966) have attempted to explain Bonte's (1962) findings that the Müller–Lyer illusion susceptibility of Europeans and Africans from the Congo differed significantly only when subjects were tested by the Herskovits, Campbell and Segall (1956) method of constant stimuli and not when the method of average error, employing a mechanical apparatus which the subjects set to produce stimulus equality, was used. They suggested that the nature of apparatus, i.e. two wooden panels fitted so that the adjustable member slides under the standard, led African subjects to misinterpret the task so that they attempted to adjust ———< until it equalled <———>. Jahoda (1966), also using an adjustable apparatus, found highly significant European–Ghanaian differences in the direction predicted by Segall, Campbell and Herskovits. He demonstrated, however, that the misinterpretation hypothesis could not account for his results on the Müller–Lyer because he failed to find the bimodal distribution of scores which would be expected if some subjects had attempted to equate the total segments of the figure while others had correctly tried to equate line segments. An advantage of the constant stimuli method is that it allows systematic inspection of the data and elimination of the subject whose inconsistency suggests failure to understand the task; it has been adopted by Jahoda (1971; Jahoda and Stacey, 1970) in his recent work.

Both the original Segall stimuli and a modified set of all black figures were used in a study employing a number of Ugandan and American samples (Davis and Carlson, 1970). A significant practice effect which resulted in decreased susceptibility was found in one American and one Ugandan sample, but the new stimuli produced points of subjective equality much greater than those reported by Segall *et al.*

Morgan (1959), on the basis of research in South Africa, emphasized the need to control the length of exposure to illusion items. Segall, Campbell and Herskovits (1966, pp. 181–3) noted that a long interval, i.e. thirty seconds, reduced the illusion effect on the Müller–Lyer and Horizontal–Vertical illusions but they considered that it could not account for their results, as the effect would only reduce the difference which they sought to explain by the ecological hypotheses. Jahoda and Stacey's (1970) report was the first cross-cultural study to state explicitly that the length of exposure was controlled, i.e. stimuli were projected for seven seconds on a screen.

Use of a controlled exposure time and one psychophysical method may yield more comparable results across cultures but progress in understanding the basic perceptual mechanisms awaits further experimental study of the effects of varying stimuli instructions and procedures, not only on the judgement of illusions but of non-illusion figures as well (Over, 1968).

Classes of illusions

The lack of an adequate theory to account for the error-inducing processes which underlie all illusion effects has hampered the development of a system to classify them. The strategy adopted by Jahoda and Stacey (1970) was to include all illusions which had been used in earlier cross-cultural studies, as well as others selected in the light of extant classifications.

The need for an adequate classification system is highlighted by Deregowski's (1967) work. Segall, Campbell and Herskovits (1966), and the researchers using their materials, have considered the T and the L (Figure 5, items b and c) as equally valid measures of the Horizontal–Vertical illusion and thus the results equally likely to be predicted by the foreshortening hypothesis. Deregowski has shown that this analysis suffers in so far as it has ignored the work of Kunnapas (1955) which indicated that two different processes operate in producing the Horizontal–Vertical illusion effect – one being attributable to the verticality of the line and a second influenced by the intersection. Deregowski demonstrated these effects with Zambian subjects and argued that while verticality alone might be responsible for the illusion effect on the L item, the second factor would affect outcomes based on the T item. Re-analysis of Rivers's (1901) data and that of Segall, Campbell and Herskovits showed that the foreshortening hypothesis predicted results on the L item much better than on the T. Deregowski indicated the need for a third hypothesis to account for results on the T item and he suggested further that a fourth factor, related to symmetry, would be necessary to encompass Rivers's data based upon the cruciform figure (+). Until there is greater understanding of classes of illusions, cross-cultural explanations will be vulnerable to the confounding errors demonstrated by Deregowski.

Cultural differences and their explanation

Cross-cultural research has usually supported Rivers's findings showing greater European susceptibility on the Müller–Lyer illusion and more illusion responses from non-Western subjects on the Horizontal–Vertical figures (Heuse, 1957; Morgan, 1959; Mundy-Castle and Nelson, 1962). Although Bonte (1962) reported negative results on the Müller–Lyer illusion when using the method of average error to compare Europeans and Congolese, Jahoda (1966) used the method to replicate overall European/non-Western differences on this illusion. He failed, however, to find differences predicted by the ecological hypotheses of Segall, Campbell and Herskovits on an inverted T version of the Horizontal–Vertical illusion among three Ghanaian groups and in European–Ghanaian comparisons. While Deregowski's (1967) work offers a possible explanation for the latter failure, studies in which carpenteredness and open vistas have varied within a single society have also failed to support the ecological hypotheses (Berry, 1966; Gregor and McPherson, 1965).

In explaining his results, Jahoda (1966) suggested that responses to illusion drawings may depend not only on ecological factors relating to rectangularity but on the ability to interpret two-dimensional representations of depth. The failure of an isolated, rural, white South African group to make three-dimensional interpretations, (cf. page 62) is related to their low susceptibility to the Müller–Lyer illusion (Mundy-Castle and Nelson, 1962). Although the white South African's environment is European in its rectangularity, his failure to make depth interpretations and his illusion responses are closer to those of non-European groups. The failure to make three-dimensional interpretation has been related to age, formal education and cultural elaboration; these factors also affect illusion responses.

The relation of age to illusion responses has been dealt with extensively by Piaget (1969) who postulated two perceptual processes – perceptual error, which leads to decreasing illusion susceptibility with age, and perceptual activity, which results in increased illusion susceptibility. His theory has been developed as part of an extensive research programme which is concerned with classifying illusions, with test procedures, but unfortunately, as yet, not with cultural differences. Dasen (1970) reported illusion results which gave limited support to Segall and which were also congruent with Piagetian interpretations of the illusions he sampled. Another developmental approach has been suggested by Berry (1966, 1968) who has related age and field dependence to illusion behaviour (Witkin *et al.* 1962). In so far as increasing age and increasing field independence have both been related to decreasing susceptibility to the Müller–Lyer illusion, Berry considered it useful to employ measures of field dependence to assess perceptual development. Berry showed, in a comparison of illusion susceptibility with two ecologies and two levels of perceptual development, that when the two factors operated in the same direction, predicted results were obtained. Berry's design was incomplete in that different groups of Eskimo subjects had experienced different ecologies but were all perceptually mature while Temne subjects shared a similar environment but their groups differed in perceptual maturity; none the less, effects of the developmental variable were clear. Thus, chronological age and other developmental variables need to be included in future studies of illusion behaviour in order to complete our understanding of the phenomena.

Berry (1968) interpreted the Kohs Block Test as an indicator of perceptual development because of its use as a measure of field dependence. Wober (1970) has used the Kohs Blocks as a measure of cognitive development and shown significant correlations between Kohs Blocks and the Perspective Illusion (Figure 5, item e) and education. He reported zero correlations between susceptibility to the Horizontal–Vertical illusions and Kohs Block scores. Indirectly, these results strengthen Berry's (1968) argument for a developmental factor underlying Müller–Lyer behaviour and Kohs Block performance, since no consistent age trends have been reported for the Horizontal–Vertical illusion and there is no correlation with Kohs Block scores. Once again evidence points to the need for some system to classify illusions; clearly the same factors do not underlie performance on the Müller–Lyer and Horizontal–Vertical illusions.

Twelve illusion figures were used in Jahoda and Stacey's (1970) study of Scottish and Ghanaian students which sought to assess the effects of special training in architecture and art on illusion susceptibility. No simple structure of illusions emerged despite cluster and principle components analyses of the twelve figures. Failure was attributed to differential effects on particular illusions produced by special training. While formal education reduced cultural differences, the authors concluded that their results still offered qualified support for Segall, Campbell and Herskovits's (1966) basic premise that particular visual inference habits arise as the result of socialization in different cultures. They were cautious in stating whether the differences, diagnosed via differential illusion susceptibility, ought to be ascribed to ecological factors or social interaction.

Jahoda and Stacey asserted confidently that learning accounted for behaviour on certain illusions, but the nature–nurture controversy is not dead. Pollack (1963, 1970; Pollack and Silvar, 1967 a and b) has offered a physiological explanation for the results reported by Segall, Campbell and Herskovits. He has argued that accuracy of contour detection and Müller–Lyer susceptibility both decrease as the *fundus oculi* darkens with age. The cross-cultural extension adds that as skin pigmentation changes retinal pigmentation also varies. Berry (1971) has re-analysed his own data on Scottish, Eskimo, Australian Aboriginal and New Guinean samples and reported a stronger relationship between skin colour and Müller–Lyer susceptibility than between carpenteredness and susceptibility; it is well to remember, however, Jahoda's (1971) reservations concerning the rating of skin colour.

Colleagues of Segall and Campbell have tested Pollack's hypothesis using the Müller–Lyer, the Sander Parallelogram and the Ames Room illusion (Armstrong *et al.* n.d.). The retinal pigmentation of black and white Americans, as determined by opthalmoscopic examination, was unrelated to illusion susceptibility. The only significant main effect was produced by age and the authors' explanation of their failure to replicate the racial differences reported by Pollack and Silvar (1967 a and b) emphasized the unusual conditions of the original testing, i.e. dim blue illumination. In the discussion of Pollack's hypothesis it may be well to recall the warning of Allport and Pettigrew (1957, p. 105) on the nature–nurture issue '. . . we do not believe that comparative perceptual studies on Western and on primitive peoples can solve this particular riddle'.

Jahoda (1971) has presented data which indirectly supports Pollack's argument. Noting recent findings on hue and brightness effects (Pollack, 1970) and the original testing conditions employed by Pollack, Jahoda compared the performance of Scottish and Malawian university students on red and blue versions of both the Müller–Lyer illusion and a spatial task. Cross-cultural comparisons failed to yield significant differences but Malawians were significantly more susceptible to illusion effects when tested with red figures. The more accurate performance of Malawians on the red spatial task could be interpreted as evidence of a physiological basis for African difficulties in spatial perception. Sherman's (1967) suggestions concerning the role of experience in male–female differences in spatial perception are worth noting. Jahoda was cautious in interpreting his results and argued against ascribing illusion susceptibility to any single factor.

There is a *déjà vu* quality to the preceding discussion. Considering the failure of subjects to discriminate the colours blue and green, blue and violet, and blue and black, Rivers wrote in 1901 (p. 46) '. . . the retina of the Papuan is more strongly pigmented than that of the European'. Recent investigators have commented '. . . as a consequence, he [Rivers] concluded, blues and greens would be strongly absorbed, resulting in corresponding insensitiveness to these colours. This explanation is almost certainly wrong, despite the considerable ingenuity it displays' (Berlin and Kay, 1969, p. 148). It is equally tempting to dismiss Pollack's explanation but the reappearance of this physiological hypothesis, albeit in relation to contour detection and illusion susceptibility rather than colour discrimination, suggests that it should be evaluated seriously.

4 Perception: Conceptually Defined

In considering the perception of time, space and emotion, greater attention needs to be given to cultural conventions. The understanding of cultural differences in the perception of colour, orientation, depth and illusions, in the previous chapter, was constrained by a limited knowledge of how these stimuli were encoded and processed in non-Western people's perceptual systems. But the perception of time, space and emotion is less immediate and less determined by the nature of physical stimulation. It can be argued that time, space and emotion are culturally defined categories and that their perception fails to satisfy the criteria suggested by Tajfel (see page 19). A debate over definitions can be by-passed as the cross-cultural literature on time, space and emotion contains a number of investigations worthy of consideration. Furthermore, the difficulties which students from non-European cultures experience in their academic pursuits when dealing with Western representations of space commends that attention is given to the perception of space.

The Piagetian studies on cognitive development in infancy suggest that the concepts of the object, of time, space and causality may arise from universal experiences in early life (Piaget, 1954). Piaget has traced the construction of elementary concepts of time, space, causality and permanent objects from the infant's sensorimotor knowledge of duration, movement and sequence. These primitive categories, which are constructed before the child acquires speech, may well be similar across different societies and serve as the broad, universal modes of thinking out of which each society fashions its own systems of time and space by emphasizing some kinds of information and ignoring others. The differential information-processing schema of adults in different societies results in the cultural variations in the perception of time, space and emotion reported in this chapter.

Time

The realization that there are many 'times' besides that seeming verity, the clock of seconds, minutes and hours is a starting point in the consideration of time cross-culturally. Biologists have sought timekeepers in body functions such as cell metabolism and alpha rhythms, while physicists have pursued time in the structure of atoms. Psychological research on the experience of time has often fallen into the trap of assuming that clock time must be the metric against which to calibrate 'subjective' experience. This particularly Western bias has, as Ornstein (1969) has argued, inhibited productive research on the experience of time.

Time is a universal experience, not only of man but of all living organisms. Behavioural evidence for sensitivity to differences in duration is found in classical conditioning studies. They indicate that the elapsed time between the to-be-conditioned stimulus and the unconditioned stimulus may vary only narrowly within defined limits if successful conditioning is to occur. Thus, without recourse to 'mentalistic' introspection, we can conclude that differences in duration are discriminated by a wide range of organisms and that duration is an important determinant of behaviour.

The study of time has beguiled men for thousands of years. Greek philosophers considered its essence in their speculations on the nature of reality; Indian thought struggled with the fall from Great Time and with life which in historical time cannot be freed from illusion; Einstein gave measured time its place in modern physics as the fourth dimension. In philosophic discussions on the metaphysics of time there is continuing debate about the importance of space in knowing time. While psychological studies focus largely on experience, discussion of this aspect of time should not be interpreted as an acceptance of Bergson's view that real time is duration while objective time derives from space (Gunn, 1929). Studies reviewed here deal with time as a psychological percept or concept, but the distinction is not clear. The guideline in collecting research findings has been concern with cultural variation in relation to time.

The psychological study of time lacks a distinguished history and a solid body of results. Many of the questions which have been asked about time were determined by developments in experimental psychology. Early psychologists sought to discover how Weber's Law fitted the experience of time. The psychophysical methods, which developed as psychology emerged from philosophy as an experimental science, have guided the questions asked about the experience of time. The perception of time intervals has been measured by the method of constant stimuli, i.e. presenting subjects with two intervals and asking whether they are the same length or different, the method of average error, i.e. asking subjects to supply the second boundary marker in order to make an interval to match a standard, or simply by rating scale procedures. Processes of short time and longer time perception, akin to short- and long-term memory, have been identified. Short time is usually defined by reference to a clock time interval of less than ten seconds while the duration of long intervals varies considerably and relates the experience of time to complex cognitive processes.

The disappointment which results have produced is emphasized by Ornstein (1969), who quoted reviews of the field by Nichols (1891) and Woodrow (1951), pointing out the conflicting nature of findings and the muddle of theory. Interpretable evidence has been replaced by speculation with recourse to terms such as 'time sense' which, Ornstein has suggested, reflects the investigation of time by methods developed in studying perception. Time is studied using a perceptual paradigm despite the absence of an organ of time perception or a dimension along which to measure psychological time. The resulting conceptual muddle has prevented progress. Ornstein has proposed a framework within which to consider the experience of time and has undertaken a series of experiments which clarify thinking about the experience of duration. The four modes of experience are (a) short-term time which included studies of the perception of short intervals (less than ten seconds) and rhythm, (b) duration which concerns the past and processes such as long-term memory, (c) temporal perspectives of a philosophical nature allowing interpretation of time experience and consideration of the future, and (d) simultaneity.

Coverage of these areas in the general psychological literature is uneven and cross-cultural studies are very limited. Anthropological analyses deal largely with (c) temporal perspectives, but have not stimulated cross-cultural psychological research directly. The cross-cultural literature uncovered by bibliographic research deals only with (b) duration and (c) temporal perspectives. The studies which appear under the heading of temporal perspectives examine questions different from those posed by anthropologists.

Duration

The studies reviewed here deal with estimates of the duration of intervals which vary in clock time from fifteen seconds to six minutes. With the exception of Meade's work (Meade, 1968; Meade and Singh, 1970) which was undertaken in North India and America, all comparisons are based on African, European and American samples (Gay and Cole, 1967; Robbins, Kilbride and Bukenya, 1968; Schwitzgebel, 1962).

Gay and Cole (1967) tested the perception of intervals, analysed Kpelle time concepts and concluded from linguistic analysis of Kpelle time terms that the temporal perception of the Kpelle was much less quantitative than that of Europeans. Their temporal analysis led them to predict less accurate perception of intervals by Kpelle subjects than by Americans. In one of their studies subjects were asked to pace twenty, forty, sixty or eighty yards and then to estimate how long it had taken to cover the distance. In the second, subjects observed a stopwatch tick off an interval which might vary from fifteen to 200 seconds in fifteen-second steps, and then estimate, without a clock, an interval of the same length. Essentially these are variations on the method of average error. Gay and Cole (1967, pp. 73–4) presented their results graphically, plotting per cent of error against distance and time in seconds. The graphs were clear and there was no need to offer statistical tests in support of the conclusion that Kpelle subjects, both children at school and illiterate adults, are more accurate than American adults who consistently underestimated duration. Not only do these results indicate the hazards of predicting behaviour in one mode of temporal experience from performance in a different mode, but also the difficulty in explaining the results. The authors noted that American subjects appeared to count to themselves but this essentially reasonable approach only led to greater errors, i.e. underestimation.

Using a reproduction technique similar to that of Gay and Cole, Robbins, Kilbride and Bukenya (1968) measured rural and urban Bagandan subjects' accuracy in judging time intervals of fifteen, thirty and sixty seconds. They presented means and standard deviations for the combined samples and for each of the rural and urban groups and concluded that there were no significant differences between the estimates of the two groups on any of the three intervals.

Bowden (1970), assuming that Robbins, Kilbride and Bukenya had come to their conclusions on the basis of *t* tests, re-analysed the data in terms of a formal criterion of accuracy. He reasoned that if individual scores were within a range equivalent to half the length of the interval, i.e. 7·5 for an interval of fifteen seconds, and if this value were equally distributed either side of the true value, i.e. $\pm 3{\cdot}75$ of fifteen seconds, a subject could be deemed accurate. Using this method to identify accurate subjects, Bowden showed that the proportion of urban Baganda classed as accurate was significantly greater for all interval estimates. Although Gay and Cole were not able to uphold such a prediction, intuitively one might expect that subjects with an urban time perspective would be more accurate. Bowden's results support such an assumption, but his re-analysis and Robbins, Kilbride and Bukenya's report are both too brief to permit firm conclusions and fail to provide a clear picture of the experimental task.

Another brief report is that of Schwitzgebel (1962). He tested Zulus and Dutch-speaking white South Africans on a variety of perceptual tasks and required subjects to estimate a named interval, i.e. one minute, which they did not experience prior to making the judgement. All subjects underestimated the interval (mean = forty-two seconds) but more Zulus (nine out of twelve) fell below the median than Europeans (one out of eleven). Although these results would appear to contradict those of Gay and Cole (1967) which showed an African superiority in estimating duration, it should be noted that Schwitzgebel's task forced subjects to rely on symbolic, verbal encoding of the length of the interval while Kpelle subjects based their judgements on comparison with an interval they had just experienced. Clausen, on whom Schwitzgebel drew in the choice of his method, stated, 'If an interval of fifteen seconds is presented to a subject, he may be able to reproduce it fairly accurately regardless of what his verbal estimation of the interval would be' (Clausen, 1950, p. 759). The two methods are expected to produce different results; they rely on different memory processes.

Meade's work on the perception of the length of time intervals is conceptually more ambitious than the studies so far considered. Meade (1959, 1963) found in America that subjects, who were working towards a goal, estimated an interval to be shorter than an interval of identical clock length in which they were idle or passively occupied with sensory stimulation such as listening to a metronome. American culture is characterized by concern with achievement and therefore Meade (1968) sought subcultures in which this need was less dominant. He compared with an American sample, seven subcultural groups in North India, known to vary in the value they placed on achievement. These subjects first sat idly for six minutes and then completed mathematical problems for an additional six minutes. They were then asked which interval felt longer. They were next told that the problem-solving interval had been six minutes and were asked to estimate the length of the other. Only for American, Kshatrya, Sikh and Parsee subjects did the estimates of the two intervals differ. The results were congruent with general expectations based upon subcultural values of achievement.

In a second study, Meade and Singh (1970) attempted to manipulate achievement motivation. Using subjects from the same Indian subcultural groups, they gave instructions designed either to involve subjects with the experimental task or to minimize their interest. Furthermore, each of these motivational groups were split so that half the subjects received feedback indicative of progress while the others had no indication of progress. Again significant differences in the estimates of interval length occurred. Kshatrya, Sikh and Parsee subjects responded to the motivational induction and to the reports of progress; these factors also interacted significantly. A significant interaction effect was reported for Vasiya subjects who came from a business and commercial community. The Vasiya can be induced to attend to achievement cues with feedback but the manipulations failed to change the temporal perception of Brahmin, Sudra and Muslim subjects.

Although five studies have here been considered, an empirical or conceptual integration is difficult. The Baganda material supports opposing conclusions depending on the statistical analysis employed, but clearly Bowden's (1970) method gives a better measure of accuracy and favours urban Baganda. On the other hand, Doob (1960), using an estimation technique, found rural Jamaicans superior in judging the length of an interview. Studies using an experienced interval reproduction design could not be expected to produce results identical with those using an estimation method relying on memory of a named interval (Clausen, 1950), but no attempts have been made to compare the two approaches in a cross-cultural study. Neither has the relationship between the experience of duration and information processing described by Ornstein (1969) been reported cross-culturally. Meade's (1968) concern lies elsewhere; he wishes to show how motivational processes influence time perception.

Temporal perspectives

Few psychologists have investigated the effects of culturally diverse temporal perspectives on behaviour. A glimpse of the anthropological approach to time perspectives was given in chapter 2; Hopi and SAE conventions for dealing with the term 'day' were discussed. The Hopi only spoke of nouns collectively when they could be assembled in reality but SAE referred to days as though they could be laid out along a spatial measuring stick. Lévi-Strauss (1963), in an analysis of Hopi kinship terminology, has suggested that the Hopi require three models of time in dealing with kin. In the first model, time is a stable and reversible dimension and is exemplified in the terms used to refer to mother's father's lineage and father's mother's lineage. Secondly, there is a non-reversible time implied in the relations specified by the Hopi terms for grandmother, mother, sister, child and grandchild. Finally Lévi-Strauss postulated a third, undulating, cyclical and reversible time captured in the use of appropriate terms for sister and sister's child when ego is male. The psychological studies presented here were found after considerable search. They are varied in their approaches to the problem but are unlike anthropological analyses of time perspectives.

In a study using the 'cross-cultural method', Zern (1967) related maternal interaction and in particular, indulgence, to the development of a differentiated time sense. His strategy was correlational; a number of child-rearing variables were related to the dependent variable, time concern. Time concern was formalized as a Guttman scale which ranged from a developed time sense (evidenced by a developed calendar of approximately a year's length, etc.) to little time sense or only a crude and general ability to differentiate parts of the day. Twenty-nine linguistically independent societies were rated on seven indicators of time concern, the highest rating being given to those societies which fulfilled all seven criteria. Significant negative correlations were found between the measure of time sense and (a) display of affection and (b) absence of pain inflicted by nurturant agent. An overall rating of infant indulgence was correlated with time sense and a highly significant negative relationship was found. Zern concluded that overall indulgence, with maternal interaction playing a minor role, was related to the failure to develop a differentiated time sense and, conversely, that the presence of frustration led to an ordered time perspective.

A number of questions can be raised about this study even at the cultural level. Zern argued for a causal interpretation of the correlations, i.e. that indulgence interfered with the development of a differentiated time sense, because he found it difficult to see how time differentiation could cause different kinds of child rearing. Zern admitted that a third factor might influence both socialization and time sense. Lambert's (1971) analysis of socialization which suggests that choices are constrained by limited resources leads one to ask whether time appears to be less strictly rationed when it is less differentiated. Indulgence may be perceived by ethnographers when mothers are less time oriented and thus less aware of temporal constraints. Criticism at a different level concerns the validity of the measure of time sense, and the question of what behaviour it might relate to at the level of individual differences. In their Kpelle study, Gay and Cole (1967) were unable to predict accuracy in judging the length of an interval from knowledge of the Kpelle temporal perspective. It is an open question whether Zern's measure of time sense would be related to measures of individual temporal performance which would allow the twenty-nine societies to be ordered as they had been by the measure of time sense. The same question, that is, the level of analysis issue, can be raised concerning the socialization variables and their interrelations.

Deregowski (1970) has successfully related an aspect of cultural experience to individual behaviour but he approached the problem of time indirectly. Impetus for his work came from a desire to integrate the apparently conflicting findings of Schwitzgebel (1962) and Doob (1960) discussed on pages 79 to 81. In particular, Deregowski sought to assess the validity of Doob's suggestion that contact with Western civilization increases awareness of time but does not improve the judgement of temporal intervals. Following the tradition of Bartlett, he developed a memory test as an indirect measure of awareness and compared recall of time concepts and others. Rural women and urban schoolboys, chosen to maximize acculturation differences, were tested for recall on eight concepts which were quantified and presented in a tape recorded story in their own language. Time concepts included time of arrival and age while the others involved number of nephews, of bananas, etc. Schoolboys' performance showed no differences when dealing with the two types of concepts but rural women were significantly better at recalling the value of non-time concepts. Highly significant differences were also found showing schoolboys much better than rural women in recalling the quantification of time. Granted that urban schoolboys are more acculturated, Deregowski's results offer indirect evidence to support Doob's hypothesis that 'civilization' leads to greater awareness of time. Before giving too much weight to these results one would like to be assured that the time concepts employed, though translated into the vernacular were not more Western than indigenous. Such a qualification is not specific to this particular experiment but is relevant whenever concepts from the Gregorian calendar or clock time are used.

In another study elaborating Doob's ideas about the effects of contact with Western civilization on the experience of time, Melikian (1969) investigated the relationship of temporal perspectives and feeling tone in Saudi-born Muslim male college students. A study of American students (Farber, 1953) had shown that Saturday and Sunday were highly preferred and that the days of the week from Monday to Friday formed a gradient increasing in positive affect as they approached Saturday. Melikian showed that Thursday and Friday, which in the Muslim week have the same function as Saturday and Sunday, were highly preferred by Saudi students. In order to investigate Doob's (1960) proposition that acculturation shifts temporal orientation from the present to the future, Melikian analysed the explanations which both students exposed to Western civilization and those unexposed offered, to support their preferences for Thursday and Friday. He found that more unexposed students preferred Friday for religious reasons and that more exposed students preferred Thursday. If we accept Melikian's interpretation that exposed subjects' choice of Thursday in terms of the anticipation of a day of rest indicates more future orientation among the acculturated, the study stands as further indirect support for Doob's analysis of the effects of acculturation on temporal perspectives.

Finally, there are two studies which have examined temporal perspective using a developmental approach (Cottle and Howard, 1969; Uka, 1962). Uka noted that only with Westernization or urbanization do Africans see time as a scarce resource. He compared American and Nigerian children on a number of time dimensions using a questionnaire to assess four areas of temporal experience. These were: *personal*, defined by questions such as how old are you?; *conventional naming*, i.e. eliciting days, seasons, months; *spatial extension*, i.e. does it take longer to come to school or to go home?; and *duration*, i.e. how long have you attended this school? Results based on the total test scores of Nigerian children six to thirteen years of age showed consistent improvement up to eleven years, superiority of children from educated families and a performance spurt after one year's formal schooling. Additional analyses showed that concepts dealing with personal time were most often correctly answered and were followed in order by conventional naming, spatial and durational concepts. It is impossible to determine whether the ordering was related to a fatigue factor because it parallels the constant order of presentation. Generally the study is difficult to interpret and inspection of his Appendix III, showing per cent of correct responses per question, raises serious doubts about the instrument. There are clear ceiling effects and age reversals with older children repeatedly performing less well than younger ones. Instructions for scoring in his Appendix II are not clear; they allow points either for Nigerian or European concepts. Younger children may have gained points for using Nigerian terms while older children, attempting to employ European ones, produced errors.

Cottle and Howard's (1969) study of the perception of time as a linear dimension in Indian adolescents stands in sharp contrast to Uka's study. It is a methodologically sophisticated investigation which required sixty-nine boys and thirty-five girls, aged twelve to twenty years, from Westernized professional families near Delhi to complete an inventory assessing their definition of the present in terms of its upper and lower boundaries, and the distant past, near past, distant future and near future, using one temporal term such as days, weeks or years. Results were analysed in terms of extension and bracketing of time zones, and four patterns of zone relatedness were identified. Some developmental trends in zone relatedness patterns were reported. Cottle and Howard considered their instrumentation carefully and compared their findings with other psychological and philosophical investigations of the nature of temporal experience but they did not elaborate on cross-cultural differences. Developmental change in temporal perspective is still a largely unexplored area in psychology. Similarly, the cross-cultural focus has added little to our knowledge of temporal perspectives.

Space

Psychological research on the concept of space reflects the epistemological ambiguities of the term. Introducing their own research on space, Piaget and Inhelder (1956) make clear the difference between the infant's ability to function adequately in a spatial medium, i.e. sensorimotor intelligence, and his capacity to represent space conceptually, i.e. as a topological, projective or Euclidean system. The distinction which Piaget and Inhelder make lies at the base of Littlejohn's (1963) argument made when confronting Hudson's (1960) work showing African failure to perceive pictorial depth (3D). Littlejohn, an anthropologist, asserted that he had no doubt that Africans perceived three-dimensionally the actual world they inhabited, but that the '"objective space" which geometrical analysis has revealed to us . . . is a not explicitly apprehended background to the space in which they are conscious of living' (Littlejohn, 1963, p. 16). In asking questions about the experience of space, we can either attempt to learn how other societies conceptualize experience or how members of non-Western cultures come to acquire the

Western systems of projective and Euclidean space with which we encode experience.

In order to show how the Temne concept of space differed from our own, Littlejohn (1963) used his own geographic introduction as a foil and contrasted Temne beliefs with our view of the earth as an object contained in the space we call the universe. Temne cosmology asserts that the earth is a flat object which God has placed on the head of a giant and that the trees are his hair and all living things lice upon it. This comparison was aimed not at ridiculing the naïveté of the Temne but at establishing the essential difference between our seemingly necessary assumptions of space as homogeneous and continuous and their complex yet manageable (on a day-to-day basis) system which they use to order their experience. Studies of this nature attempting to present a systematic formulation of space and other concepts radically different from our own are generally carried out by anthropologists. The few investigations of space undertaken by psychologists cross-culturally have focused upon the adequacy with which non-Western people employ our primarily geometric and physical representations of space (Cowley and Murray, 1962; Hudson, 1967; Kidd and Rivoire, 1965).

The traditional problems which have concerned psychology in the study of space have been the techniques by which a two-dimensional medium is used to represent spatial distance and the fundamental question of how we can know space and distance. The cross-cultural contribution to research on pictorial depth was considered on pages 61 to 66. The conclusion there, that the ability to interpret line drawings in 3D is primarily a function of education and general cultural experience, implies a tacit acceptance of the empiricist view of perception. The empiricist argument asserts that we know depth and distance as the result of experience and that it is from our memories, including those of movement in space, that we develop images which allow us to interpret sensations as clues to depth and distance.

In recent years the empiricist view of perception has come under repeated attack. The developmental literature includes Fantz's (1961) work showing systematic visual pattern preference in very young infants, Hubel and Wiesel's (1963) demonstrations of differential cell responsivity to contour in young kittens, and Tauber and Koffler's (1966) findings on perception of apparent movement in newborn infants. The cross-cultural literature on the development of visual perception does not reflect this renewed interest in innate mechanisms. Attention has focused instead on the experience of different cultures, ecologies and formal learning situations. Adherence of the cross-cultural researcher to the empiricist position may stem from feeling that biological explanations of perceptual processes can lay him open to attack as a racist. Whatever the reasons, the result has been little recent cross-cultural developmental research on spatial perception.

The most coherent explanation of the development of the concept of space has been that of Piaget and Inhelder (1956). They contend that the development of conceptual knowledge of space, which they argue is based upon practical, sensorimotor schemata, follows a prescribed course. First the child represents space according to topological principles, i.e. proximity, separation, order, enclosure and continuity, but the final property, that of continuity, is only fully understood in adolescence when the child is no longer tied to concrete actions and can entertain notions of the possible and thus infinity. Once basic topological principles develop they become the foundation upon which the spatial characteristics of the projective and Euclidean geometries develop. These properties which include spatial invariances, overcoming shifts in viewpoint in the projective system and distance, parallelism and angularity in the Euclidean system, develop along with other concrete operational skills. Thus, Piaget and Inhelder (1956) show both that children can manually explore unseen objects and match them to a visible standard on the basis of open-closedness before they can match in terms of rectangularity and that projective interpretations depend upon conservation of length.

An intensive investigation of spatial concepts in pre-operational English children was undertaken by Lovell (1959). He studied children aged between two years eleven months and five years eight months and his results raised a number of important questions about the Genevan stage formulations. English children were less talkative than Piaget's Swiss children but they were able to discriminate shapes not only on the basis of topological properties but were also able to identify Euclidean shapes based on circularity though less often those with long straight sides and few angles. Lovell (1959) concluded that the validity of the stage sequence postulated by Piaget and Inhelder (1956) remained an open question.

Unlike Lovell who concentrated on a limited age range, Cowley and Murray (1962) investigated spatial development in each year between five and twelve, but sampled only forty Zulu and forty white South African children. There were ten children, five from each cultural group in each year. Consistent cultural differences were found overall, with white South Africans performing at higher levels on all subtests; but despite the apparent superiority of white South African children they were responding at lower levels than similarly aged Swiss children. None the less these investigations led Cowley and Murray to conclude that the topological, projective and Euclidean stage sequence postulated by Piaget and Inhelder (1956) provided a valid description of the development of the spatial concept in all the South African children.

Cowley and Murray used three subtests to investigate topological space, eight in the study of projective space and seven to measure Euclidean space.

…mance of Zulu and white children showed fewer significant …s on the Euclidean subtests. The authors ascribed this failure to …ficance to the unreliability of small numbers and to highly variable …ance. Another plausible hypothesis suggests that a Euclidean view …ce, more than any other, may be susceptible to the effects of school… …chooling may induce similarly variable behaviour when dealing with Euclidean concepts.

A study of American children which in part supported the stage theory of Piaget and Inhelder (1956) was reported by Rivoire (1962). Although she found that, at varying age levels, characteristics specific to the test tasks interacted with the stages of spatial representation, she concluded that basic spatial concepts were not highly susceptible to cultural influences. Kidd (1962) in a psychometric investigation of Anglo- and Mexican-American children from differing social classes, found that certain items on Cattell's test of *g* and Raven's Matrices failed to reflect cultural and class differences. Examination of these culture-fair items led Kidd to hypothesize that these items sampled basic perceptual variables.

Kidd and Rivoire (1965) together considered the characteristics of culture-fair items and compared them with items reflecting cultural and class differences. They showed that the nineteen culture-fair items could be ordered in three series which represented topological properties of spatial succession, equivalence and continuity. A mathematician supported their classification of the culture-fair items. Analysis of the items susceptible to cultural influence indicated that successful discrimination depended on projective, affinal and Euclidean characteristics in addition to basic topological properties. Although the cross-cultural data was not extensive, Kidd and Rivoire (1965) concluded that it was the basic topological properties of items sampling elementary spatial concepts which were least susceptible to cultural influence. The data cannot be marshalled to support or refute the empiricist or innate theories of perceptual organization but they are congruent with the Piagetian assertion that psychological development follows logical necessity in the primacy of the topological system.

The conclusions of Kidd and Rivoire and of Piaget gain additional support from recent cross-cultural research in Australia. As part of a larger study of cognitive development, Dasen (1970) administered three Piagetian spatial tests, Order, Rotation and Horizontality, to children aged six to sixteen. The performance of Aboriginal children from two milieux, one having considerably more contact with European culture, was compared and contrasted with that of children of European origin living in Canberra. Dasen reported that all groups were most successful on the Order test which involved only topological relations. The differences between the Aboriginal samples were minimal and the performance of European and Aboriginal children was most similar on this test. The other tests which understanding of projective and or Euclidean relations were more di for all subjects and cultural differences were magnified. Knowledge topological relations remains the prime area of common cultural understanding in the perception of space.

Emotion

The origins of the comparative study of the perception of emotion can be traced to the writings of Charles Darwin (1872). Darwin examined the expression of emotion in an effort to support an evolutionary argument, but his work nevertheless remains a useful source of naturalistic observation documenting pan-human as well as mammalian similarities of expression. Psychologists have approached the problem of judging persons together with the sub-area, the perception of emotion, using controlled experimental techniques. Early psychological research sought simple explanations but the last twenty years have seen considerable progress in the field of person perception. Psychological researchers are sensitive to the intricacies of the judgemental process and the uniqueness of other persons as stimulus objects, i.e. that both persons are in turn perceiver and object (Tagiuri, 1969).

In the discussions of perception, hitherto, attention has centred on the nature of the stimulus material, the context in which it was presented and, when possible, on the organizational principles employed by subjects in the perception of this material. In considering emotion it becomes necessary to take account of the meaning of the context to the stimulus object, i.e. the person who is being perceived. The observer may interpret a situation as one which provokes aggression, but it is important to ask whether the situation is perceived and coded by the stimulus person in a similar way. In a sense the emic or insider's view appears once again as an issue.

A review of the literature on person perception, or even on the sub-area concerned with the judgement of emotion, is beyond the scope of this discussion. The focus here is on the cross-cultural generality of the perception of emotion. While some attempt is made to review the scattered research on this topic, greater emphasis is placed on the studies recently undertaken by Ekman (1972). This work has links with ethological studies (e.g. Eibl-Eibesfeldt, 1970) illustrating pan-human dimensions of emotional expression; Ekman, however, investigates both the perception and expression of emotion in a more systematic and rigorous manner.

The question, 'Do people who are socialized in different cultures interpret emotions based upon facial expression (as displayed in photographs and line drawings) in the same manner or differently?' has been explored in a direct and methodologically simple fashion in a series of studies by Vinacke and Fong (Fong, 1965; Vinacke, 1949; Vinacke and Fong, 1955). Vinacke (1949) investigated the judgemental accuracy of Japanese, Chinese and Caucasian subjects living in Hawaii following an American paradigm (Woodworth, 1938) which showed that subjects were relatively successful in judging emotions from facial expressions. Vinacke (1949) used twenty photographs of Caucasian faces expressing a range of emotions. These were pilot tested for clearness and lack of ambiguity and presented in two conditions, one with supporting context and the other with just the face on a blank background. The photographs were projected on a screen and groups of subjects required to complete checklists which included such common affect terms as fear, curiosity, interest, joy and no emotion, as well as the appropriate identification for each photograph. Analysis was based upon agreements and showed little difference in the performance of the three ethnic groups. The context complete, or situation condition, produced greater agreement in all ethnic groups and females showed higher levels of agreement in this condition than males.

In a second study, the stimulus material was changed to include twenty-eight photographs of Japanese, Chinese, Korean and Chamorro faces prepared as in the earlier study (Vinacke and Fong, 1955). Again the stimuli were presented in the situation and face only conditions in group testing with checklists. Considerable agreement was found for Japanese, Chinese and Caucasian subjects; the situation condition again produced higher agreement and females in all three groups produced more similar judgements. A slight Caucasian superiority had been observed in the accuracy of judgements of Caucasian faces (Vinacke, 1949); but an opposite effect occurred in the second experiment (Vinacke and Fong, 1955). Both Chinese and Japanese subjects produced more agreement on Oriental faces than Caucasians. Vinacke and Fong (1955, p. 194) explained the second, stronger effect in terms of social learning and suggested 'that Japanese and Chinese in Hawaii are more familiar with Caucasians than vice versa'.

Focusing on intra-cultural differences in the interpretation of emotion another psychologist, Fong (1965), has studied groups of Chinese who differed in their exposure to Western civilization. He sampled first to fifth generation Chinese living in America and Chinese who had lived in Hong Kong for varying lengths of time. He used line drawings of human stick figures as stimulus material instead of the photographs used in the earlier studies. Each drawing was presented with a checklist of five adjectives and a blank space to be used in case none of the supplied words were appropriate. The responses of Chinese subjects were scored as correct in relation to the modal responses of a Caucasian-American sample (Sarbin and Hardyck, 1955). The significant differences found in the accuracy of Chinese subsamples related to friendship patterns, ability to speak Chinese, residence in America or Hong Kong, as well as area of residence within the different places. Although this result differs from those of the earlier studies it is explicable. Stick figures employ only minimal cues of gesture and posture in order to indicate emotion and even these are encoded in a representational system whose validity was explored only for Caucasian-American subjects. Cultures, no doubt, differ in their stylized representation of emotion and arguments for cultural differences in the expression of emotion have received support from other evidence based on different representational systems. Thus, Klineberg (1938), an advocate of the social learning position as regards the expression of emotion, has quoted Chinese literature to show that facial expressions are differently associated with particular emotions in East and West.

Conclusions from this series of experiments could be used to support either the relativistic or universalistic position on the expression of emotion. The first two studies (Vinacke, 1949; Vinacke and Fong, 1955) offer some evidence of cross-cultural universality in the recognition of emotion while the later study (Fong, 1965) documents the effects of social learning. The failure of psychological research to find consistent evidence that specific emotions are related to definable facial expressions has predisposed acceptance of a relativistic or social learning view (Tagiuri, 1969). Facial expressions have been conceptualized as language and it has been suggested that these expressive languages vary as widely as spoken languages (Birdwhistell, 1963). Birdwhistell has been challenged, however, by ethologists (Eibl-Eibesfeldt, 1970) and recently by psychologists (Ekman, 1972).

Filming with a side lens in fast motion, Eibl-Eibesfeldt has photographed subjects unaware of his activity. From initial analyses of films made in Europe, Kenya, Tanzania, Uganda, India, Siam, Bali, Hong Kong, Japan, Samoa, the United States, Mexico, Peru and Brazil, he has concluded (Eibl-Eibesfeldt, 1970, p. 416):

> ... we have filmed enough to say that some of the more complex human expressions can be traced back to the superposition of a few fixed action patterns which do not seem to be culturally determined. To give just one example, we found agreement in the smallest detail in the flirting behavior of girls from Samoa, Papua, France, Japan, Africa (Turcana and other Nilohamite tribes) and South American Indians (Waika, Orinoko).

Eibl-Eibesfeldt uses an etic technique, determining by his own criteria whether a behaviour sequence implies flirting, etc. Thus, his evidence can only offer partial support for universal expressions of emotion.

Ekman (1972) has approached the problem both in terms of the perception of emotion from facial expression and the registering of emotion in facial expression. He has traced the positions of relativists and universalists in a review paper which presents his own integrative theory and the research work which has developed from it. Ekman's 'neuro-cultural' theory postulates both universal and culturally specific determinants of emotional expression. On the innate or universal side, Ekman contends that certain emotions trigger the firing of particular patterns of facial muscles and that these patterns are largely unlearned and require minimum cognitive control. The results of social learning are seen in the cultural determinants of emotional expression. These include three broad categories: the stimuli which elicit emotion, the rules governing the actual facial display of emotion and the behavioural consequences of a particular display for the actor.

The universal or pan-cultural aspects of emotional expression are formalized in Ekman's (1972) concept of a 'facial affect programme'. He postulates that the programme is a link between primary emotions and distinctive sets of patterned neural impulses to particular facial muscles but he makes no attempt to locate the mechanism precisely within the nervous system. The seven primary emotions which Ekman identifies are happiness, sadness, anger, disgust, fear, surprise and interest. His prime concern is the link between primary emotions and distinguishable facial expressions. Although he has related the primary emotions he has identified to research on categories of emotion (Ekman, Friesen and Ellsworth, 1971) he has not sought to establish the precise number of primary emotions.

Problems in identifying facial expressions linked to primary emotions arise because social learning modifies the elicitors of emotion, their display rules and the consequences of their display. Ekman suggests that certain non-interpersonal events may trigger particular facial expressions, i.e. bad smell, but adds that the majority of interpersonal elicitors are learned. Although the facial affect programme may link certain facial expressions with particular primary emotions, the display of the linked expressions is governed by rules which can prevent its appearance, reduce its strength, truncate the performance or mask it with another expression. Although there is an innate link between primary emotion and facial expression the learned display rules have sufficient potency to interfere radically with display. Social learning patterns the response to expressed emotion as well as the elicitors and display rules.

Ekman's research has aimed at identifying pan-cultural aspects of emotional expression and his theoretical formulation is useful in pointing to methodological pitfalls along the way. Using the example of a funeral he shows how confusions concerning the learned or culturally patterned, elicitors, display rules and consequences can arise. If funerals are always assumed to be sadness elicitors, then one is forced to conclude that singing and dancing at a funeral are cross-cultural variants of the sadness response. Similarly, one can be misled unless aware that some cultures permit the display of sadness by men in public while others prohibit it. Finally, it is possible that people learn different responses to the experience of sadness, i.e. some react with disgust while others feel angry. With all these caveats and many more in mind, Ekman and his colleagues have carried out a series of cross-cultural experiments designed to offer support for the hypothesis that the association between particular facial muscular patterns and discrete emotions is universal (Ekman and Friesen, 1971; Ekman, Sorenson and Friesen, 1969).

In the first experiment Japanese and American subjects were required to identify facial expressions which had been made while watching a stressful, emotion-inducing film and those made in response to neutral films. The stimulus material was the spontaneous expressions of Japanese and American subjects who were unaware of being videotaped while watching films. Statistically significant accuracy levels were recorded and there were no significant differences relating to the cultural origin of observers or expressors. Although the study offers some evidence for cross-cultural comparability in the perception of emotion, it is incomplete because the emotional response was diffuse, i.e. not the identification of particular emotions, and extensive culture contact introduced the possibility of cross-cultural learning to identify culturally different expressions each signalling emotion.

The second experiment attacked the latter problem by specifying the precise nature of the facial expressions. Using the Facial Affect Scoring Technique (FAST) devised by Ekman, Friesen and Tomkins (1972), the facial behaviour of the Japanese and American expressors recorded during stressful and neutral films was assessed. Results indicated that the facial expressions in the two cultures were highly similar in the stress situation. At a behavioural level, then, stress elicited similar expressions although the emic question, whether the expressions were triggered by the same subjectively experienced emotion, remained.

Subjects from Brazil, Chile, Argentina, the United States and Japan were required to identify thirty single emotion photographs in a study designed to answer the question posed in the first experiment by the diffuse nature of the emotional response. Both posed and spontaneous facial expressions were selected using the rationale of FAST to represent happiness, anger, sadness, fear, disgust and surprise. No differences were found in the identification of faces with emotion words across the five cultures and analysis of variance also failed to show any culture by emotion interaction effect. Only on one happy face and one angry face did the response of Japanese subjects differ from the predicted. Judgements of intensity of emotion similarly showed no cultural variation.

Still concerned lest shared visual traditions and hence social learning account for the observed similarities, further investigations were undertaken in remote areas of New Guinea (Ekman and Friesen, 1971). Subjects were required both to identify a picture which represented the emotion described in a story and to produce a described emotion. Adults and children from the Fore group in the South East Highlands were successful in both these tasks but there were no significant differences in the performance of acculturated and traditional people. The only failure was a confusion of fear and surprise. It is possible that among the Fore fear is the learned behavioural consequence of surprise. While this series of studies is valuable for the framework for further cross-cultural comparisons which it provides, it may well be that learned cultural differences will provide the most fruitful area for future research. Cross-cultural psychologists interested in the effects of social learning on the expression and perception of emotion should view specification of the rule systems of elicitors, display and response to emotional cues as a challenge.

Before leaving the topic of emotion it should be noted that research inspired by Osgood's (1955) formulations based on the Semantic Differential and Schlosberg's (1954) dimensional theory of emotion has also met with success in identifying possible pan-cultural factors in the perception of emotion. Unlike the Ekman position, this formulation stresses the role of general attitudes and activity patterns in the recognition of emotion (Frijda and Philipszoon, 1963). Situational cues are invoked to specify particular emotions. Although these approaches differ in their assumptions and techniques, they share a common faith in the cross-cultural similarity of emotional experience. Each would reject the extreme social learning position which makes emotional expression unique to every culture, but would view the expression and perception of emotion as an interaction of innate and learned factors.

5 Cognition: Micro Models

The results of cross-cultural research on cognition are presented in two chapters. Unlike the discussion of perception which was also divided into two parts, one using the nature of the stimulus material as a focus and the other ordered in terms of concepts, this analysis of the effects of cultural variation on cognitive processes is organized according to levels of explanation. Relatively simple processes such as memory and learning are considered under the heading 'micro models' in this chapter. Cross-cultural studies of comparatively more complex processes such as intelligence and cognitive style are reviewed in chapter 6.

The view that research on micro models of cognition is necessarily prior to research on macro models is unwarranted. Such a relationship may be implied by a reductionist logic but a research strategy of such a nature has characterized the development of psychological research neither generally nor in the cross-cultural area. Historically, socialization and personality were the foci of much cross-cultural investigation. The nature–nurture controversy within psychology gave impetus to numerous comparative studies of intelligence (cf. Porteus, 1931, for an early example; Vernon, 1969, a recent review), but perception attracted only limited notice mainly about the turn of the century (Rivers, 1901).

Investigation of macro models has received sustained attention. Piagetian concepts of intelligence have been studied as well as psychometric formulations. Just as Freud's comprehensive theory provoked early tests of its universality (Malinowski, 1927), so Piaget's theories were quickly subjected to trial in non-Western cultures (Mead, 1932). Studies of cognitive style are the exception and research on these processes has only recently been stimulated by the work of Witkin and his colleagues (Witkin *et al.*, 1962).

Studies of cognitive processes at a micro level have little history in cross-cultural psychology and receive scant attention currently but they must be undertaken if cultural differences are to be thoroughly understood. Memory is the only topic of those considered in this chapter to which historically psychologists have contributed. Bartlett (1932), in a classic monograph, considered the reputedly phenomenal memory of Africans; and Louttit (1931), in an early controlled study of immediate recall, compared the performance of adolescents from four cultures. The lack of research into the basic cognitive processes of peoples from diverse cultures is beginning to be noticed and research programmes to correct the deficiency have been initiated (e.g. Cole *et al.*, 1971; Gay and Cole, 1967; Heron, 1968).

Intellectual inspiration for the research examined here has often been drawn, in the absence of relevant psychological material, from the writings of anthropologists and philosophers. Impetus to cross-cultural investigation of basic thought processes has come from the work of Lévy-Bruhl (1922) who argued that civilized thought is characterized by reason, logic and scientific argument, while that of primitive man is emotion-laden, poetic and mythical. Lévy-Bruhl stressed the role of language and of cultural learning in producing different concepts and mental schemata in Western and non-Western man. Horton (1967 a and b), an anthropologist, has suggested that traditional thought attempts to solve the same problems as scientific theory but that the former is constrained by an inability to tolerate contradiction or ignorance. Horton has argued that while fundamental values or content may vary, the cognitive processes of non-Western man might be similar to those of Western man. He has suggested that the question can only be answered after considerable study of the basic cognitive processes of peoples from diverse cultures. Only then would it be possible to determine whether content and values differ while cognitive processes are universal or whether processes also vary in the face of diverse cultural experience.

Memory

Memory is an essential component in many of the perceptual tasks already reviewed. It may be recalled that clear support for the Whorf–Sapir hypothesis came only from work such as the Brown and Lenneberg (1954) investigation which showed a relationship between memory and colour codability.

In experimental studies using English subjects, Bartlett (1932) showed both that the cultural concerns of a group determined which aspects of experience would be recalled and also provided a context or schema into which these elements could be placed. Bartlett's cross-cultural investigations were spurred by visits to Africa and the repeated comments of Europeans on the prodigious memories of the Bantu peoples. He reported, only in passing, on the results of picture and story reproduction tests carried out on African subjects. He found their performance similar to that of English subjects and described in detail a naturalistic experiment with a twelve-year-old Swazi boy who, when asked to carry a message and recall it, performed no better than an English twelve year old. On the other hand, Bartlett was impressed when a forty-year-old Swazi herdsman could recall almost perfectly the details of his employer's complex series of cattle purchases of the previous year but compared this to some Englishmen's memories of sports statistics.

He noted the effect of cultural concerns on memory in a Swazi chief's account of a visit to England. The hand signals of English policemen, similar to those of a Swazi greeting, had been particularly salient. The evidence led Bartlett (1932, p. 267) to conclude, 'What is beyond dispute is that remembering, in a group, is influenced, as to its manner, directly by the preferred persistent tendencies of that group.' Although Bartlett did not employ a content-process distinction but wrote rather of matter and manner, it is clear that he considered recalled content to be determined by cultural experience within a particular social group. It is less certain whether the mechanisms of memory which he postulated to replace an atomistic associationism were intended to have cross-cultural validity or whether they were subject to modification as the result of cultural experience.

Several researchers have employed Bartlett's reproduction method to study the memory of Africans. The anthropologist, Nadel (1937), used his own stories and photographs in a study of secondary-school educated Nupe and Yoruba in Nigeria. He tested Nupe himself having learned the language while carrying out fieldwork in Nupe country, and trained two Yoruba teachers to test the Yoruba subjects. From his knowledge of the art, religion and ritual of the two cultures, Nadel devised qualitative categories into which to score the written recall material of his subjects. The procedure was used to identify themes such as (a) rational, logical and meaning intent interpretations, (b) numerative interpretations concerned with spatial and temporal arrangements, and (c) emotional and impressionistic interpretations. Nadel considered the first category most characteristic of Yoruba culture while the second and third included elements derived largely from Nupe culture.

The three types of responses occurred in the written recall material of Nupe and Yoruba subjects but their distributions differed. The evidence supported Nadel's hypothesis of a relationship between psychological and cultural differentiation. In part the study gave an affirmative answer to Bartlett's (1932, p. 255) question, 'Whether the preferred persistent tendencies of the group ever pass into the individual members . . .', but Bartlett's queries about the precise nature of the social transmission remain unanswered.

In a monograph primarily concerned with communication, Doob (1961) reported results of memory tests with Baganda and Zulu subjects. His main finding was a positive relationship between quality of recall and education. He also noted that skill in recall was correlated with knowledge of English, adherence to a world religion rather than an indigenous religious system and to rejection of other traditional beliefs. The latter variables probably co-vary with education. The brevity of Doob's reference makes assessment of these unique results difficult.

European/non-European comparisons are examined in a study of the recall of oral prose. Ross and Millsom (1970) contrasted the performance of Ghanaian and New York University students on two of Bartlett's original stories and a third tale presented in seventeenth-century English. The first recall trial took place without prior warning thirty-five to forty minutes after the story had been read, while the other two tests occurred after intervals of several weeks. The hypothesis of Ghanaian superiority, based upon the strong oral tradition of African societies, was tempered by consideration of the difficulty of the story in archaic English, the unfamiliarity of Ghanaians with the American accent of the experimenter and by the Ghanaians' use of English only as a second language. Analysis was carried out in terms of a theme count, a simple word count and the three temporal recall conditions, which produced six comparison conditions for each story. The performance of Ghanaians appeared significantly better on all comparisons on the first Bartlett story and in four out of six comparisons on the second. Only on the story in seventeenth-century English was there no Ghanaian superiority but on only one of the six comparisons were New York students significantly better. Unfortunately, Ross and Millsom did not discuss the cross-cultural differences beyond saying that the Ghanaian superiority had been predicted. Analysis of the material recalled led Ross and Millsom to suggest that accurate recall of meaningful content may be based on an inherent serial order in the narrative and that in the case of folktales their survival may attest to the strength of event sequence effects.

No firm conclusions can be drawn from cross-cultural studies which have utilized the Bartlett reproduction paradigm. Although Bartlett (1932) was not able to document an African superiority in recall, Ross and Millsom did find such an effect but it was tied to particular stimulus materials. Doob has shown that educated Africans have more precise recall than uneducated Africans and Nadel related the quality of the themes recalled to the concerns of the cultures he studied.

Cross-cultural findings based upon Bartlett's paradigm are inconclusive as is other cross-cultural work on memory. In 1954 Klineberg argued that it was impossible to comment on laws of learning and forgetting cross-culturally because of the scarcity of material. The situation was similar more than ten years later. The only experiment which Harari and McDavid (1966) drew upon in planning their cross-cultural study of memory was that of Louttit (1931).

Louttit used four tasks to assess the immediate recall ability of white, Chinese, Japanese and Hawaiian children of twelve and of about eighteen years living in Hawaii. 'The Marble Statue', a story reproduction task, was one of Louttit's auditory items while the other was a digit span test. He used two forms of visual assessment: one employing matrices composed of three rows and four columns of consonants presented on large cards and the other using cards with digit strings of various lengths. On none of these tasks was Louttit able to present significant cross-cultural differences and only on ten out of twenty-four comparisons was there a white superiority. Sex and age differences were greater than cultural differences.

Harari and McDavid drew upon Louttit's work in a study of twelve-year-old Israeli and American children. They used the Marble Statue Test as a method for assessing the recall of meaningful material but developed their own non-meaningful symbolic task. This test involved the presentation of cards which had two digits opposite a simple geometric figure. Theoretical impetus for the study came from the observation that American educators use recognition methods when assessing achievement while in Israel much greater stress is placed on reconstruction or recall procedures. Furthermore, American psychologists have consistently reported better scores on recognition measures than on recall measures of memory (e.g. Anastasi, 1932; Burt and Dobell, 1955). Recall and recognition measures were employed either immediately or forty-eight hours after exposure. Statistical problems made it difficult to assess the differences in recognition scores or to compare recognition and recall scores. Analysis of recall scores, however, showed the Israeli children's superiority to be highly significant. Although Harari and McDavid's final results were incomplete, they were sufficient to indicate the effect of experiential and training factors on measures of retention and to lead the authors to urge caution in the interpretation of cross-cultural comparisons. Their study highlights the culture-bound nature of the conclusion that recognition tasks are necessarily easier than recall measures.

The final group of studies investigating memory employs paradigms which derive from the study of verbal learning. The most extensive of these studies are those of Gay and Cole (1967; Cole and Gay, 1972). Gay had ample occasion to observe the heavy reliance placed on rote learning in African education while teaching in Liberia. He and Cole studied rote learning and memory using a free recall technique. The method is particularly suitable for cross-cultural research because it allows subjects to structure their responses as they wish. It is also easy to administer and adaptable in permitting as much practice as necessary. Subjects are presented with a series of stimuli to learn and told that they will be required to reproduce them in any order they wish.

Cole and Gay (1972) used the reliable differences in the free recall of Kpelle and Americans as the starting point of their investigations. When twenty common nouns drawn from four concept groups – food, tools, kitchen utensils and clothes – were used, the performance of American subjects improved with practice and showed recall based upon conceptual clustering, while that of Kpelle subjects failed to improve and showed no clustering.

To guard against ethnocentric bias in the definition of clusters, Cole and Gay investigated the validity of their concept categories for Kpelle culture. When the stimulus material and its organization proved meaningful in the Kpelle context they turned their attention to other conditions of the experimental situation. The manipulation of one physical cue and one linguistic constraint on recall eventually produced change in the free recall performance of the Kpelle. Clustering occurred when the experimenter asked Kpelle subjects to give all the words of a particular concept category, i.e. food items. The physical cue which aided recall was the use of chairs. When objects themselves rather than words were first used, Kpelle performance improved only slightly but when the objects were held up over four chairs, one for each concept category, performance improved markedly. Great ingenuity was shown by Cole and Gay in manipulating the experimental situation in such a way that the performance of American and Kpelle subjects became equivalent. There is still a long way to go in offering explanations of these effects but the work suggests that caution should be exercised in formulating the basic problem in the cross-cultural investigation of cognitive processes. The question, 'Do the thought processes of Europeans and non-Europeans differ?' may be too vague, and questions of the order 'Under what conditions are the performances of Europeans and non-Europeans similar and different?' may prove more meaningful and researchable.

Two doctoral dissertations which also employed verbal learning paradigms to investigate recall should also be noted before going on to examine learning. One, a study which compared the performances of Anglo-American and Mexican-American eleven year olds, found no cross-cultural differences in paired associate learning; in the other, an investigation of eight-, ten- and twelve-year-old American Indian and white American children reported better performance by Indian children (Doan, 1967; Purdy, 1968). Doan hypothesized that the use of meaningful (high association value) nouns, and consonant–vowel–consonant nonsense syllables would facilitate the performance of Anglo-Americans but not that of Mexican-Americans because the latter had difficulties with English. In fact, Doan found that meaningful material produced improvement in both groups. If the Mexican-Americans had any English language difficulties these did not interfere in the rote learning and recall of his material. In the second study Purdy used pictures in a paired associate paradigm to test American Indian and white children who had been matched on the Otis Quick Scoring Test of Mental Abilities. At all age levels the performance of Indian children was superior and at the twelve-year age level this difference was statistically significant. Rather than consider that Indians might have more efficient learning and memory processes, Purdy suggested that the original matching on the Otis Test was in error. He suggested that the Otis

Test had underestimated the intelligence of these Indian children and that they learned faster and remembered better (i.e. required fewer trials and committed fewer errors) because they were more intelligent. In terms of the scheme being used to organize the discussion of cognition, Purdy explained Indian behaviour at the micro level by resort to a macro concept, intelligence. Neither of these studies offers the last word on rote learning and memory but they do indicate that cross comparisons do not always support a European superiority in basic cognitive skills.

Learning

The meagre cross-cultural literature on discrimination learning is buttressed by a large and conceptually sophisticated research effort in experimental psychology. Evidence of this theoretical development is clear in the set of papers examining the reversal shift phenomenon in various cultural settings (Cole, Gay and Glick, 1968; Knowles and Boersma, 1968; Rapier, 1967). The authors aimed at exploring parameters of the reversal shift effect in non-Western settings but they were also forced to consider problems of stimulus definition. The question of what the stimulus means to the subject or along what dimensions he codes it is essentially an emic problem.

The remaining studies in this section do not fall neatly into a pattern. In so far as these additional reports share a common theme, it is the effect of stimulus processing rules on equivalence grouping, discrimination learning and classification. Any of the studies in this section can be structured etically in terms of the experimenter's definition of variables or emically according to the importance of dimensions for subjects.

Experimental psychologists have known for some time that adults learn a reversal shift more quickly than a non-reversal shift (Kendler and Mayzner, 1956) and that learning shows a developmental trend with reversals becoming easier and more frequent with increasing age (Kendler and Kendler, 1959). Thus subjects initially trained to match a to a′ and b to b′ will learn to match a to b′ and b to a′ more quickly than they will learn to match x to x′ and y to y′. A widely used experimental procedure combines exposure to two dimensions during initial training but makes one dimension irrelevant to the initial discrimination. Figure 6 illustrates this training procedure. Initial training makes colour relevant with black positive, while form is irrelevant. A reversal shift (RS) occurs when white becomes positive, while the non-reversal shift (NRS) makes form relevant, that is, circles become positive while colour becomes irrelevant to reinforcement. The Kendlers attribute the ease of reversal learning to a symbolic mediating response system which, they contend, results in a flexible self-regulating capacity for problem solving that only appears at an age of about seven years (Kendler and Kendler, 1970). Other theorists ascribe the facilitating effect of reversal

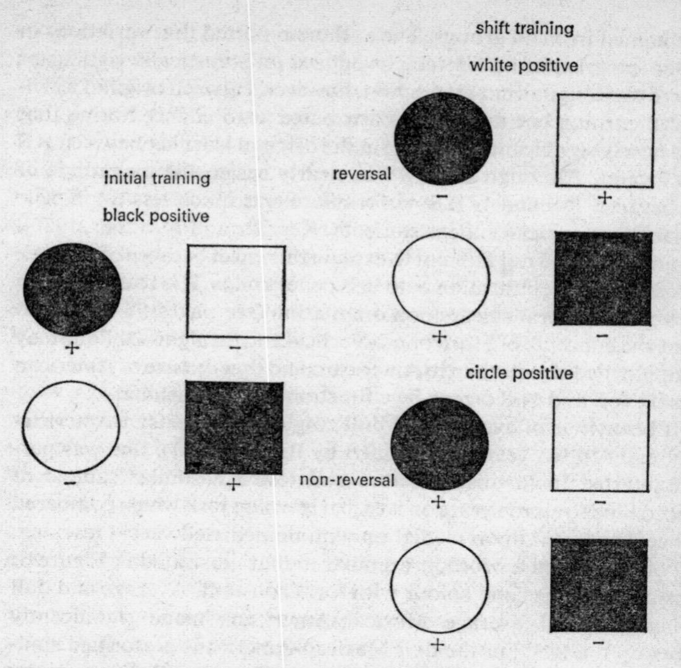

Figure 6 Reversal and non-reversal shift training (adapted from Kendler and Kendler, 1962, p. 5)

shifts to the positive transfer of a central selective attentional response intermediate between the external stimulus array and the instrumental response (Shepp and Turrisi,1966). Efforts to determine whether mediation is of a verbal-symbolic or attentional nature has led to the further differentiation of non-reversal shifts into those involving intradimensional (ID) and extradimensional (ED) transfer. While this controversy has exercised experimental child psychologists, the cross-cultural studies reviewed here have tacitly accepted the Kendlers' formulation.

The reversal shift performance of illiterate Kpelle adults and children and of Kpelle school children was investigated by Cole, Gay and Glick (1968) using a matching procedure in which subjects were initially trained either on a Horizontal–Vertical match or a Straight–Oblique match. In the RS condition the concept remained the same but targets and reinforcement were reversed. NRS subjects learned a new concept match; thus, those trained on the Horizontal–Vertical match learned the Straight–Oblique match and vice versa. Clear evidence of superior performance on the reversal shift was obtained from all groups. The authors reported that variations in acculturation experience, i.e. literacy, produced no statistically significant effects. There was a significant interaction, however, between original learning and shift learning but the authors attributed it to chance noting that there was a nearly significant difference in the original learning between R S and N R S groups. Although the R S was clearly easier, the magnitude of difference between R S and N R S performance was much less for Kpelle subjects than for American college students (Kendler and Mayzner, 1956). Cole, Gay and Glick did not attempt to explain this effect because of the lack of differences due to acculturation among Kpelle groups. It is reasonable, in the light of cross-cultural research on orientation (see pages 57 to 58), to suggest that the concepts of Horizontal–Vertical and Straight–Oblique may be newer to Kpelle subjects than to Americans and that the size of American differences on R S and N R S may be a function of overlearning.

The shift behaviour of average and dull Anglo- and Mexican-American children of eight to ten years was studied by Rapier (1967). She was particularly interested in linguistic factors and tested a similar sample of children aged nine to eleven years on a verbal learning task which compared performance dependent upon mediation with unmediated verbal learning. Her study of shifts used a procedure similar to that illustrated in Figure 6; the dimensions were size and colour with form constant. Average and dull Anglo-Americans and average Mexican-Americans made significantly fewer errors on the R S, but the dull Mexican-Americans performed similarly on the R S and N R S. Accepting the position that R S superiority depends on mediating responses and noting that the dull Mexican-Americans performed better than dull Anglo-Americans on the verbal task which supplied mediators, Rapier suggested that dull Mexican-Americans' deficit may be related to lack of verbal experience in developing mediators and not a process difficulty in making associations. It should be noted that the shift study and verbal learning study employed different subjects with only ten children in each category in each. The suggestion that the performance similarity of dull Mexican-Americans on R S and N R S can be accounted for by 'the lack of a reservoir of verbal associations which [they] can evoke in any new learning situation' (Rapier, 1967, p. 47) cannot be distinguished from an attention theory explanation hypothesizing low initial probabilities for dull Mexican-Americans to attend to dimensions of size and colour. The problem of the unfamiliarity of the dimensions critical for discrimination is an issue in either interpretation.

The optional shift procedure (Kendler, Kendler and Learnard, 1962) which enables classification of responses in terms of preference for reversal, non-reversal and inconsistent strategies was employed by Knowles and Boersma (1968) in a study comparing eight- to eight-and-a-half-year-old

Canadian-Indian and middle-class Canadian children. Initial training was similar to that shown in Figure 6 but size and brightness were the relevant dimensions with form constant. After initial training to a criterion of nine correct out of ten consecutive responses, subjects were given optional shift training. In this sequence only one pair of the stimuli employed in initial training is used and the reward contingencies reversed. Thus a subject, trained as indicated on Figure 6 to choose circles, might have a black circle and a white square during optional shift training but the white square would now be reinforced and not the black circle. In the test series after this training both pairs would appear, and reinforcement could be obtained either by an RS or an NRS strategy, i.e. by the choice of squares or of white figures. Inconsistent preference is not frequent by eight years of age.

Knowles and Boersma employed the optional shift procedure because they were particularly interested in the mediation process. They assumed that mediation would be facilitated for Indian children by the use of familiar, concrete stimuli and thus employed large and small tin cans with white and black labels on them as well as the usual drawings of large and small, black and white squares. Significantly more middle-class children chose RS solutions but there were no differences in RS and NRS preference with concrete stimuli. Both cultural groups showed slightly more preference for RS with abstract stimuli. The failure to confirm the prediction of an Indian preference for RS using concrete stimuli may lie, as the authors suggested, in the choice of stimuli. They seem to have failed to find stimuli which differentiate between the groups in the elicitation of verbal responses. The possibility of an attentional difficulty is also raised by the suggestion that in handling cans, cues for dimensions other than those of brightness or size may be evoked. Perhaps the most noteworthy finding was the failure to show any relationship between speed of learning and shift preference. There was also a failure to show a difference in the speed with which Indian and middle-class children reached criterion. Although middle-class children preferred RS more often than Indian children, Indian children reached criterion in the same number of trials by their preferred strategies. There was no deficit in the performance of this sample of non-Western children, given a procedure which allowed success by more than one strategy.

Linguistic factors have been considered indirectly in the discussion of mediation in reversal shift studies but Cole, Gay, Glick and Sharp (1968) attacked the problem directly in a study comparing transposition of a discrimination by Kpelle and American children. They noted that, in the Kpelle language size comparisons were usually made by placing the larger member first: 'John is bigger than Mike' is common, but not its inverse, 'Mike is smaller than John.' This led to speculation on the outcome of transposition training. The stimulus material was a series of ten white plastic squares each differing in size from the next by a factor of 1·4. Illiterate Kpelle children four to five and six to eight years, school-going Kpelle six to eight years and American nursery-school children three to five years were trained on the fifth and sixth squares in the series to choose either the smaller or the larger. Immediately after the criterion of nine correct out of ten consecutive responses was met, children were tested on either a near, i.e. squares 4 *v.* 5, 6 *v.* 7, a medium, i.e. squares 3 *v.* 4, 7 *v.* 8, or a large transposition, i.e. squares 1 *v.* 2, 9 *v.* 10. A strong form of the Whorf–Sarpi hypothesis predicts that Kpelle children would learn the bigger discrimination more quickly and would be more successful on the up transpositions, i.e. choosing 2 over 1 or 10 rather than 9. There was no evidence of cultural difference in acquisition but the older and school-going Kpelle learned more quickly and made more accurate responses on the first transposition trial. The linguistic factor affected performance only on initial choice before training began. Here Kpelle children chose the larger stimulus more often than would be expected by chance. When children were required to explain their choice behaviour after satisfying the performance criterion, Kpelle and American children gave the same proportion of relevant explanations for the down transposition but Kpelle children gave almost twice as many correct relevant explanations of up transposition. These results are congruent with those presented in chapter 2 when considering the Whorf–Sapir hypothesis. On an ambiguous task such as the initial trial in discrimination learning, or when memory is involved, as in recalling the choice principle, language affects cognition. In the learning sequence constrained by experimenter-determined reinforcement patterns, no linguistic effect appeared.

Tribal, rural non-tribal and urban Asian-Indian children were trained to discriminate similar geometric figures. One set of subgroups learned to respond differentially to circles and ellipses and rectangles and parallelograms. The other subgroups were trained on obtuse and acute angled triangles and circles with triangles inside or outside them. Nanda, Das and Mishra (1965) argued that their six- to ten-year-old subjects would not have verbal labels available to mediate these discriminations and questioned whether differential past experience would affect learning none the less. Chi square analysis based upon numbers of subjects from each environmental group who failed to learn the discrimination showed highly significant differences. Urban children consistently outperformed rural and tribal children. An analysis of variance based on trials to criterion failed to show any significant differences. The authors concluded that 'the level of performance and not the speed of learning turns out to be a reliable measure for use in the cross-cultural samples' (Nanda, Das and Mishra, 1965, p. 200). This is a curious conclusion as there were no tests of the reliability of either measure and even if validity is the intended term, it is difficult to understand why the authors place greater faith in a measure which shows differences than in one which indicates similarities in performance. Their faith could be partially justified, as the failure of the analysis of variance to produce significant differences may result from the non-normal distributon of trial scores. Heterogeneity of variance is also likely as sixty-two out of eighty subjects in the tribal group failed to learn the discrimination and hence were arbitrarily assigned scores of 16, which are equal to the number of training trials. It does seem likely that tribal, rural and urban children learn to discriminate similar geometric figures at different rates but the report is not conclusive and gives no indication of the factors underlying the differences.

The learning task, which Evans and Segall (1969) presented to Baganda children from rural and urban environments with differing amounts of schooling, was a concept discovery problem. The discovery technique employed required subjects to select from four cards two which could be the same either in colour or function. Thus, a set of four objects might include a blue book and a blue cup as well as a non-blue bottle, which is a second container, and a non-blue hat. For a given series subjects were required to match to the concept which the experimenter held, either colour or function and only reinforced when their choice matched the concept he held. Verbal feedback served as reinforcement for choices deemed correct by the experimenter.

All groups, whether from urban, semi-urban or rural backgrounds, unschooled or with primary 1, 2 or 5, learned the colour concept with ease. Of the 270 children tested, only thirty-five failed completely to discover the colour concept in twenty trials and the overall mean trials to the criterion of four consecutive correct responses was 7·51 for those who solved the problem. Results from function learning were different with eighty-four failures. These occurred predominantly among unschooled and primary 1 children from rural and semi-urban areas. However, only for primary 5 children was function as easy as colour matching and then only when it was the first discovery task. Interest in the effects of schooling and environment prompted Evans and Segall to replicate the study with groups of rural and urban Baganda adults. Those with fewer than four years' schooling did not learn the function concept. For adults able to learn a function to the criterion of four consecutive correct responses, colour was easier and learning first on colour again appeared to interfere with function. To investigate the inhibiting effect of learning colour first drawings of shaded and unshaded objects rather than those differing in hue were used in a study with thirty urban primary 3 children. In the main study twenty-eight children had reached criterion with colour; only eleven subjects in the second study succeeded using the shading concept. Trials to criterion on function remained stable indicating that though shading was a more difficult task, function was not easier.

Evans and Segall offer little theoretical explanation apart from suggesting that colour and function concepts have differing primacy in Baganda subjects' habit hierarchies depending on environment and schooling. Colour concepts receive perceptual support as they noted and have high attentional value (Serpell, 1968b; Suchman, 1966). The function concepts used in the study may not only receive no perceptual support in the stimulus material but also be unfamiliar in Baganda culture. Unlike the Cole and Gay (1972) free recall study, no effort was made to investigate Baganda concepts of superordinate categories. The clear effect of schooling on function matching both in children and adults indicates not only that these categories or equivalences are traditionally unfamiliar but that they are only acquired after considerable tuition. The failure of children over age for their class placement suggests further that this type of learning, i.e. function matching, is as difficult as the acquisition of academic skills.

A concern for using function concepts appropriate to their cultural settings is related to issues examined by Greenfield, Reich and Olver (1966) in their cross-cultural studies of equivalence. Using data gathered from Mexican, Eskimo and Wolof children in Senegal, they concluded that form and function equivalence depended upon Western education. In particular they suggested that schooling forces the use of language to analyse perception and that, without this impetus, restructuring divorced from perceptual support fails to occur. Their conclusion 'that modern technical societies demand of their members a fundamental cognitive change as their capacities change with biological growth; whereas traditional non-technical societies demand only the perfection and elaboration of first ways of looking at the world' (Greenfield, Reich and Olver, 1966, p. 318) suggests that the search for function concepts appropriate to Baganda is not useful. Their approach is thoroughly etic and Western modes of classification are viewed as necessary for cognitive growth. The Bruner *et al.* (1966) formulation also contains a variant on the old argument that primitives are concrete thinkers while Western man is abstract, but it is one buttressed by some empirical evidence and an elaborate theory of the interrelation of language and cognitive development. Non-Western subjects were tested using a free sort technique to determine whether they employed colour, form or function superordinates which were defined by the experimenters. Thought processes were identified as concrete or tied to perception when they employed colour primarily or when their performance only showed evidence of modification as the result of Western education. Emphasis on the role of schooling indicates that symbolic representation is potentially accessible to all. The question remains, however, whether an etic approach is sufficient in studying equivalence or classification cross-culturally.

Classification has been studied by psychologists using an emic approach, i.e. employing the concept hierarchies of subjects studied rather than those of experimenters. Price-Williams (1962) used indigenous plants and models of animals to study Tiv children's classification strategies and reported no major differences in the skills of schooled and unschooled children six and a half to eleven years. Kellaghan (1968) explored classificatory behaviour of eleven- to twelve-year-old Yoruba schoolboys from rural and urban backgrounds on two standard psychological tests and another test composed of twenty-six objects familiar to Yorubas. All three tests required abstraction from colour and form attributes. Only with the familiar objects was the performance of rural and urban boys similar; on the Goldstein–Scheerer Cube Test it differed a little and it was markedly different on the Colour Form Test. Kellaghan noted that Yoruba children, especially those in the rural sample, learned during assessment on the Cube Test but generally they showed poorer abstraction ability on the standard tests than did Irish children whom he also tested. Kellaghan concluded that Yoruba children were more colour dominant than Irish children and that differing attentional strategies allowed Irish children to employ more alternative methods of classification. Low intercorrelations on the standard tests for Yoruba children but evidence that the tests were measuring a common ability among Irish children led him to question whether the three procedures were each measuring the same underlying process of abstraction.

Deregowski and Serpell (1971) have examined this question from a different perspective in a study of Zambian and Scottish children. Subjects were required to sort models of animals, colour photos of the models and black and white photos. The performance of Zambian and Scottish children was equivalent in sorting models but not when sorting photos. These differences led Deregowski and Serpell to conclude that the nature of the stimulus affected experimenter judgements about the nature of the classificatory process. For the experimenter the dimensions along which animals can be ordered remain the same but the mode of representation was clearly shown to affect the ability of Zambian children to sort.

Further studies which show the advantage of using familiar materials include those of Okonji (1971) and Irwin and McLaughlin (1970). Using a Piagetian conceptual framework, Okonji found no differences in the number of classes produced by Nigerian and Scottish children when sorting animals but he found a Nigerian superiority at age eleven when both groups were required to sort objects familiar only to Nigerians. Okonji concluded that for English children able to perform the necessary logical operations, i.e. concrete operational eleven to twelve year olds, the absence of appropriate superordinates inhibited their performance.

A similar point is made in a study based upon within group comparisons. Irwin and McLaughlin found that illiterate adult Manos (Liberians) were highly skilled at sorting, shifting sorts and describing the bases of classification when the materials used were bowls of rice which differed in three ways held to be functionally important in Mano culture. This performance contrasted with their ability to sort geometric figures of differing colour and number. On the geometric figures children with four to six years' schooling excelled adults and children with less schooling. The authors showed that preference for a particular kind of sort, i.e. colour, form, number or function, need not be isomorphic with ability and used initial sort as a measure of preference and later shifts to other bases of classification as indicative of the subjects' range of ability. Irvine and McLaughlin also noted that the ability to explain a previous sort was indicative of sucessful completion of the next sort and suggested, following Brown and Lenneberg (1954), that codability may play an important role in flexible equivalence grouping. Gay and Cole (1967) in a similar study also undertaken in Liberia concluded that sort preference was an area requiring further cross-cultural investigation. Their advice still seems timely.

It is clear from the studies reviewed here that we must refine Horton's appeal that more information on basic cognitive processes be collected before an attempt is made to decide whether non-Western and Western men employ the same strategies in thinking. Studies of equivalence, classification and discrimination learning indicate that similarity or difference in performance of European and non-European subjects can be modified by experimental procedures and particularly by task content. Although differences can always be ascribed to the unfamiliarity of test material and although the ideal of equally familiar tasks can never be completely realized, the studies cited indicate that some researchers are conscious of the problem and seeking solutions to it.

6 Cognition: Macro Models

In the best of all possible worlds this final substantive chapter would be empirically as well as conceptually integrative. The discussion thus far has dealt with individual cognitive skills. Intelligence, as conceived either by psychometricians or by Piagetians, is a concept at a higher level. Butcher's (1969, p. 25) definition makes this point in a manner particularly appropriate to the cross-cultural perspective.

It is quintessentially high level skill at the summit of a hierarchy of intellectual skills. It will always function in the integrating manner described, but on different material and with different hierarchies and with varying ceilings of complexity according to the experience of the individual.

Psychometric and Piagetian formulations of intelligence will be examined here in relation to cross-cultural research on cognition and perception. The third macro level model to be considered, cognitive style, can be viewed as the most integrative of the three. Through the use of concepts such as field dependence and differentiation, Witkin *et al.* (1962) take account of individual difference and developmental change in a theory dealing with both higher and lower level cognitive processes.

Psychologists differ in choosing to pursue either micro or macro level strategies in their studies of cognition. Experimental psychologists prefer to investigate 'simpler' cognitive skills, while other psychologists, attracted by molar concepts, invest their energies in studies of intelligence and cognitive style. In Euro-American psychology both enterprises flourish and while interaction between these groups of researchers has hitherto been limited, more is now developing. Thus Ferguson's (1954) work on skills and particularly transfer effects, has offered theoretical insights for understanding the structure of intelligence (Anastasi, 1970). Cross-cultural study of micro level cognition and perception currently offers little hope of producing similar support for macro models. Analysis thus far has revealed that the Emperor has, if not 'no clothes', at best very few. Theories currently being developed at a macro level can expect little buttressing from micro level cross-cultural investigation. This statement is valid in terms of empirical description as well as of theoretical development. It is difficult to state a theoretical principle which derives from micro level cultural explanations of cognition but it is equally embarrassing to look for a behavioural law whose cultural parameters have been systematically marked. For instance one might examine studies of visual illusions (Segall, Campbell and Herskovits, 1966) but many questions have recently been raised concerning this work (see pages 70 to 75).

Psychometric intelligence, Piagetian intelligence and cognitive style are examined independently in this chapter. The separation of psychometric and Piagetian intelligence is pragmatic rather than conceptual; indeed, the last decade has seen a steady *rapprochement* of these positions (Green, Ford and Flamer, 1971; Hunt, 1961). Psychometric research is reviewed first because it has a longer history in cross-cultural studies. The early investigations of Piagetian concepts in non-Western settings tended to deal with topics such as animism (Mead, 1932) which are not central to the later theory of Piaget discussed here. Despite the disclaimer of interaction between levels of analysis in the cross-cultural study of cognition, reference to perceptual and cognitive skills will be made where possible and especially in so far as they pertain to the discussion of cognitive style.

Psychometric intelligence

Intelligence is at the same time one of the most widely used psychological terms and one of the most misunderstood. Cynics, following the controversy occasioned by Eysenck's (1971) book on intelligence and race, might add 'even by its practioners'. Research on intelligence in other societies has stirred debate since the turn of the century and intrigued laymen with the possibility of a racial hierarchy of intelligence.

In a remarkably contemporary paper published in 1936, Goodenough made the point that intelligence referred to high level cognitive skills which were evidenced in adaptive functioning in particular environmental settings and that tests only sampled a limited range of skills in order to make inferences about intelligent behaviour within that setting. From this perspective Goodenough understood the folly of testing people of diverse cultures with instruments designed to sample middle-class Euro-American intellectual capacities – inventories such as the Stanford Binet or the Weschler Adult Intelligence Scale.

The discussion thus far raises two fundamental issues: one concerns the culture-bound nature of definitions of intelligence, the other, the biological or genetic basis of intelligence. At a general level there is also a need to understand the nature of intelligence. These themes recur throughout the discussion of psychometric intelligence but the first section will briefly examine each of them specifically. Next an analysis will be undertaken of results from cross-cultural investigations aimed at exploring the structure of intellectual abilities. Finally, the practical problems of intelligence testing and selection for further training will be considered.

The concept of intelligence

Some steps toward a definition of intelligence have been taken in considering intelligence as a macro model of cognition, in the quotation from Butcher and the review of Goodenough's position on cross-cultural testing. A completely operational definition of intelligence, which would tie it to specific tests was rejected because it seemed particularly foolhardy in cross-cultural research where instrument modification to suit new environments is common. Intelligence is viewed rather as an integrative high level skill manifested in a range of operations applied to a variety of materials.

The need to explicate the relationship of intelligence and experience is clear; both Cattell (1963) and Hebb (1949) have examined the question. Biological endowment has been described by these theorists respectively as 'fluid' intelligence and intelligence A. The realization of this potential, through experiences in specific environmental settings, is labelled 'crystallized' intelligence and intelligence B. The major difference in the formulations of Cattell and Hebb lies in the belief of the former that each of these components can be directly assessed. Cattell holds that fluid intelligence can itself be measured. Vernon (1969) has argued that Cattell's test of fluid intelligence, while not bound by the verbal restraints of a particular culture, is none the less tapping skills which have been modified by cultural experience. Vernon has provided the term intelligence C to specify that sample of behaviour which is actually measured in efforts to infer intelligence B (Vernon, 1955); he suggested that it was possible to measure directly neither intelligence A nor B.

Cattell's formulation of fluid intelligence places him in one of the major debating arenas of intelligence testing; this is the nature–nurture controversy. Its protagonists align themselves according to the outcomes of efforts to assess the relative importance of the components of potential and experience in functional intelligence. Behaviour geneticists have developed analysis of variance techniques which, along with systematic assignment of sibs to rearing conditions, yield estimates of the effects of genetic potential and nurturance for given situations (Hirsh, 1967). Cattell (1963) has also offered an analysis of variance procedure which employs within- and between-family variation in order to assess, for a given population, the contribution of genetic and environmental factors. Assignment for human rearing is unlikely and even the extension of Cattell's family analysis across cultures is problematic. Efforts to assess the relative contributions of potential and environment are premature in the cross-culture sphere where it can be validly claimed there is still doubt about what is to be measured and how to do it.

Cross-cultural intelligence testing has been undertaken with culture-free and culture-fair tests. Anastasi (1968) has described a number of the instruments which have been developed to meet these aims and offers an explanation of their underlying assumptions and shortcomings. The inventories which she discussed include the Leiter International Performance Sacle, Cattell's Culture Fair Intelligence Test, Raven's Progressive Matrices and the Goodenough Harris Draw-a-Man Test. The attempt to produce culture-free tests was initially bound up with the view that innate potential and the results of experience could be separated and assessed directly. General recognition that, throughout development, potential and experience interact has shifted efforts from devising culture-free tests, which would peel away cultured experience, to devising culture-fair tests; these would allow less biased measurement given the lasting but diverse effects of cultural experience.

The strategy in developing culture-fair tests is to avoid, or modify, those variables along which behaviour in different cultures varies markedly. The assumption that pictorial material rather than words was culturally fairer was only recently challenged by Hudson's work on depth perception (see pages 61 to 66) and it is now appreciated that different cultures produce different rule systems for interpreting drawings. Other strategies have been to use untimed tests and to exclude content items tied to particular cultural experiences, i.e. references to snow or television.

The Leiter International Performance Scale, for example, has no time limit and requires almost no instructions either verbal or mimed, but it introduces each subtest with training tasks which allow the subject to learn what is required. The cognitive skills sampled include number memory, colour and form matching, seriation, classification, analogies and spatial relations. These tasks are similar to those employed in micro level studies but the aim of their administration in the Leiter Scale is to produce an overall assessment of intelligence – mental ages (M A) and intelligence quotients (I Q) – rather than to investigate particular cognitive skills. To intelligence testers, particular cognitive processes are secondary; their strategy is to seek overall measures. They wish to assess the products of perception and cognition, i. e. intelligence.

The aim of producing tests fair to individuals with differing cultural experience has met with varying success. The more that is known about micro level cognitive functioning across cultures, the better test construction should become. In so far as we are unable to assess the effect of culture upon memory, we cannot be certain that a test of number memory is fair. The *reductio ad absurdum* is reached in a parody by Bernardoni (1964) from which the point emerges that if a test is to be truly representative of the cultural context in which it is developed it may not lend itself to genuine comparison in different cultures. Bernardoni's suggestion can be entertained because we are in the dark concerning basic cognitive functioning.

If the core problem being attacked in the construction of culture-fair tests were the ranking of the societies of the world in terms of intelligence it would be necessary to heed Bernardoni's warning. However, intelligence testing is usually undertaken in non-Western settings either to further understanding of cognitive function or to solve practical problems of selection.

A more precise model of the nature of intelligence is necessary as a tool for understanding the literature of cross-cultural testing. Pages can be filled describing theorists' models of intelligence but these will only be examined in so far as they furnish a paradigm useful in cross-cultural analysis.

In the early days of intelligence testing conflicting trans-Atlantic traditions developed in the analysis of intelligence test results. Led by Spearman and then Burt, English workers interpreted the intercorrelations of test results in a hierarchical fashion. Thus, in their factor analyses of a battery, effort was first made to extract that portion of the variances which was common to all subtests. This factor was identified as a general intelligence dimension and was labelled by Spearman as the *g* factor. It was customary, having extracted the *g* factor, to group the next set of factors in terms of test characteristics and to identify a verbal-educational group (*v:ed*) and a spatial-perceptual-practical group (*k:m*). Similarly, these factors were analysed into more specific components. At the bottom of the factor tree were those portions of variance specific to particular tests (Vernon, 1969).

In America, factor analysis of intelligence test scores was guided by different assumptions. Thurstone argued that, in a diverse battery, a single high level cognitive skill could not be expected to influence performance on every subtest. In his analysis he set out to identify a set of basic cognitive functions or, as Thurstone (1938) later labelled them, 'Primary Mental Abilities', i.e. spatial ability (S), perceptual speed (P), numerical ability (N), verbal meaning (V), memory (M), verbal fluency (W), inductive reasoning (I) and deductive reasoning (D). American theorizing has pursued the course set by Thurstone and culminated in the work of Guilford (1959). His three-dimensional representation of intellect has five operations, six products and four kinds of content. Thus Guilford has suggested 120 factors of intelligence. The focus of his research effort has been in devising specific tests to measure each of these factors.

The problem for cross-cultural research is in choosing a model of intelligence which will facilitate meaningful comparisons. Vernon (1969) argued for the hierarchical formulations suggesting that the detailed factor approach with its need to identify a host of dimensions in specific subtests stood little chance of immediate success. Whole new test batteries would have to be devised and there is little likelihood of comparability. By and large, published cross-cultural studies of intelligence support Vernon's argument. The choice of a structural model may be problematic, but cross-

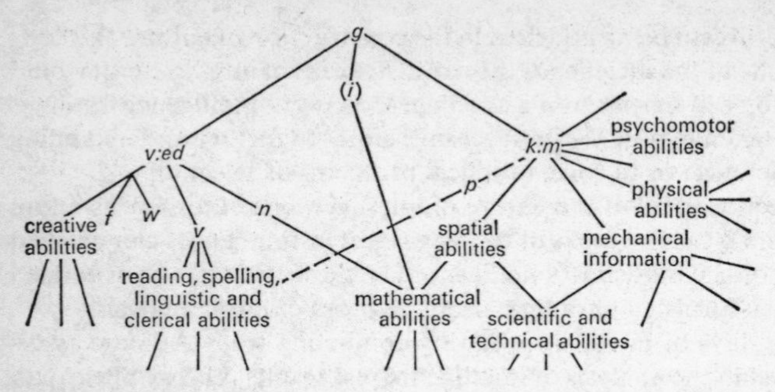

Figure 7 The structure of main general and group factors underlying a variety of ability tests applied to Euro-American adults and adolescents (from Vernon, 1969 p. 22)

cultural comparisons seeking differences in organization have positive advantage over older approaches. Early cross-cultural investigations of intelligence focused on mean differences across societies and lent themselves readily to the ranking of societies for intelligence. Structural analyses disregard mean levels but examine, instead, the intercorrelations of test results. Both of these strategies consider cognition at a molar level but the structural approach is more liable to raise theoretically interesting issues and less likely to lead to invidious comparisons. It is adopted in the section below which considers results of cross-cultural research.

Cross-cultural testing: the structure of abilities

Structural interpretations of intelligence are based upon factor analyses of correlation matrices of batteries containing a range of tests presumed to tap a variety of cognitive and perceptual skills. Thurstone (1938) employed fifty-six tests with a sample of 240 college students when he presented his set of Primary Mental Abilities (P M A). The first cross-cultural factor analysis was probably that of Macdonald which was based upon tests administered during the Second World War to hundreds of East African army recruits. Loadings on the first two factors which Macdonald extracted for thirteen tests have been presented by Vernon (1961, p. 106).

Vernon has suggested that the first factor was related to the adaptability of individuals to the strangeness of the tests. In an experimental study varying administration procedures, Irvine (1964) has shown that it is possible to remove this test adaptability source of variance. This first factor is not like general intelligence or Spearman's *g* since it loads heavily on form board and dexterity tests while *g* would normally be expected to load on tests involving logical relationships. In fact the highest loading on this first factor is 0·77 on the screwboard dexterity test. The only loading to fall below 0·40 is that of 0·27 on mechanical comprehension. The second factor loads positively on the subset of tests which can be construed as cognitive, i.e. including matrices and arithmetic, and negatively on a manipulative and physical subset. The positive pole can be identified as *g* but its opposite pole is closer to *k:m*, the spatial-perceptual-practical group. This result raises the interesting question, as Vernon points out, of whether, on the basis of these East African results, it is legitimate to regard *k:m* as a 'descendant' in the hierarchical sense discussed earlier, of *g*. *k:m* may arise initially from man's physical abilities and only later be incorporated with higher level cognitive skills.

Though burdened with the problems of a limited range of suitable tests, pre-computer age statistical analysis and lack of cultural identification of subjects, this early study emphasizes the value of cross-cultural research on the structure of intelligence. While a comparison of performance means might lead to the conclusion that East Africans are more, less or equally intelligent as a sample of Europeans, these results raise fundamental questions about the development of the structure of intelligence. Later work by Hofstaetter (1954) has shown that the primacy of factors changes with age; Macdonald's data show that it may also vary developmentally with cultural experience.

Despite this early success (possibly because it was little known until Vernon's report), the number of factor analytic studies, in a growing literature on cross-cultural cognition, is not great. In a general article on trait organization, Anastasi (1970) lists only six cross-cultural studies concerned with structure. The most geographically diverse, that of Vernon (1969), compares the structure of intelligence in samples tested in Africa, the West Indies, Canada, England and the Hebrides. Using tests of Philippine and Chinese-American students, Guthrie (1963) and Vandenberg (1959) deal with the effects of bilingualism on factor structure; while Das (1963), Vandenberg (1966) and Guttman and Guttman (1963) report on the structure of intelligence of subjects who speak Indo-European languages. Irvine (1966, 1969a to c), in a series of studies has analysed much of the available test material for East and Central Africa.

Guthrie's (1963) study undertaken in the Philippines is an example of research designed to investigate Whorf–Sapir inspired questions on the nature of linguistic determinants of cognition in relation to the structure of intelligence. Subjects were bilingual college girls aged between nineteen and twenty-two who spoke Tagalog, a Malayo-Polynesian language and related Philippine dialects at home but who were educated in English. The battery included tests in English and Tagalog and was designed to measure a general verbal factor and ideational and verbal fluency in Tagalog. The total battery of fifty tests, administered in eight hours of group testing, sampled verbal, numerical, spatial and visualization factors, and included tests of motor and perceptual speed, inductive, deductive and general reasoning, and rote and meaningful memory. In view of Vandenberg's (1959) work on bilingual Chinese students, Guthrie expected to find a factor specific to the Tagalog language and unique reasoning factors.

These earlier findings were, in fact, paralleled in Guthrie's results. Numerical, verbal, rote memory, visualization, motor and perceptual speed, and ideational fluency factors were found which showed similar patterns to American studies. Separate English and Tagalog vocabulary factors replicated the Chinese and English factors of Vandenberg. English spelling emerged as a factor distinct from verbal facility and digital facility was separate from numerical facility. These factors may relate to an overlearning of spelling and counting, a recognized feature of Philippine education. The failure to find any of the memory factors loading on the scholastic assessment measure was surprising. As in Africa, outside observers have stressed the emphasis on memory in Philippine education. Guthrie accepted the validity of this finding and explained it by suggesting that observations concerning the importance of memory may reflect only a lack of spontaneity in speech deriving from deficits in English, a second language for Philippine students. The work on Philippine and Chinese bilinguals suggested considerable overlap in factor structure with American models of organization. Of course these American-trained researchers used the models which they knew and there was no implication that a hierarchical model had been tried and rejected.

In a study which is virtually unique in the cross-cultural literature, Vandenberg (1967) has assessed statistically the degree of congruence in the factor structures which he derived from results with Chinese and South American students. He administered similar batteries to the two samples; of the thirty-one scales, twenty came from Thurstone's (1938) study of P M A, seven were numerical and figural tests while four were specially constructed verbal tests in Chinese and Spanish. Despite known cross-cultural difficulties with timed tests, this method of testing was retained in order to maintain similarity with the original Thurstone conditions. In addition, subjects were students with complete secondary-school education accustomed to test conditions. In both studies Vandenberg followed the factor analytic procedures laid down by Thurstone but he suggested that the first factor he extracted 'resembles the British idea of a "general" intelligence factor, even after rotation' (Vandenberg, 1967, p. 184). While this is an intriguing sidelight, the major consideration here is the comparison of the two samples after the transformation of the South American data according to Ahmavaara's (1957) method. This involved rotating the South American results towards the position of factors found in the Chinese study and then employing Tucker's Index of

Congruence. Vandenberg has promised a further comparison in which both results are rotated and neither is assumed to be the model. Using the Chinese data as a model the congruence indices for the seven common factors ranged from 0·953 to 0·780. The factors identified were (a) native language, (b) verbal ability, (c) memory, (d) spatial visualization, (e) perceptual speed, (f) number ability and (g) a poorly defined reasoning component. With the exception of the native language factor these results are similar to Thurstone's PMA.

Vernon (1965 a and b, 1966, 1967 a and b, 1969) has undertaken an ambitious comparative study of the range and structure of intelligence, relating it to differences in cultural environment. He has not, however, employed statistical tests of congruence across cultures. His battery of twenty-three tests included verbal and educational measures, induction, concept development and creativity tests, Piagetian scales, as well as assessment of spatial and perceptual functioning. It was administered to schoolboys usually in groups. The test results from a sample of 100 English boys of ten to twelve years were used to derive distributions of Deviation Quotients (similar to I Qs) which served as norms for each test. The non-English samples also ranged from ten to twelve years. Of the forty Scottish boys examined individually in the Hebrides, half were from homes in which Gaelic was spoken while the remainder spoke English at home. The ninety Canadian boys included Eskimos and Indians; twenty-eight of the fifty Ugandans were from the dominant Baganda kingdom, but this sample also included students from fifteen other ethnic groups. The fifty Jamaican subjects included boys from rural and urban backgrounds but it was biased in favour of the urban environment.

The traditional first order *g* factor was recognizable in the factor analyses of the test batteries for Jamaicans, Eskimo and Canadian-Indian boys but the tests which loaded on *g* and the size of loadings varied across the cultures. Vernon (1969) suggested that the Eskimo showed the highest *g* loadings due to sample heterogeneity but he also reported that the same subjects showed high *g* loading on a number of group intelligence tests administered by MacArthur (1967). The first factor in the Canadian-Indian results was similar and loaded, as expected, on tests of abstraction and matrices, but these tests also showed a substantial loading on a verbal educational factor (*v:ed*) and a spatial factor. The Porteus Maze, picture recognition and form board showed low *g* loadings while the sorting test and creativity measures failed to load on *g*. Jamaican results on the other hand showed first order loadings on matrices, sorting, Piagetian conservation and visualization tests combined but also loaded on arithmetic, information learning and Kohs Blocks.

Although Canadian-Indian and Eskimo factor structures were similar, there were marked differences in the relation of the factors to environmental variables. The Indian *g* factor is related 0·65 to an initiative rating which reflects encouragement versus over-protectiveness, 0·47 to a cultural stimulus variable which measures home support for the aims of education, and 0·38 to family socio-economic level. The Eskimo *g* factor showed no significant relation to any of these factors. The Jamaican *g* factor related to the three familial environment dimensions already listed and to a planfulness of home variable and a male dominance scale, all within the range of 0·25 to 0·33. The considerable correlation of age and amount of schooling with *g* in the Eskimo sample leaves open the question of whether the relevant family background dimensions were assessed or whether schooling and general experience with age are for Eskimos sufficient to override differential family environments.

The Hebridean and Ugandan samples are similar in failing to show a clear *g* factor. In the Ugandan study the first factor loaded on information learning, vocabulary, spelling and English and less strongly on arithmetic, word learning and Piagetian tasks. It was identified by Vernon as a verbal ability, *v:ed*, and it correlated with the familial background variables. The first factor in the Hebridean study loaded on English, spelling, information learning, group vocabulary, abstraction, matrices, Piagetian tasks and Gottschaldt Figures. The reasoning component was inseparable from the verbal education dimension and Vernon labelled the entire factor *g:v*. There were strong correlations with the usual familial environment variables ranging from a high of 0·72 on cultural stimulus to 0·50 on initiative. Linguistic factors in the family were ruled out as the major factor inducing this unusual factor structure as an English versus Gaelic dimension correlated only 0·29 with *g:v*. Vernon ascribed the effect instead to a general differential effectiveness of a sophisticated, modern environment as compared with a more traditional, limited social setting of the Hebrides.

The factor structure of the Jamaican sample is not a clear replication of English analyses. Although Vernon identified a general factor it does not load widely and the second, verbal educational factor loads not only on all written tests but on the design reproduction and Draw-a-Man tests as well. The diffuse nature of the *v:ed* factor in both the Hebrides and Jamaica is ascribed to the failure of the home to provide enough relevant verbal experience. The effect of the home appears in the Jamaican sample, not in the *v:ed* factor, but in relation to a factor identified as oral English and strongly evidenced in the individual vocabulary test. This factor correlated 0·46 with cultural stimulus and 0·41 with linguistic background.

By focusing on structural findings, this discussion only hints at the variety of material available in Vernon's monograph and the influential nature of his research in cross-cultural intelligence testing. He has identified a range of factors, related them to environmental variables and considered differences in levels of performance. Vernon attempted to relate his findings to the needs of developing countries but concluded that our knowledge is not yet sufficient to furnish a sound foundation for practical advice. Theoretically his results offer only partial support for a hierarchial interpretation of factors in intellectual functioning.

A study of Australian Aboriginal school children draws on Vernon's earlier published work on the Jamaican sample (Vernon, 1965a and b). David and Bochner (1967) attempted to validate Vernon's conclusion that the Porteus Maze Test was a useful measure of *g* in cross-cultural testing. Twenty-six children were rated on intelligence by school teachers and these ratings correlated with Maze scores. The significant correlation of the two measures was interpreted as supporting Vernon's conclusion that the Maze Test was a measure of *g*.

Irvine has produced a series of papers in which he re-examined many factor analytic studies of African intelligence and raised fundamental questions about the nature of intellect (Irvine, 1966, 1969a to c). He concluded that although the tests which have been administered have a Western bias, similar theoretical factors could be identified in results from different cultures. The loadings of particular tests on these factors were not identical across cultures and the appearance of a general or *g* factor varied with the heterogeneity of the sample tested. The lack of consistent support for a hierarchical interpretation with homogeneous samples parallels findings with English and American samples (Vernon, 1961).

One of the major issues raised by Irvine is the failure to find consistent environmental influence on the factors which have been identified as similar. Vernon's work is cited as evidence of this inability to identify the familial variables which are related to intellectual factors. Irvine argued that this shortcoming indicates either that the relevant environmental variables are not being measured or that the structure of intelligence as it has been described fails to take adequate account of African intellectual functioning.

Irvine has developed this line of thought in two directions. On the one hand he has accepted test results and shown how they relate to certain environmental variables, while on the other he has questioned the concept of intellect as defined by Euro-American psychology. In accepting the conclusion that factorial analyses of cross-cultural results can be meaningful, Irvine was careful to show that the factors which are regularly identified are closely related to cognitive skills developed in the course of a Western-style education. (In almost all the testing reviewed above subjects were children with at least five years' schooling.) Thus factors which reflect close drilling in school, i.e. spelling and arithmetic, have stable factor loadings. European and African children may even have the same median scores on arithmetic achievement tests at the end of primary schooling (Heron, 1966), though attending school in the same country is no guarantee of similar education.

Factors usually dependent upon non-verbal tests of reasoning or of visualization show less stability and they are less likely to be influenced by school curricula. However, when Lloyd and Pidgeon (1961) coached African, Indian and European children on material of this nature, the African children improved markedly suggesting that some learning deficits could be corrected with limited training. Why the Indian samples failed to improve is not clear but the authors suggested that the skills tested were not valued in Indian culture. Other motivational factors which have been shown to influence improvement in the test performance of lower-class and black American children (Rosenham, 1967) have yet to be investigated systematically in cross-cultural settings. A study by McFie (1961) showed that the performance of Ugandan students on figural tests improved after two years' education in a technical college; it lends further support to the hypothesis that the shortcomings of an African home in providing training on Western cognitive skills can be remedied. Vernon's (1967a) studies on the effects of coaching in Tanzania place some doubt on the effects of training but Wober (1969) has suggested that Vernon's results are subject to a number of interpretations.

The second point which Irvine has pursued is the meaningfulness of the concept of intellect as currently formulated. He has argued for the premise that there are kinds of intelligence which present tests have not sampled at all. One of his discussions focuses on results of testing with Raven's Matrices which are used extensively in cross-cultural research; he showed in a comparative factor analysis based upon item difficulty that the interaction of items and cultural groups was statistically significant. These findings suggest that the Matrices are less independent of cultural variation than had been supposed. Furthermore, in an analysis of individuals, Irvine has shown that three different strategies may lead to the same overall score. Test performance can be analysed in terms of perceptual speed, flexibility of closure and two reasoning components. Ultimately he asserted that it was impossible to comment on the suitability of particular tests for cross-cultural use unless a good deal more was known about the effects of cultural variables on perception, learning and reasoning. Shortcomings in knowledge of cognitive processes at the micro level restrict efforts to evaluate the Matrices as an instrument of cross-cultural comparison.

Finally, Irvine has examined anthropological accounts of the thought systems of African societies, analysed sayings and proverbs of the Shona peoples of South Africa and studied, in general, the cultures of Central Africa. As a result both of this work and of his traditional psychometric investigations, he has concluded that there may be a culturally and linguistically conditioned primary African thought mode which is not encompassed by usual definitions of intelligence. Although Irvine has proposed a hypothetical factorial study which might begin to expose these African abilities no research has, as yet, been reported.

Intelligence testing and selection

Irvine (1969a to c) and other researchers have serious reservations about the concept of intelligence and the appropriateness of tests when used in diverse cultural settings; but some selection procedures are necessary if students are to be chosen for further education, workers for training and employees for promotion. Many Euro-American psychometricians still their doubts in order to undertake these necessary testing chores, but it is intriguing to find an African psychologist much less disturbed by the problem of cultural differences and highly aware of the needs for skilled manpower.

Dogbeh, a Dahomean trained in France, has argued that measured differences in intelligence must not be viewed as the result either of the exclusive results of maturational tendencies or of learning (Dogbeh, in Wickert, 1967, pp. 40–46). He sees the interaction of maturation and culture as crucial, but in defining culture asserts, 'Education opens the way to culture. . . . We were saying that scholarly knowledge, because of the culture it permits one to acquire, explains the superiority of cultured subjects over uncultured ones' (ibid., p. 41). Although this position is extreme in praise of Western-style education, it mirrors the enthusiasm for it of people in developing countries. Selection becomes a necessity because cost dictates that higher education cannot be provided for all. In discussing entrance criteria for secondary schooling in Uganda, Somerset (1968) noted that while the national *per capita* income was £30 per annum, the cost of training a single secondary-school student was £100. Until developing countries are much richer, screening will be maintained. But even in industrial nations with a high national income, selection procedures are employed to ensure that only those who can benefit from particular training receive it.

The need for systematic selection, both for educational and occupational placement, has been a matter of urgency in developing countries for over a decade. One of the main points arising from a conference held in Ghana in 1960 (Taylor, 1962) was the need for research to establish both the requirements of the positions to be filled and the best selection procedures to adopt. Research in this field is in some ways less difficult than 'pure' cross-cultural investigations of cognition. Nagging doubts that the measures are not really tapping intelligence as defined in a particular exotic culture need not arise. Criteria are more readily available; they are measures such as the number of screened candidates who successfully complete the training or the number of passes at school certificate. There is a great need for research in this area; it is easier to carry out and results can be sharper and less subject to ambiguity than in theoretical studies of intelligence.

The need for trained manpower has dictated the speed with which research on personnel selection has been undertaken. For example, in Nigeria, the Ford Foundation supported research into selection for technical training was undertaken in the early 1960s; currently the West African Examination Council carries out extensive selection services. In South Africa, sophisticated selection techniques have been developed; the impetus for this achievement has come not only from industry but from Simon Biesheuvel the Director, for many years, of the National Institute for Personnel Research. His writings summarize the studies carried out in South Africa and also work throughout the world. Biesheuvel's chapter in the *Annual Review of Psychology 1965*, and in the Handbook which he prepared for the International Biological Programme (Biesheuvel, 1969) are particularly useful for gaining an overview of this field.

In the past decade the cross-cultural use of objective tests has grown considerably. Rérat (1963a and b) has reported on occupational selection problems in French Africa while a number of authors have contributed to an international conference on educational testing (Ingenkamp, 1969), with reports on West Africa, Argentina, Chile, the West Indies, Japan, Malaysia, Pakistan, Iran, Israel and Australia. By and large these studies are concerned with describing methods which have been used for evaluating candidates for further study in terms of past achievement and current ability. The test batteries may include tests of memory or block designs and the like, but the aim is not to analyse the cognitive skills involved in the test. Cognitive skills are treated here as indicants, just as glucose levels are used in the diagnosis of diabetes. The more fully the cognitive requirements of the criterial performance are understood, however, the greater success should be experienced in selecting appropriate diagnostics.

Evaluating the success of tests in selecting appropriate candidates, that is predictive validity studies, lies outside the scope of this discussion of intelligence. Reports of personnel selection studies are of interest, in so far as they shed light on our understanding of cognition and its development. Thus, Somerset's (1968) account of his efforts to evaluate the success of secondary-school selection procedures used in Uganda in the early 1960s includes material of general interest for the study of cognition. He found that there were significant differences between schools in the level of performance on school leaving achievement tests taken at the end of primary education, i.e. the Junior School Leaving Examination (JSLE). These differences correlated with the overall quality of the schools. In selecting pupils for secondary training he reasoned that if individuals from schools of differing quality were equated for JSLE performance, it could be assumed that individuals from the poorer schools were more intelligent in the sense of Intelligence A or fluid intelligence since they had overcome the handicap of poor education in gaining their scores. Furthermore, he argued, individuals who came from poorer quality primary schools might be expected to gain more from a good secondary education since they were more intelligent. Success on the school certificate examinations at the end of secondary training did not support Somerset's hypothesis about intelligence and schooling. He concluded instead that the effects of inferior primary training may be irreversible and suggested that they may set a limit to later performance.

The notion implicit in this argument, i.e. that intellectual growth and especially linguistically constrained skills may become less flexible after puberty receives support from diverse sources. Lenneberg (1967) asserted this position and cited as evidence brain damage to the dominant hemisphere which results in little permanent deficit if it occurs before puberty but irreversible loss if damage occurs after puberty. Bloom (1964) has shown that intelligence test performance at eighteen years is largely predicted (80 per cent) by performance at eight years of age. Follow-up studies of adult literacy programmes suggest that there is considerable loss when training ceases and even a return to illiteracy. Findings of this nature are of interest to a developmental psychologist in that they begin to outline the course of cognitive development but they must be a source of concern to policy makers faced with difficult decisions about the allocation of financial resources for education.

Piagetian intelligence

The developmental theory of Piaget occupies a position of prime importance in contemporary psychology. Its focus on cognition is congruent with the *Zeitgeist* and its aspirations to universality, in describing epistemological development within individuals and societies, make it particularly attractive for investigation in other cultures.

Clearly a full introduction to Piagetian psychology is beyond the scope of this review. Discussion is here organized around three topics: (a) a comparison of psychometric and Piagetian intelligence, (b) a review of cross-cultural research on the concrete operational period, because this stage has inspired the majority of investigations from outside the Genevan school, and (c) a consideration of formal operations. Before examining these themes it is useful to clarify Piaget's position on cross-cultural investigations.

Piaget's stage theory which postulates four major invariant periods of development – identified as the sensorimotor, the pre-operational, the concrete operational and the formal operational – has been held to imply that Piaget views intellectual growth as mainly a question of maturation; but this is not so. Piaget has repeatedly argued for an active view of knowing (cf. Furth, 1969) and has explicitly presented the case for cross-cultural research in a paper which draws upon work carried out in Iran by one of his students (Mohseni, 1966; Piaget, 1966). He lists four factors which influence development and argues that only through comparative research will it be possible to assess the effects of each of them. The first two factors are intra-individual: they are biological constraints determining physical growth, and equilibration variables, the regulatory factors which underlie biological organization and which are seen in the development of intelligence. The third and fourth, inter-individual factors, Piaget divides into those which are general to the human social condition, i.e. parameters such as cooperation and conflict, and those which are specific, being due to particular educational and cultural experiences. Piaget argues, in reviewing Mohseni's material, that biological constraints determine the order of stages even though they appear at different ages in the rural and urban Iranian children, and that the second and third factors account for the later development of conservation among the rural children. The general Iranian deficit of almost five years in performance on standard psychometric tests, Piaget ascribes to the absence of Western-type schooling or his fourth factor. This explanation contains an important premise for cross-cultural research on cognition: operational intelligence or intelligence as conceptualized by Piaget is held to be less susceptible to the effects of formal education than intelligence as measured by standard tests. It is appropriate, then, to consider the similarities and differences in the two formulations of the concept of intelligence.

Psychometric and Piagetian intelligence

A simple definition of psychometric intelligence was not offered in the first section of this chapter but a view of intelligence emerged which focused on efforts to assess individual differences in performance on a range of cognitive tasks. While debate surrounds the exact structure of these intellectual skills it is clear that some overall score representing high level cognitive functioning was sought which would distinguish, according to certain criteria, the performance of individuals and groups. Psychometric intelligence is end-product orientated and assessment is judged successful in so far as it can identify individual differences.

Intelligence is used by Piaget to describe a system and thus he can consider sensorimotor intelligence or operational intelligence each as potentially coherent adaptations. The concept of intelligence is more often used in an adjectival form and Piaget usually means adaptive behaviour when he writes of intelligent behaviour. A core concept for Piagetian theory is the adaptive process and the biologically given, functional invariants of assimilation and accommodation. Consideration of adaptation leads straight to the heart of Piaget's theory of development. Piaget was initially trained as a biologist and he uses adaptation in the sense of a biological system which implies both process and structure. The human organism is seen as having adaptive structures for dealing with the world at birth – these are the reflexes, i.e. sucking, looking, etc. The sucking reflex may be used to explore different objects, that is, to assimilate the thumb or the teat to the sucking reflex. The reflexive structure will itself be modified, i.e. accommodated to these diverse objects, and it is through interaction – assimilation and accommodation – between the physical world and cognitive structures that development occurs. The sensorimotor schemes are in time modified by this interaction and representation develops leading to the formation of pre-operational functions. Out of these schemes and through continuing adaptive interaction these functions become organized and reversible giving rise to operational intelligence. Two emphases are dominant throughout this formulation; one is the cumulative nature of intellectual growth and the other is the focus upon regularity and normative behaviour. The age at which conservation of substance first appears may separate the gifted child from the subnormal but, despite Piaget's early research experience in working with Binet, his attention is on the regularities of development and not on individual differences.

In discussions of psychometric intelligence, the role of hereditary or genetic factors is a controversial topic. Earlier in this chapter, innate potential was mentioned briefly without any attempt to make claims about what proportion of the variance in tests scores could be attributed to genetic determinants (cf. Jensen, 1969). It has usually been assumed that the hereditary component in individual differences is invariant while environmental effects are considered mutable. Thus differences in the performance of monozygotic or identical twins reared apart are ascribed mainly to environmental factors while differences between foster children reared in the same home are considered genetic. In the Piagetian system, as seen in the analysis of Mohseni's Iranian data, genetic factors are held to account for regularity, i.e. for the invariant sequence of stages. Piaget considers the process of physical development a constraint which regulates adaptive interaction. Fundamentally there is no contradiction; psychometricians are engaged in seeking differences in individual rates of development while Piaget has disregarded individual differences in a search for universal laws of development. Confusion has resulted because the term 'genetic factors' has been used in different senses in these two endeavours. A further source of ambiguity is Piaget's use of the term 'genetic' as a synonym for 'developmental'. English speakers are likely to confuse this usage with genetic in the sense of genes and chromosomes.

The psychometric concept of *g*, a general reasoning factor, and Piaget's view of formal operations as the final equilibrium of cognitive development, share a rationalist view of intelligence but none the less differences in theory construction and method separate these approaches. The psychometric method is essentially pragmatic and empirical. Choice of test items is only minimally guided by theory and the retention of items is determined by statistical criteria. Psychometric descriptions of mental development are based upon curves generated by the repeated testing of a sample over the course of its growth. The resulting 'theory' is the by-product of statistical analysis.

Contemporary Piagetian theory has developed from a two-pronged attack on developmental problems. Inhelder and Piaget (1958) describe in the introduction to their monograph on formal operations how Inhelder carried out empirical studies of children in a wide age range while Piaget developed a logical apparatus combining propositional logic and the four transformation rules of the mathematical four group. The applicability of the logical model to Inhelder's empirical results led to further collaboration and the studies which they published together. Their empirical investigations are often described as clinical in method, in the sense that children are placed in standard problem situations but interviewed in a flexible manner about their solutions. Scores of right and wrong are not the major concern, but rather the experimenter seeks to learn about the reasoning which underlies children's performance. Undoubtedly one of Piaget's major contributions to psychology has been his vast quantity of insightful observation and controlled data on cognitive skills; but it is important to remember that in these empirical investigations Piaget has been guided by a professional training as a logician coupled with expertise in biology. If the terms do not jar too much – he might be described as a theoretical empiricist!

Cross-cultural research on concrete operational thinking

Piaget's theory of cognitive development has spurred a great deal of research in recent years, some of it sympathetic and aimed at offering support for his conclusions but much of it designed to show limitations in his formulations (e.g. Sigel and Hooper, 1968). A characteristic of both strategies has been concentration on the developmental stage known in the Piagetian system as that of concrete operations. In this third major stage of development, unified though limited logical structures first make their appearance. This coherent organization arises from the internalization of action sequences modified through adaptive, i.e. assimilative and accommodative, interaction and representation. Piaget has formalized these structures in terms of groupings and semi-lattices, i.e. derivatives of mathematical groups and lattices. Flavell (1963) presents a comprehensive, explanatory summary of Piaget's model.

Piaget has described the structure of concrete operations in terms of nine groupings, one of which is concerned with identity or equivalence, i.e.

relationships of the order, if A=B and B=C then A=C. To most five year olds the final proposition is not obvious but to a child of eight or nine, diagnosed as concrete operational, the conclusion has logical necessity. The remaining eight groupings are identified by Roman numerals; I to IV set forth the transformation rules of class addition and multiplication and V to VIII describe the same operations as applied to relations. Of course Piaget's formalization is an abstract account of cognitive structures which have been inferred from observations of the behaviour of European children – its cross-cultural validity is a major issue.

Cognitive development is only complete when the equilibrium of formal operations is reached. A reorganization takes place which results in new combinatorial skills whose theoretical description Piaget based upon propositional calculus and the transformations of the mathematical four group. With this final change the concrete operational child is freed from the limited and reality-based internalized action sequences which characterized the third stage of development.

The description of concrete operational thought presented thus far has focused only on the organization of logical structures, but Piaget has also described arithmetic groups and measurement as well as producing stage-by-stage accounts of the development of concepts such as time, space and causality.

Piaget separates operational thinking which is based on actions or transformations from figurative knowledge which has a sensorial content. Perception, an example of the latter, because of its immediate dependence on reality is considered incapable of the developmental potential of thinking; but its growth has also been documented (Piaget, 1969). The aspect of Piaget's research on the concrete operational period which has most often captured the attention of other workers has been his experiments on conservation. Conservation, be it of quantity, weight, volume, length, area or number, is dependent on reversibility, which, for Piaget, is one of the hallmarks of concrete operational thought.

Conservation experiments have three essential phases. First an identity must be established, i.e. a child's attention drawn to the weight of a ball of plasticine. Next the child must observe as this object is transformed in some way which leaves its defining characteristic (its weight) intact; thus the ball is pressed into a pancake. Finally the child is asked, 'Is the ball still the same weight?' The concrete-operational child, undisturbed by the shape transformation replies that the plasticine is the same weight whether a pancake or a ball. Logic determines the operational child's answer, not perception. The pre-operational or transitional child may be deceived by the altered appearance and say that it now weighs more or less. This paradigm is based upon conservation of identity but another assessment procedure commonly employed uses two initially equal objects; one, the standard, remains the same, but the other is transformed without altering its criterial identity. The child is then asked whether the standard and the transformed object are still the same. This method of testing is based upon equivalence and identity and thus requires an additional logical operation (Elkind, 1967).

The unified structure of the groupings is presumed necessary for conservation; and it follows that all the conservations should appear at the same time along with the other concrete operational skills of seriation and class inclusion. This is not the case. There appears to be an order of difficulty, or 'horizontal *décalage*' as this phenomenon is termed by Piaget. In studies with Genevan children the conservation of quantity appeared first along with space, and was followed by weight and then volume (Piaget, 1950). Twenty years ago replication studies questioned whether the different conservations appeared at all and if so whether at the same ages as they did in Genevan children. Recent emphasis on the horizontal *décalage* has shifted attention to examination of the order in which the different conservations first appear (Elkind, 1961; Lovell, 1969). The maturational emphasis of Piaget's theory has also raised questions about the effects of experience on cognitive development (cf. Sigel and Hooper, 1968).

Cross-cultural research has reflected these interests. It is currently possible to survey more than a dozen individual studies of conservation in different settings and consider questions of practice effects, language, schooling and acculturation on the appearance of concrete operational thought. Goodnow (1969, 1970) has already presented two excellent summaries of the effects of different cultural environments on cognitive development, while Peluffo (1967) has reviewed studies of European researchers. In the discussion of cross-cultural research on concrete operational thought three topics will be considered. The first is the universality of concrete operational thinking. The second concerns the *décalage* or ordering in the appearance of conservations. The final and most extensive section will examine factors which affect the development of concrete operations.

Peluffo (1967) has considered the question of the universality of cognitive development up to the level of concrete operational thought. Although his review of the literature had not been exhaustive he has suggested (Peluffo, 1967, p. 193) that

> ... the general level of a culture in which the techniques of agriculture and handicraft are developed, is a sufficient support for a complete conservation of substance, while for the notion of weight, the transformation into certain forms can sometimes produce figural reactions.

This conclusion was based upon examination of Price-Williams's (1961) material showing conservation in Tiv children similar to that described by

Piaget, of his own comparisons of unacculturated Sardinian, Northern Italian, and immigrant children to Northern Italy from rural communities in the South, and of Ponzo's reports of difficulty with conservation among adult Indian groups living in the Amazon basin. Although a minimal level of concrete operational skill was reached by these subjects, Peluffo argued that cultural factors may inhibit the formation of organized structures necessary for combinatorial reasoning.

A long list can be compiled which displays evidence for various conservations in differing proportions of samples drawn from a range of cultures: Ghanaian (Beard, 1968), Aboriginal (Dasen, 1970; De Lemos, 1969), Yoruba (Etuk, 1967; Lloyd, 1971), Chinese (Goodnow, 1962), Wolof (Greenfield, 1966), Zambian (Heron and Simonsson, 1969), Aden (Hyde, 1970), Igbo (Okonji, 1971), Hausa (Poole, 1968), New Guinean (Prince, 1968). As yet there is no counter-evidence. None the less, the search for such evidence might be facilitated by Peluffo's suggestions. Once a society develops agriculture and handicraft, conservation of substances is expected; but before this development, for instance in hunting and gathering societies, evidence of conservation or other concrete operational skills may not be found. Societies such as that of the Eskimo depend upon complex spatial skills in hunting which appear to be a spur to development, particularly of spatial concepts (Berry, 1966; Vernon, 1969). Although Aboriginal culture and that of New Guinea may once have satisfied the cultural requirements of hunting and gathering economies, the particular samples investigated have had considerable Western contact and some Western-style education.

In considering the question of the order of appearance of conserving responses in respect of number, length, weight and so on, it becomes necessary to take account of a range of variables. The issue is discussed in great detail in Hyde's (1970) report of her own research in Aden in which she compared European, Arab, Indian and Somali children, aged six to nine years, on a variety of Piagetian tasks in order to assess their abilities with number and quantity. Hyde reported that, in terms of age, results were in the direction described by Piaget, with older children showing more conservation; however the appearance of conserving responses for substance was dependent on the material used. Many children who produced responses indicative of conservation of substance when water was used failed when tested again with plasticine (twenty-nine out of a total of 144 children tested) but six reversed this effect, failing with water and passing with plasticine. Thus the materials used in assessing conservation influence the occurrence of responses which can be interpreted as evidence of concrete operational thinking.

Differences in test materials make it difficult to compare De Lemos's

(1969) results with those of Hyde. De Lemos substituted sugar for liquid, following the use of sand by Price-Williams (1961) in the test of continuous quantity or substance. She used bags of tea to assess conservation of weight and found more Aboriginal children able to conserve weight than substance. Of the seventy children showing weight conservation, twenty-seven failed to conserve quantity, while more conserved length than quantity. De Lemos presented other cross-cultural evidence to support the validity of her results which challenge the order of emergence of the various conservations described by Piaget. She also quoted Boonsong's (1968) finding of the simultaneous appearance of quantity and weight conservation in Thai children. He had used the same materials as Piaget and Inhelder and counterbalanced order of presentation to compensate for any practice effects. Together these studies stand as a challenge to the Genevan order of appearance of the various conservations. Although it would appear from these results that order is affected by particular cultural experience or Piaget's fourth factor, Dasen (1970), also working with Aboriginal children, failed to replicate De Lemos's results. His order followed that reported from Geneva.

An additional order contradiction discussed by De Lemos concerned conservation of area. She noted that the late appearance of area conservation in Aboriginal children could be interpreted as congruent with Genevan results in research on space. Dependence on the understanding of a co-ordinate system of references suggested area conservation would develop later in the concrete operational period. Although an argument based on Piagetian research can explain the late appearance of area conservation in the Aboriginals, it was observed early in the concrete operational period in Genevan children. Genevan results which have been described as the horizontal *décalage* are challenged by cross-cultural evidence collected thus far but more systematic studies of conservation can be expected to explicate the mechanisms of these reorderings.

A number of factors which affect performance were highlighted in the examination of cross-cultural evidence for conservation, and by the order in which children appeared to understand the transformations. The most straightforward of these factors concern the materials and procedures employed in assessing conservation. Of the more wide ranging and less easily controlled variables are those of schooling, contact with Western industrial societies and language. The effect of each of these variables will be examined in at least one study.

In the attempt to compare De Lemos's results with those of Hyde, the question of different stimulus materials arose because De Lemos used sugar as a continuous quantity while Hyde used water. Systematic investigation of the effects of using different materials has been undertaken in tasks assessing conservation of number and continuous quantity (Lloyd, 1971). The materials were red and yellow inch cubes and local sweets wrapped in red and blue paper. Despite the fact that the Yoruba language only encodes colours on a dimension of red–blue and thus red and yellow are labelled together *pupa*, in a counterbalanced design order was significant but not differences in test materials. Thus, for Yoruba children aged three and a half to eight years the ability to conserve was affected by practice but not by the use of materials differentially codable in Yoruba. Few cross-cultural studies have systematically assessed the impact of different stimulus materials.

Procedural modifications in testing also raise questions of comparability. Heron and Simonsson (1969) used a non-verbal technique developed by Furth (1966) for testing deaf children, to study weight conservation of Zambian school children aged five to seventeen years. A characteristic of this technique is an initial training in the use of signs for equal and heavier. Heron and Simonsson sought evidence for the validity of their procedure in comparisons with the performance of Genevan children on the assumption that, if the non-verbal method is equivalent to orthodox Piagetian techniques, the performance of Zambian children will be very similar to that of Genevan children. In fact by ten years of age performances were identical for both samples in terms of percentage showing conservation, although Zambian children reached the 50 per cent level a year later than their Genevan counterparts. By thirteen years 100 per cent of Zambian children showed conservation of weight. The authors were reasonably satisfied that their non-verbal method gave an accurate estimate of operational thinking in the conservation of weight.

In a study examining the effects of schooling and modification of testing procedures, Mermelstein and Shulman (1967) reported a highly significant difference in results on non-verbal and verbal measures of conservation of continuous quantity. Explanation of the differential success of these two studies in employing non-verbal techniques may lie in part in the nature of the task imposed by the Mermelstein and Shulman method. Once the child had established that two 150 millilitre jugs held equal amounts of water, the experimenter began to pour the contents of one jug into a 1000 millilitre bottle. Unknown to the child, liquid also flowed into the bottle from a hidden source controlled by the experimenter. The contents of the bottle rapidly exceeded 150 millilitres and the child's response to this was observed and rated. Surprise or puzzlement was interpreted as evidence of operational thinking while the absence of expression change was considered preoperational. The authors admitted that transitional children could not be reliably identified, but the non-verbal method produced significantly more conservers than the standard method of assessing conservation of discontinuous quantity. The logic of this comparison, when the authors might have contrasted the two methods of measuring conservation of continuous quantity, is a mystery despite their explanation. The non-verbal procedure is unusual but it is a variant of a method of assessing cognitive development described as a 'phenomenal trap' by Piaget's co-workers (Morf, 1962) and labelled a 'contrary cue' by Smedslund (1963). These results fall within the general problem area concerned with interpreting conflicting evidence of concrete operational thinking when this evidence is gathered by different techniques. One advantage of working on Piagetian tasks is that a great deal of effort has already gone into working through these difficulties.

The problem of interpreting task and response similarities and differences served as the starting point for an essay by Goodnow (1969) in which she argued that fundamental questions of method and theory were raised by the transposition of tasks to different cultural settings. She offered the suggestion that tasks and responses must be analysed separately, pointing out that the precaution of using the same task with European and African subjects was not a sufficient guarantee that it would be similarly construed by all subjects. Viewed from the response side, the appearance of identical answers should not be interpreted as evidence that they were the product of identical psychological processes. The latter point has been argued by Greenfield (1966) who contended that while Wolof and American children both conserve continuous quantity, they may well employ different strategies.

Schooling is one of the more definable experiential variables which have been shown to affect performance on Piagetian tasks. The extent of its influence is debatable. Greenfield and Bruner (1966, p. 104) after examining results of conservation testing stated that:

> . . . it is always the schooling variable that makes qualitative differences in directions of growth. Wolof children who have been to school are more different intellectually from unschooled children living in the same bush village than they are from city children in the same country or from Mexico City, Anchorage (Alaska) or Brookline (Massachusetts).

Limited contradictory evidence is available from studies of Chinese boys in Hong Kong (Goodnow, 1962; Goodnow and Bethon, 1966) and of black American children who were deprived of public education during desegregation controversies in Virginia (Mermelstein and Shulman, 1967). It is clear from Goodnow's work that tests for conservation of weight, volume and area are not affected by schooling but the quality of instruction, in particular, poorer science tuition and an anti-empirical approach, is reflected in the explanations produced. Heron and Simonsson (1969) have suggested that the apparent regression in Zambian children's ability to conserve weight may be the product of poor teaching in upper primary school. By way of contrast Goodnow found that a combinatorial task was sensitive to schooling and other experiential differences such as the family's standard of living. In trying to explain why schooling should have these differential effects on cognitive skills, Goodnow (1969) suggested that the conservations may be more closely tied to immediate experience such as counting money while shopping but combinational tasks require reasoning or the ability to work things out in one's head.

Strong claims for the effects of schooling come from a survey by Prince (1968) of 2700 school children in Papua and New Guinea. His test procedures differed markedly from those considered thus far. Children were tested in groups and required to mark correct answers on paper. The five conservations measured along with other science concepts included continuous quantity, substance, weight, volume and area. Prince argued that years of schooling was a better predictor of performance than either chronological age or particular aspects of the educational experience, i.e. a superior science programme or non-English instruction. Prince failed to provide an adequate test of the environmental hypothesis in the Papua and New Guinea setting. His report of the testing of seven members of an adult literacy class is vague and he stated in a contradictory fashion that while testing produced a number of conserving responses subsequent interviews revealed few real conservers.

Mermelstein and Shulman (1967), in the study already discussed, were not able to demonstrate any significant differences in the performance of black children with varying amounts of formal schooling. Although Greenfield and Bruner (1971) might argue that even the eight months of schooling the children had received just prior to the testing would improve their linguistic skills, a follow-up study cited by Mermelstein and Shulman showed considerable linguistic deficit in the Prince Edward Country children after schooling had resumed. Goodnow's formulation stressing the need for greater specificity in linking experiential factors to particular cognitive skills promises to be a fruitful direction for research on concrete operational thought to pursue.

An example of this strategy is the study by Price-Williams, Gordon and Ramirez (1969) of conservation in Mexican children. Boys from a town and a village were matched for age, schooling and social class but were differentiated in that half the groups were composed of the sons of potters. All the children were tested for conservation of number, continuous quantity, weight, volume and substance, the latter using plasticine as the test material. The hypothesis that the experience with pottery making would lead to earlier conservation, at least of substance, was borne out in the village and town samples. Only the differences on conservation of substance reached statistical significance but the sons of potters gave more conserving type responses generally. Experience in manipulating clay appears to spur cognitive development in potters' sons and leads, a Piagetian might argue, to the internalization of action sequences reflected in the development of concrete operational thought.

Greenfield and Bruner (1971) have suggested that in non-Western settings schooling modifies thought through the medium of written language. Using Greenfield's data from Senegal they have argued that experience of the printed word frees the child from word–thing bondage and allows the development of thought beyond a unitary realism. In chapter 2 the contrasting views of Cambridge and Geneva were reviewed. The analysis of language and schooling follows from Bruner's position on the role of language in the development of thinking. Furby (1971) has drawn extensively on the conservation research of Bruner's group in formulating a theory of cognitive development in which reasoning and perceptual flexibility are determined by cultural background and degree of technical advancement. Unfortunately further cross-cultural evidence which might clarify these positions is lacking.

The evidence examined here to assess the universality of concrete operational thought has focused only on the conservations. Other material on concrete operational thinking has been reviewed in earlier chapters. Results of investigations with Anglo- and Mexican-American, and black and white South African children were analysed and found to support Piaget's claim that topological concepts of space develop before Euclidean or projective systems (see pages 86 to 88). The discussion of classification (see pages 106 to 108) included two studies carried out in Nigeria (Okonji, 1971; Price-Williams, 1962). Dasen (1970), in his study of Australian Aborigines investigated seriation, space and perceptual behaviour at the same time as he studied conservation; he urges other investigators to follow his example, arguing that the effects of ecological, cultural and educational variables may be seen more sharply in their differential effects on various concrete operational skills.

Initially Piaget accounted for the development of thought in a highly descriptive theory, but in recent decades he has produced formal statements characterizing the structures and process of development in mathematical and logical notation. In his early work the thought of the pre-operational child was described as realistic and was marked by failure of the child to perceive the boundaries of the self (Piaget, 1928). The shift to what is now described as concrete operational thinking was conceptualized along three dimensions: objectivity, reciprocity and relativity. The operational child is objective in so far as he is aware of his own separate identity, reciprocal in his ability to entertain another person's viewpoint and relative in his awareness that all substances and qualities lack absoluteness. Terms such as animism, artificialism and finalism describe aspects of thought processes before they become objective or operational. At first glance, the older descriptive formulation of cognitive development appears particularly suitable to an understanding of phenomena in non-Western cultures.

The ambiguities inherent in the early descriptions become apparent when the terms are used by other authors. Greenfield and Bruner (1971) use concepts deriving from Piaget's description of ego-centric thinking in discussing the failure of unschooled Wolof children (as evidenced by their explanations on a conservation task) to distinguish between their own psychological reactions and external events. While Piaget suggested that pre-operational thinking was characterized by an inability to distinguish self and others, or internal and external, Greenfield and Bruner (1971, p. 42) go a step further and state that, 'A more developed ego-centrism then follows, in which the child can distinguish between inner and outer but still confuses the two.' The superficial contradiction in this statement can be resolved easily but in the following discussion it is difficult to determine how the analysis relates to Piagetian theory and to measure the extent to which the authors, in applying Western reference points, failed themselves to understand the unschooled Wolof children's definitions of inner and outer.

Jahoda (1958) has surveyed the cross-cultural literature and carried out studies on animism in Ghana. His research indicates the care and effort which must be expended if meaningful study of Piaget's older, descriptive concepts is to be carried out successfully. The popularity of conservation for cross-cultural investigations may lie, in part, in the accessibility of the procedures and rationale to those not fully steeped in the Piagetian tradition.

Formal operations

The essence of development in the Piagetian system is its cumulative nature and the re-ordering of old structures which results in the appearance of qualitatively new ones. In *The Growth of Logical Thinking*, Inhelder and Piaget (1958) have presented evidence of the changes in operational thinking which can be observed in normal Genevan children around puberty and which result in the appearance of the adult thought structures which they have called the 'formal operations'. The limitations of the groupings or concrete operations are such that while the ten year old can easily construct a two-by-two matrix of leaves which vary in size and colour, he is unable to produce a similar structure based upon hypothetical elements or abstract variables. The final equilibrium of formal thought is signalled by the ability to order abstract entities and to employ complex combinatorial rules.

Another way of expressing the nature of the change is to consider concrete thought as based upon 'first order operations', i.e. internalized actions which are tied to empirical reality, while formal thought is characterized by 'second order operations' or the coordination of first order operations. Three features distinguish the second order operations. These are the ability to entertain the possible, i.e. not only to note empirically evident variables but to conceive of hypothetically relevant variables, to operate on sets of propositions and to invoke complex combinatorial rules. The propositional logic of formal thought develops from simple classification but results in skills which allow the further ordering of classes and relations. The result of the coordination of reversibility by inversion and reversibility by reciprocity is the appearance of the integrating transformations of the four group. The adequacy of Piaget's formalizations of propositional logic and combinatorial thinking is a matter for debate among logicians (Parsons, 1960). The questions of concern to psychologists are whether the three attributes of formal thought can be observed functioning together and what the nature of their developments is.

Psychological evidence of the formal operations has been reviewed by Lovell (1971). One of the major questions he raised concerned replications of Inhelder and Piaget's (1958) original work. In their monograph two sets of experiments on formal thinking were described; one related to the use of hypothetical variables, the other was concerned more directly with combinatorial skills. Lovell was satisfied that empirical evidence from other researchers' studies supported the Piagetian assertion that the two groups of experiments were linked by a common intellectual complexity which could be described as the necessity for second order operations for their successful solution. He reported, however, inter-individual differences in the ages at which evidence of formal operational thought could be elicited and marked intra-individual variability in the materials which allowed the operation of second order processes. Evidence of formal thinking is found at earlier ages in English students if they are questioned about physics rather than history. These age differences probably reflect differing approaches to training in the two subjects.

Of particular relevance to cross-cultural research is Lovell's conclusion that the experiential factors of culture and education which facilitate the transformation of concrete operations into the formal structures are little understood. His search of the published literature revealed few cross-cultural studies dealing with development up to the formal operations. Few replications of the Genevan experiments on formal thinking have been carried out in Europe or America (cf. Lovell, 1961). The procedures are complex by Western standards and the probability of their survival in meaningful form after the necessary translation and adaptation to other cultures is slight.

Cross-cultural evidence on combinatorial thinking is available from tests which were parts of two larger studies of operational intelligence. Goodnow and Bethon (1966) reported poorer performance on reasoning tasks than on conservation for both unschooled boys and for students at Chinese language schools in Hong Kong. Peluffo (1967) found that lack of formal education and a simple cultural environment interfered with the development of anticipatory and combinatorial thinking.

The importance of education for cognitive development is highlighted in Lovell's (1971) account of a study undertaken in Malawi by Kimball. Boys and girls in grades 1 to 8 were tested on concrete operational tasks, e.g. conservation, and reasoning problems. Years of schooling was a better predictor of performance than chronological age and there was a weak relationship between total score and years of science training. Lovell has suggested that the items designed to assess development towards formal operational thought may have strengthened the relationship with schooling.

The concrete operations may not depend on schooling since experience of a practical nature can support thinking about reality but the abstract thought of formal operations probably depends heavily on Western-type schooling. This is hardly surprising; the structures of formal thought, the propositional calculus and the mathematical four group are products of Western thinking. Their universality, as the goal of mature cognitive development, is an open question. The possibility of geometries other than that of Euclid was realized only centuries later in the development of Riemannian geometry. The possibility of other calculi and other theories of the structure of mathematics is largely speculative at the moment. The major conclusion for the cross-cultural study of cognition is that sensori-motor intelligence and some aspects of concrete operational thinking may develop in the absence of contact with Western culture but the appearance of the formal operations and of abstract thinking as defined in the Piagetian system probably depends on Euro-American education.

Cognitive style

Cognitive style is a concept on the one hand more inclusive of diverse aspects of behaviour than either psychometric or Piagetian intelligence, and on the other less specifically tied to a particular theoretical position. Theorists of cognitive style share the view that individuals cannot be understood solely in terms of intellectual functions, and typically they spread their nomothetic nets to include personality, socialization and/or language. In this discussion three approaches to the analysis of cognitive style will be considered. Gardner's (1953) research is cited as an example of an attempt to relate cognition and personality. The work of Hess and Shipman (1965) shows the effort to link language and cognitive style. Witkin *et al.* (1962) have provided the major theoretical formulation of cognitive style used in cross-cultural research and have related socialization, personality and cognition.

Equivalence range, i.e. the preferred span of objects or qualities usually considered to form one unit, was shown by Gardner (1953) to relate to a number of perceptual tasks. He argued that the same underlying tendencies which led individuals to use a few abstract categories, rather than many specific ones in sorting objects or qualities, would lead them to judge brightness accurately and to maintain object constancy. In addition, he contended that individuals with narrow equivalence ranges would show less tolerance of affective differences and would employ a critical and negative mode of social interaction. Gardner's claim to have shown that individual preferences in equivalence range were related to perceptual behaviour was challenged by Sloane, Gorlow and Jackson (1963). In a study testing the generality and construct validity of equivalence range, they assessed subjects on a series of sorting tasks (including group administered procedures), on the constancy and brightness problems as well as on measures of response style, verbal associations and personality. Although the factor analysis of their battery led them to identify a first factor which represented a sorting equivalence range, it failed to load on the perceptual items. Two further factors were clearly identified: one related to willingness to make wide concept associations while the other was concerned with the ease with which ambiguity would be tolerated in associations. The second factor was independent of the sorting equivalence range factor, as was the third which had a large verbal component. The authors concluded that while their study had produced limited evidence for the validity of the concept of equivalence range in sorting tasks, it was important to recognize that a limited range could be the result either of a failure to differentiate or of an awareness of differences masked by a willingness to overlook them in forming abstract and inclusive categories. Gardner's theory of cognitive style offered no developmental explanation but the remaining positions considered, those of Witkin and Hess, include explanations of the genesis of the patterns which lie at the heart of their ideal types.

Hess and Shipman (1965) investigated cognitive functioning and mother–child interaction primarily in working-class black American families. Their theoretical framework derived from Bernstein's (1961) studies of English children in which he identified two modes of interaction. The elaborated or formal code was seen as the dominant pattern of speech in middle-class families, while the restricted code was considered typical of working-class interaction. Hess and Shipman showed that socialization variables could be classified along these dimensions and they measured differences in the manner in which mothers interacted with their children and offered them help in learning situations. Although the approach has been successful in identifying related aspects of language, socialization and cognitive functioning in subgroups in the United States and England, it has not prompted wider cross-cultural investigations.

Extensive studies of cognitive style in African societies have been based upon the theoretical formulations of Witkin and his colleagues (1962). Witkin (1967, p. 234) has been explicit in asserting that cognitive style is a more general theory. His unit has worked on problems relating differences in cognitive style both to personality and socialization. Summaries of the development of Witkin's position and of the cross-cultural research which it has inspired are provided by Witkin (1961, 1967). A résumé of the major aspects of Witkin's theory and some critical comments on his 1962 formulation are presented here, followed by a discussion of the cross-cultural studies which it has inspired.

Witkin's work on cognitive style has roots in the approach described as the 'new look in perception' which appeared in the 1940s. It was an effort to relate personality variables to responses elicited in standard perception experiments. Witkin derived his models of field dependent and field independent cognitive styles from analyses of individual differences in three test situations. He has described these as measures of perceptual functioning. In the first situation, the Body Adjustment Test, the subject is required to indicate when his body is vertical while seated in a chair, which the experimenter can tilt, in a room specially constructed so that it too can be tilted. Witkin found wide individual differences in responses; some subjects could correct experimenter-induced tilt while others appeared unable to make body corrections when the physical context supported the deception. The second situation, the Rod and Frame Test (RFT), explores the same principles but in objects outside the subject's own body; a luminous rod and frame, each of which can be tilted, are manipulated in a darkened room. A body alignment variable can be introduced by testing subjects in a chair which can also be tilted. The third measure, the Embedded Figures Test (EFT), requires subjects to locate a simple geometric figure in a complex pattern. All three situations are held to assess the common ability of an individual to isolate either his body, an object or a design from its context. Individuals who are able to do so are described as field independent while those whose judgements are largely determined by context are considered field dependent.

Reliability studies showed that, in adults, the measures were stable for periods up to seven years; research on children indicated a developmental progression with young children first finding difficulty on all three tasks but improving with age. Studies have also found that males are generally more field independent. Sherman (1967) and Vernon (1969) have suggested that male field independence may be related to better spatial ability in men. In a test of this hypothesis, Mayo and Bell (1972) compared student teachers of art, held to be high in spatial ability (Smith, 1964), and found no sex differences on Witkin's EFT or on his Figure Drawing Test (FDT). Moreover, they found no evidence of sex differences in student teachers of other subjects but the explanation they offer, that student teachers are generally high on spatial ability, is *post hoc*. Zigler (1963) has argued that the correlations of measures of field dependence are inflated by general intelligence. Witkin

(1963) has answered that the intelligence factor which correlates with cognitive style derives from block design, picture completion and object assembly subtests and not those tapping a verbal factor, i.e. vocabulary, information and comprehension. Thus differences in spatial ability remain the best explanation of sex differences in cognitive style.

The discussion of Witkin's research thus far has centered upon ways of assessing modes of cognitive style. Important claims are made about the relation of these differences to other aspects of psychological functioning. Witkin (1967, p. 235) argues:

> . . . they are not discrete achievements of separate channels of growth but rather diverse expressions of an underlying process of development toward greater psychological complexity. To the extent that an articulated cognitive style is an outcome of differentiation of the psychological system as a whole, the effects of socialization upon development of cognitive style must be sought not only in social processes acting directly on the cognitive sphere but also in social processes which influence the overall development of differentiation.

The socialization variables which have been examined are those relating to the child's development of an autonomous identity and thus an articulated or field independent cognitive style. These include independence training, the handling of impulses, especially aggression, and the imparting of constraints either through conformity or internalization.

The series of cross-cultural studies which Witkin's theory have inspired will be examined even though the variables they include extend beyond the bounds of perceptual and cognitive processes. These studies furnish more information on problems such as the perception of space and orientation while at the same time attempting integrations across many levels of psychological analysis.

Cross-cultural studies using Witkin's model

The first studies to employ Witkin's model were undertaken by Dawson (1963, 1967 a and b) in Sierra Leone. Two types of variables, physiological and societal, were of particular interest to Dawson. He had observed that severe infant malnutrition and kwashiorkor, the illness associated with it, had in some Sierra Leonian men resulted in an endocrine dysfunction and the appearance of secondary feminine sex characteristics (gynaecomastia). Linking the physiological factors and the possibility of its inducting a more feminine socialization, with Witkin's findings that in America women were more field independent, lower in spatial and numerical abilities but higher on verbal skills, Dawson predicted that men suffering from gynaecomastia would display a feminine pattern of intellectual functioning. He also noted marked differences in the socialization practices of the two major cultural groups in Sierra Leone. Temne mothers were much harsher and controlling than Mende women and were also more dominant in the family. Temne–Mende differences in socialization linked with Witkin's results showing that repressive socialization aimed at producing conformity was related to an undifferentiated, field dependent cognitive style. The harsher socialization of the Temne, it was predicted, would produce more field dependent responses among the Temne.

The Embedded Figures Test and Kohs Blocks were used to assess field dependence but Dawson also measured spatial ability using an adaptation of Hudson's test of three-dimensional perception and the Sander Parallelogram illusion. Furthermore, individual reports of socialization experience as well as estimates of age, intelligence, education and family background were collected. The major hypotheses were supported; Temne were more field dependent than Mende subjects and gynaecomastic men more field dependent than unaffected males. In addition, Dawson found that men from highly polygamous homes in which their fathers had had many wives and were seen by the sons as less dominant in the socialization processes, were more field dependent. Those men from monogamous homes who reported greater paternal dominance were most differentiated and field independent. Individual differences in socialization experiences were congruent with societal variations in their relation to the development of a differentiated cognitive style.

Interest both in the possibility of training 3D interpretations of 2D drawings and the relation of cognitive style to 3D perception led Dawson to carry out a learning experiment. His successful efforts to improve 3D performance have already been discussed in terms of depth perception (chapter 3). Of note here is Dawson's assertion that the high rank order correlation of initial Kohs Block performance and 3D scores after training indicated that the effects of training were constrained by differences in cognitive style. The evidence presented is insufficient to evaluate the effects of training. It would be necessary to examine the correlation of Kohs Block scores with initial 3D performance before accepting the implication that field dependence limited improvement. Should this correlation be high, it would suggest that training only added equally to the performance of the twelve experimental subjects but a low coefficient would indicate that the effects of training and cognitive style were related. Even the coefficient based upon pre- and post-training 3D scores would be useful, for a low value would support Dawson's view that subjects were differentially affected by training. The limited evidence on these points prevents comment on the relationship of cognitive style to improvement in depth perception as the result of training.

In reviewing cross-cultural studies of cognitive style, Witkin (1967) took care not to place too strong a biological interpretation on the appearance of sex differences in intellectual functioning. He did not deny the possible effect of genetic factors but he argued that the differences in genetic factors and socialization experience as the result of sex differences should both be considered. Dawson (1970) has recently been pursuing the question of sex differences in cognitive style in men and rats in terms of an interaction between sex hormones and socialization.

The interaction argument which Dawson presented for his African data is difficult to understand because the hormonal imbalance resulting from kwashiorkor can lead to observable feminization at such an early age that it would be bizarre in either sex and probably result in unique socialization problems. Furthermore, Dawson was only able to show a reversal of sex-appropriate cognitive behaviour in male rats and this required two administrations of feminizing hormones. His suggestion that future research should utilize animals treated at birth makes the human argument all the more difficult to support as kwashiorkor is an illness associated with weaning and generally appearing, in Africa, in the second year. At this stage in the development of cross-cultural psychology the wiser strategy would seem that of Witkin, stressing the combined effects of social learning and genetic endowment. If anything, the psychological literature on sex differences should serve as a warning about the pitfalls of assuming biological differences before they are reliably assessed (Maccoby, 1971; Sherman 1967).

Evidence to support the view that social learning is an important variable in the development of sex differences in intellectual functioning comes from two studies of field dependence in Eskimo. In extensive cross-cultural comparisons examining responses of Eskimo, Temne and Scottish subjects to the EFT, Kohs Blocks, Morrisby Shapes, Raven's Matrices and tests of closure, Berry (1966) found predicted male–female differences in Scottish and Temne samples but not among Eskimo subjects. MacArthur (1967) tested the generality of these findings for other Eskimo groups. Berry's work was undertaken among Eastern Eskimo but MacArthur's results, based on the EFT with Western Eskimo school children, supported Berry's evidence of similarity in the perceptual differentiation of Eskimo men and women. MacArthur's earlier findings are reinforced by his report (MacArthur, 1971) of a large-scale, on-going study of Eskimo mental abilities and environmental variables. Again he has found no male superiority on tests of spatial relations or field independence.

The position that comparability in differentiation or field independence of Eskimo men and women reflects social learning is supported by Berry's description of cultural variables: these include the detailed spatial reference system available in the Eskimo language, the extensiveness of complex art works, the mild socialization of children and the freedom of women in Eskimo society. Cultural conditioning appears to negate any biological predisposition to differential perception among Eskimo men and women. Work with Eskimo offers in addition the opportunity to study an ecological extreme. Survival for the traditional Eskimo depended upon success in hunting and the frozen landscape of the north required considerable skill in tracking and navigating to ensure success.

Eskimo results showing failure to support previously consistent reports of sex differences in perception are important; but the major focus of Berry's study was on differences within and between cultures. Berry explored two levels of Westernization in Temne and Eskimo society and rural/urban differences among the Scots. His hypotheses based upon ecological and cultural analysis were supported. Temne responses were consistently and significantly below those of Eskimo and Scottish subjects at all ages and improvements with age were more marked in the latter groups. However, in both Eskimo and Temne society, those subjects with greater Western experience performed at higher levels. Thus ecological and cultural factors ensure an Eskimo performance similar to that of European subjects but additional advantages are gained from exposure to Western culture. An additional factor, years of education, related positively to success on all four tests of spatial ability in all six groups, with the exception of the traditional Eskimo sample where it was correlated significantly and negatively with performance on the Morrisby Shapes and Kohs Blocks. MacArthur's finding (1971) that acculturated Eskimo perform better than unacculturated Eskimo only on school-related skills but not on tests of spatial relations emphasizes the impact of traditional Eskimo culture on the development of complex spatial skills.

In addition to discussing the effects of ecological, cultural and educational factors on perceptual performance, Berry considered questions of measurement. From the relatively high intercorrelations of scores on Kohs Blocks, EFT, Morrisby Shapes and Raven's Matrices, Berry concluded that these admittedly Euro-American tests could be used meaningfully in their cultures. Support for this argument is available in the structural pattern of inter-test correlations. Although the size of correlations varies across samples, the rank ordering of coefficients within samples remains the same, i.e. performance on Kohs Blocks is more closely related to performance on EFT than to the other two tests in all six samples while Shapes is generally least closely related. Although these tests had been successfully used by Dawson and Berry, Wober (1966, 1967) doubted whether they offered optimal measures of non-Western perceptual performance.

The four measures employed by Berry all depended to a large extent on the processing of visually received information. Wober (1966) has argued that cultures vary in the emphasis which they place on information from different sensory channels. He contended that the Igbo and Edo cultures of Southern Nigeria placed greater emphasis than Western culture on proprioceptive and aural cues through reliance on tone and rhythm in their languages and the customs of tying young infants on the mother's back, encouraging walking and dancing at early ages. The standard tests devised to assess field dependence in the essentially visual culture of Euro-American men do not explore the perceptual differentiation which might occur in other sense modes. Wober suggested that analysis be directed towards uncovering those sensory modes in which a culture encouraged the most complete differentiation and he coined the term 'sensotype' to denote differences in modes of cultural elaboration.

Intuitively Wober's notion of sensotype is appealing and it avoids the ethnocentric implication that one culture produces differentiated and field independent individuals while in another there is little prospect of cognitive growth. The evidence on which Wober claims to have found differing sensotypes is contained in two articles. In his 1966 paper, Wober argued from Nigerian workers' performance on the Rod and Frame Test (RFT). Two findings supported his claim: (a) subjects gave significantly more accurate estimates when the frame was not tilted, but the angle of the chair did not affect performance, and (b) results on the RFT were significantly and positively correlated with an employer's rating of job efficiency but failed to correlate significantly with results on the EFT, Kohs Blocks, the Raven's Matrices or with education. Wober concluded that failure to find differences under conditions of chair tilt indicated that proprioceptive cues could be adequately processed but that a visual deficit was indicated by improvement in performance when the visual demands of the test situation were reduced, i.e. the frame was not tilted. The correlation of the RFT with job efficiency, in a sense a validity measure, was used to underline the necessity for valid assessment procedures which allow individuals of differing sensotypes to display their own particular skills.

In his 1967 article Wober explored similarities among the responses on the RFT and EFT of normal American subjects, of those trained specially to attend to proprioceptive cues – professional dancers, and of Nigerians. The main assertion is that the lack of correlation between dancers' responses on RFT items involving body tilt and the EFT shows the effect of proprioceptive differentiation on the RFT. For normal American subjects there was a positive relationship between scores on the RFT and the EFT. Difficulties in interpreting this argument arise from the use of different types of data to support the assertion that proprioceptive cues are important in RFT performance. Wober (1966, pp. 183–4) stated, 'When the frame is not tilted, errors are about one-tenth the size of errors occurring when the frame is tilted, and are about the same regardless of the tilt of the chair.' In his discussion about dancers, the lack of correlation between body tilt items and EFT is taken as similar to the lack of correlation between RFT and EFT for Nigerian subjects. Many alternative hypotheses can be put forward to explain these findings. First of all Wober's procedures in producing body tilt are very different from those of Witkin. Wober placed a wood block either under the two right or two left legs of an ordinary chair fitted with a footrest, while Witkin's apparatus allowed him to rotate subjects in a chair and bring them to rest without their knowing whether the chair had been righted or not. Secondly, training in the dance may produce such a high level of accuracy in interpreting proprioceptive cues that individual differences are lost and the correlation thus reduced to zero. Further hypotheses can be entertained but this exercise should not be construed as negation of the role of proprioceptive cues for African subjects or professional dancers. Wober found precedent for emphasizing the role of proprioceptive information in the Beveridge (1939) study discussed on page 56 which indicated that male Ghanaian students rotated in a dimly lit cupboard were better able to right a rod than English men and women.

The relationship of the RFT and the EFT as measures of field dependence is intriguing. Berry (1966) and Dawson (1967 a and b) relied on the EFT and Kohs Blocks to assess perceptual differentiation but Okonji (1969), working in Southern Nigeria as Wober had done, used both the RFT and the EFT. Okonji studied Igbo villagers and university students of both sexes.

Okonji's analysis is complex as it involves the examination of sex differences, rural and urban differences, the interactive effects of rural and urban environment and literate and illiterate parents on university students as well as comparisons with Witkin's own data. When the EFT proved too difficult for villagers, the children's version (CEFT) was substituted and, with this, sex differences in the performance of villagers were found; these, however, were not replicated on the RFT. Among university students, sex differences were found on the RFT but not on the EFT. The two tests failed to correlate significantly in the rural sample but the coefficient for performance on the EFT and RFT was highly significant in the student sample. Furthermore, all urban-reared university subjects appeared more field independent when measured on the RFT but not on the EFT. Unlike American results, no significant differences appeared for Igbo females; but rural-reared Igbo males were more field dependent on the RFT and both urban- and rural-reared males were significantly more field dependent than American males when measured on the EFT.

The failure to replicate the village CEFT sex differences in undergraduate performance was explained in terms of education and intelligence. While all university students in Nigeria are selected for high intelligence, or *g*, a factor which effects success on the EFT, it is safe to assume that students who reach university from a rural home are particularly high in *g*. Furthermore, as Dawson noted in Sierra Leone, EFT performance is influenced by education. The effects of Westernization are also seen in the similar performance of female Nigerian and American students and in the correlation of the EFT and the RFT. Okonji considered that an even simpler version than the CEFT might have yielded a correlation with the RFT but, in general, he supported Wober's argument that the RFT measured something unique, especially in so far as the more usual pattern of sex differences was preserved despite the effects of education and intelligence on the performance of university students.

Okonji was careful to show that while it was not necessary to invoke ecological, physiological, genetic or linguistic factors in explaining his data, the results could be only partially accounted for by the demographic, educational and socialization variables which he considered. These he suggested needed finer analysis before their role in the development of cognitive style would be thoroughly understood. In a challenge to Western psychological theory, Okonji suggested that the personality variables associated with field dependence in Euro-American studies may need careful scrutiny. He speculated that the warm–cold dimension of interpersonal relations may well need revision if the personality theory associated with the perceptual measures of cognitive style were to be successfully transplanted.

Okonji (1972) has recently reported additional research which he has carried out on the socialization antecedents of cognitive differentiation in children born in Kampala, Uganda. Aware of the limitations of Witkin's formulations and the conflicting nature of the evidence which it has yielded, Okonji supports the theory as the one which is currently best able to identify the effects of child-rearing practices on cognitive development. His confidence is reflected in his suggestions for the establishment of early education programmes in Africa, especially in rural areas, in order to train children in more articulated cognitive styles.

The range of human behaviour which has been included in this brief review of research on cognitive style supports the assertion that this is the most macro of all the approaches to cognition. Unfortunately, it is also clear that unresolved issues at a micro level, such as those concerning the rules employed by subjects in determining the orientation of lines and preferential sensory modes, still cloud the understanding of notions such as perceptual differentiation. One hopes that multi-level attacks on the problems of perception and cognition will rapidly fill the many crucial gaps in our knowledge.

7 Prospects for Cross-Cultural Research

Our journey through the major cross-cultural investigations of perception and cognition has been long and demanding. The aim of this final chapter is to draw together positive results and re-examine unsettled issues. The two major themes of chapter 1, theory and method, are considered once again and to these is added the problem of application. It is essential to ask what contribution cross-cultural findings can make to the practical issues confronting those planning education and development in the Third World.

A major lesson to be learnt from this survey is that of the impact of basic assumptions on the search for cultural differences and their explanation. In the late nineteenth century, evolutionary theory led serious researchers to view non-Western peoples as less developed or less evolved than their European or American observers. Analysis of the historical and sociological roots of this racist anthropology lies outside the current discussion but the assumption, coupled with a second that an individual's capacity to perceive is reflected in the encoding characteristics of his mother tongue, led to the research on colour perception described in chapter 3. Armchair scholars examined reported colour vocabularies or the colour imagery of Homeric verse and commented on the perceptual capacities of non-Western peoples or of the ancient Greeks. The points concerning the study of perception have already been made. At issue here is the interplay of theory and method following upon certain basic assumptions. The evolutionary and linguistic hypotheses resulted in research which today seems highly speculative but at the time appeared to be empirically grounded.

Historical perspective simplifies the task of identifying basic assumptions, criticizing methodology and confronting contradictions. My aim is to carry out a similar, though by its contemporary nature more hazardous, analysis of the research which has been reviewed here.

An inquiry of this nature was undertaken in the monograph which collates and synthesizes the Kpelle studies, some of which have been reported earlier – on time perception in chapter 4 and on learning and memory in chapter 5; but this report did not include all the cross-cultural studies considered here (Cole *et al.*, 1971). The authors reviewed the major theoretical orientations to thinking in non-Western peoples and analysed in detail the role of language. They identified two archetypal positions: one, which assumes 'the psychic unity of mankind', was traced to the anthropologist Boas (1911), while the other, that of 'primitive mentality', has already been linked with its author, Lévy-Bruhl, in chapters 1 and 5. The current viability of the two positions is evidenced in the discussion of equivalence and discrimination learning. Bruner's position, which holds that major reliance on symbolic representation results from education in a technological society (see page 106), is a variant on the theme that basic thought processes diverge with cultural differentiation. Bruner has since modified his views (cf. Cole and Bruner, 1971). The underlying assumption of those researchers who select objects to be sorted in order to show that non-Westerners can classify as well or better than Europeans is that thought is constrained by the material on which it operates (Okonji, 1971; Price-Williams, 1961). It is clear again that the nature of empirical research is influenced by basic assumptions about the nature of culture and cognition.

A position is emerging (cf. Cole and Bruner, 1971; Cole *et al.*, 1971; Glick, 1969) which considers the two hypotheses – that of psychic unity and primitive mentality – incomplete in so far as each of them ignores the cultural context of cognition. These recent formulations have stressed rather the interactive nature of culture and cognition. It is argued that the psychologist's traditional aim of describing universal processes has only seemed to be fulfilled because the subjects he has studied have shared his cultural assumptions. A necessary question to ask is how far the studies which have been reviewed here also fall into this trap. In the search for the impact of cultural variables on psychological processes the assumption is often made that process is invariant, that it may function or not depending upon situational constraints. Cole *et al.* argue that the existing literature on culture and cognition is unclear about the postulated relationship and that an adequate theory and methodology is yet to be developed which would allow evaluation of the culture–cognition model.

In discussing issues raised by cross-cultural research in chapter 1, we noted the censure which Doob (1965) passed upon those researchers who failed to identify the cultural background of the people they studied. In chapter 2 a paradigm was described which would allow outsiders to take account of the perspective of a particular culture. Yet, when all the studies cited here are reviewed, it is surprising how little sense of understanding emerges of the influence of specific cultural variables on thinking. Admittedly Serpell (1969b) proposed a scheme which accounted for the orientation processing strategies employed by Zambian children (see page 60), Dawson (1967 a and b) and Berry (1966) invoked general cultural variables to explain psychological differentiation (see chapter 6) and Vernon (1969) has reported on efforts to relate background measures to the structure of abilities (see pages 117 to 118). The Kpelle studies are an obvious exception. In general, however, the cross-cultural literature fails to make the most of cultural information. Triandis, Malpass and Davidson (1972) consider that many researchers acknowledge the problem, but their studies might none the less be described as *pseudo-emic*, i.e. imposing outsiders' views rather than fully utilizing the perspective of the particular, non-Western culture.

Cole *et al.* have proposed a new field of study, that of experimental anthropology, and they have argued for the need to identify and manipulate specific situational factors much more thoroughly than has been done to date. Their monograph demonstrates the feasibility of such an approach. Behind their proposal lies the assumption that all human behaviour is adaptive and unless one understands another culture, in the manner of the anthropologist, it is not possible to explore the interaction of situation and psychological process. Random or nonsense responses, they argue, indicate failure to present a meaningful task to the subject. Their analysis is congruent with Campbell's view that gross differences in comparative research generally indicate a failure in communication between the experimenter and his subjects. With a knowledge of specific cultural variation, Cole *et al.* believe, it should be possible to employ the experimental method in any setting and to make meaningful inferences about cognitive functioning in that specific and well-defined situation. The competence–performance distinction of modern linguistics was used to clarify their views. They assumed that men shared a similar competence and that the cultural differences or performance variations which they sought to explain were influenced more heavily by situational and cultural variables than by major differences in skills.

An additional point made by Cole and Bruner (1971) is that, unless cognitive functioning within different societies is understood as ordered and adaptive, it becomes all too easy to view non-standard, usually non-middle-class and non-Western behaviour as somehow defective or deficient. The pervasiveness of such an interpretation is evidenced in enrichment programmes which range from increasing protein calorie intake to hanging coloured mobiles over the cots of neonates. Clearly under-feeding is a problem which merits attention but even here the precise nature of the supplement is debatable. The analogy with cognitive development and especially the easy comparison with increasing intake is suspect unless one assumes that the nature of thinking in middle-class Western culture is the goal towards which all growth should be guided. This is a powerful assumption and one which Cole and Bruner argue against. Although they urge that teachers in particular be freed from the assumption that difference is equated with deficit, they believe that all individuals should have access to the intellectual tools of the dominant culture if they so choose.

At the more mundane level there remains the question of interpreting the various cultural differences which have been reported in the preceding chapters. From the general summary thus far it is clear that a deficit interpretation can but point to variables such as education and Western contact which will allow differences to be erased as non-Europeans become more like those who devise the tests which measure their inadequacy. For certain purposes, as noted in the discussion of selection procedures (see pages 121 to 122), this is necessary in so far as all societies wish to share in modern technology. However, an alternative approach – to accept differences as indications of the adaptation psychological processes in different cultural situations – may lead to fuller understanding of cognitive functioning.

Generally it has been assumed that cognition is more susceptible to the impact of cultural variation than perception. None the less, the evidence reviewed in chapter 3 illustrated cultural diversity in perceptual processing rules. While the presence of similarities as well as differences in behaviour is reassuring, the major problem lies in accounting for the differences.

The studies which focused on colour, orientation, depth and illusions have generally been coherent. It appears that while human beings in all societies can discriminate colour, the salience of colour and the persistence of colour as an attention-eliciting dimension varies with cultural experience. Again the perception of orientation appears to develop similarly in American and Zambian children but when orientation cues are presented in complex drawings and photographs they are differentially interpreted. In a similar fashion the representation of depth in varying pictorial modes increases perceptual difficulty. From this evidence one draws the general conclusion that the rules of representation vary culturally. The data underscore the need for more systematic studies which would allow specific analyses of the rule systems of pictorial perception employed by individuals who have been socialized in other cultures. The possibilities which such studies present are illustrated in the work of Wober (1972) who offers results which suggest that Africans infer sequence and temporal relationships from figural repetition. This inference may seem bizarre as well as complex to Westerners but it is of more than antiquarian interest. Given the current stress on education in most societies, there is a need to plan tuition which takes account of the cognitive skills which children have already acquired when they begin schooling. This is also a problem in European and American societies. Educators planning Western schools, who assumed that they shared the cultural traditions of a majority of their pupils, have only recently begun to appreciate the insights offered in Piaget's descriptions of the cognitive structures of children at different stages of development.

A further problem which cross-cultural psychologists encounter, in seeking to explain intellectual functioning as it varies from one cultural situation to another, is illustrated by results from the study of illusions. Although experimental psychologists have investigated illusions since the turn of the century and have demonstrated illusion responses in chicks and chimpanzees as well as in men, there are still difficulties in accounting for the underlying perceptual processes and as a result no adequate system exists by which to classify illusion figures. It is tempting to speculate that the difficulty in finding psychological accounts of illusion responses increases the attractiveness of physiological explanations such as those of Pollack and Silvar (see page 74).

Similar problems are raised in the cross-cultural study of the perception of time, space and emotion (see chapter 4). The results also lead to renewed consideration of the possibility of universal categories of experience, first mentioned in discussing colour perception. Piaget's theorizing on intellectual development in the first two years of life, before the appearance of language, offers suggestions about the growth of concepts of time, space, causality and permanent objects, albeit in European children. Although Piaget does not deal explicitly with emotion it is clear that cognitive development is also reflected in the differentiated perception of emotion. Cross-cultural evidence offers support for Piaget's views on space perception from workers outside Geneva; topological models of space are, as Piaget has suggested, the first to develop and topological features can be easily discriminated. Euclidean and projective models of space develop later, as Piaget also hypothesized, but their appearance is limited by experience in particular cultural settings. The latter statement does not imply that they appear only in European and American environments, as data collected from Eskimo subjects have shown not only sophisticated spatial abilities but also the absence of male superiority on spatial tasks, a usual feature of European and American results.

Over all the results from the study of time, space and emotion are disappointing. It is reasonable to expect researchers to explore cultural definitions in studying these concepts since they are not tied to specific physical stimuli to the same degree as the perception of colour or illusions. However, even skilled investigators such as Gay and Cole (1967) have difficulty in moving from the level of cultural analysis to the psychological and they were unable to predict accuracy of time estimations from a knowledge of Kpelle culture. They could but speculate why the counting by Americans led to estimates less accurate than those of the less quantitatively time-orientated Kpelle. Again the constraints imposed on cross-cultural research by the general methodological and theoretical development in the area cannot be overlooked. The psychological study of time has made little progress (cf. Ornstein, 1969); Piaget's theory of space has had only limited support in European studies, while the investigation of the perception of emotion is just beginning. Ekman's (1972) work, like much cross-cultural research, is fascinating in the promises it holds out for future achievements. If the elicitors of emotions, the display rules and the consequences of emotional display could be specified, it would be feasible to evaluate Ekman's claims about biological universals and cultural specifics. Currently, they are attractive possibilities.

There are disappointingly few studies, in the cross-cultural literature, of cognitive processes at a micro level but chapter 5 includes some important studies such as that of Cole *et al.*, illustrating their approach to culture and cognition. Reports on memory ranged from those which show that non-Western peoples can perform as well as Americans (cf. Louttit, 1931), to others showing that memory is constrained by cultural concerns (e.g. Nadel, 1937) and to yet other work indicating that memory improves with Westernization (Doob, 1961). The inconsistencies are obvious. The Kpelle studies stand as an example for future researchers, because the finding that Kpelle subjects were unable to use clustering principles to recall culturally suitable material served only as the starting point for further studies. Here one again sees the impact of basic assumptions on research strategies. Dissatisfied with concluding that the Kpelle, unlike American subjects, do not use clustering principles in recalling information, Cole *et al.* carried on their investigations until they were able to vary the experimental situation in ways which enabled Kpelle subjects to cluster items. Analysis of these situations led to a more thorough understanding of memory processes.

Micro level studies seem a particularly promising area for further research. Not only is there already evidence that success is possible and the considerable expertise of experimental research available, but basic assumptions are easier to identify and evaluate. At a number of points in the book the potential of structural, i.e. factor analytic, techniques has been mentioned. The method was used in Heider's studies of the structure of the colour domain in the lexicon and in memory (Heider and Olivier, 1972); it was alluded to in the brief comments on other approaches to the study of emotion and discussed in the review of research on the structure of abilities in chapter 6. All these reports have thrown up interesting possibilities but they share a common difficulty. In order to undertake factor analysis, powerful assumptions about the nature of the original data are often necessary especially when more advanced techniques are employed. Often these assumptions are not made clear. Rather than dismiss the potential which these techniques hold, it is to be hoped that cross-cultural researchers who employ them will take care to make known the inferences about their data on which their analyses depend.

By now it is apparent that the question with which we started – are cultural differences just a passing stage on the road to a universal technological society? – was very naïve. A guess, based upon the failure of that great experiment in cultural homogenization, the American melting pot, would suggest that cultural differences in cognition, as well as in emotion and other aspects of life will remain for a long time.

Some light has been shed on how to interpret these differences. Two related assumptions allow fruitful study. The first asserts that men are fundamentally similar in their intellectual skills but that these skills are differentially realized in culturally diverse settings. The second argues that no one setting should be acclaimed as superior. From these premises it follows that psychological research should aim at explicating the effects of differing cultural situations on basic skills. Thus evidence of cultural differences in response to a particular task becomes the starting point rather than the goal of cross-cultural research, and performance on a task should be scrutinized to determine whether it is a meaningful response or attempt to satisfy the arbitrary whim of an alien investigator.

Clearly the cross-cultural study of cognition presents a challenge to the serious psychologist. It is obvious that it is no longer an area of study which requires only a passport and air-plane ticket. Since the aim is not only the demonstration of cultural differences, but rather their explanation, the field requires dedicated workers willing to immerse themselves in another culture and painstakingly unravel the effects of situational variables on psychological processes. The reward for this effort is that the cross-cultural perspective may highlight processes overlooked in familiar situations.

Many psychologists might feel that their obligation rests with explicating the effects of cultural situations on cognitive skills but the problem of offering advice to planners in developing countries remains. The literature which has been reviewed raises questions and suggests possible future solutions but as yet there are no unambiguous answers. The two basic assumptions which were shown to offer direction for future research can also be applied when thinking about practical issues.

People in developing countries are demanding a rapid increase in Western-type education. Studies reviewed here indicate that children from Westernized homes with educated parents will be at a distinct advantage in such a system and it can only be hoped that those without these privileges will not be stigmatized as deficient. Secondly, in the rush to acquire Western skills it is possible that the unique indigenous adaptations to particular situations will be lost or treated merely as stumbling blocks. Psychological research directed to uncovering the assets of particular cultural environments may at first glance appear a luxury but it could prove the means to avoid some of the mistakes which are currently posing serious problems in many culturally diverse modern societies.

References

AHMAVAARA, Y. (1957), 'On the unified factor theory of mind', *Annals of The Finnish Academy of Science*, Series B106, Helsinki, Finland.

AL-ISSA, I., and DENNIS, W. (eds.) (1970), *Cross-Cultural Studies in Behavior*, Holt, Rinehart & Winston.

ALLPORT, G. W., and PETTIGREW, T. F. (1957), 'Cultural influence on the perception of movement: the trapezoidal illusion among Zulus', *J. abnorm. soc. Psychol.*, vol. 55, pp. 104–13. Reprinted in I. Al-Issa and W. Dennis (eds.), *Cross-Cultural Studies in Behavior*, Holt, Rinehart & Winston, 1970.

ANASTASI, A. (1932), 'Further studies on the memory factor', *Arch. Psychol.*, vol. 142, p. 60.

ANASTASI, A. (1968), *Psychological Testing*, Macmillan, 3rd edn.

ANASTASI, A. (1970), 'On the formation of psychological traits', *Amer. Psychol.*, vol. 25, pp. 899–910.

ANTONOVSKY, H. F., and GHENT, L. (1964), 'Cross-cultural consistency of children's preferences for the orientation of figures', *Amer. J. Psychol.*, vol. 77, pp. 295–7.

ARMSTRONG, R. E., RUBIN, E. V., STEWART, M., and KUNTER, L. (n.d.), 'Susceptibility to the Müller-Lyer, Sander Parallelogram and Ames Distorted Room illusions as a function of age, sex and retinal pigmentation among urban Mid-Western children', unpublished research report, Department of Psychology, Northwestern University, Evanston, Illinois.

BARTLETT, F. C. (1932), *Remembering*, Cambridge University Press.

BEARD, R. M. (1968), 'An investigation into mathematical concepts among Ghanaian children: I', *Teacher Education in New Countries*, vol. 9, pp. 3–14.

BERLIN, B., and KAY, P. (1969), *Basic Color Terms*, University of California Press.

BERNARDONI, L. C. (1964), 'A culture-fair intelligence test for the Ugh, No and Oo-La-La cultures', *Personn. Guid. J.*, vol. 42, pp. 554–7.

BERNSTEIN, B. (1961), 'Social structure, language and learning', *Educ. Res.*, vol. 3, pp. 163–76.

BERRY, J. W. (1966), 'Temne and Eskimo perceptual skills', *Int. J. Psychol.*, vol. 1, pp. 207–29.

BERRY, J. W. (1968), 'Ecology, perceptual development and the Müller–Lyer illusion', *Brit. J. Psychol.*, vol. 59, pp. 205–10.

BERRY, J. M. (1969), 'On cross-cultural comparability', *Int. J. Psychol.*, vol. 4, pp. 119–28.

BERRY, J. W. (1971), 'Müller–Lyer susceptibility. Culture, ecology or race?', *Int. J. Psychol.*, vol. 6, pp. 193–7

BERRY, J. W., and DASEN, P. (1973), *Culture and Cognition: Readings in Cross-Cultural Psychology*, Methuen, in press.

BEVERIDGE, W. M. (1939), 'Some racial differences in perception', *Brit. J. Psychol.*, vol. 30, pp. 57–64.

Biesheuvel, S. (1949), 'Psychological tests and their application to non-European peoples', in G. B. Jeffrey (ed.), *Yearbook of Education*. Reprinted in D. R. Price-Williams (ed.), *Cross-Cultural Studies*, Penguin, 1969.

Biesheuvel, S. (1952), 'The study of the African ability: a survey of some research problems', *Afric. Stud.*, vol. 11, pp. 105–17.

Biesheuvel, S. (1965), 'Personnel selection', in P. R. Farnsworth, O. McNemar and Q. McNemar (eds.) *Annual Review of Psychology*, Annual Reviews Inc.

Biesheuvel, S. (ed.) (1969), *Methods for the Measurement of Psychological Performance. A Handbook of Recommended Methods Based on an IUPS/IBP Working Party. IBP Handbook No. 10*, Blackwell.

Biesheuvel, S., and Liddicoat, R. (1959), 'The effects of cultural factors on intelligence test performance', *J. Nat. Inst. Personn. Res.*, vol. 8, pp. 3–14.

Birdwhistell, R. L. (1963), 'The kinesic level in the investigation of emotions', in P. H. Knapp (ed.), *Expression of the Emotions in Man*, International Universities Press.

Bloom, B. S. (1964), *Stability and Change in Human Characteristics*, Wiley.

Boas, F. (1911), *The Mind of Primitive Man*, Macmillan, rev. edn, 1938.

Bonte, M. (1962), 'The reaction of two African societies to the Müller–Lyer illusion', *J. soc. Psychol.*, vol. 58, pp. 265–8.

Boonsong, S. (1968), 'The development of conservation of mass, weight and volume in Thai children', unpublished M.Ed. thesis, College of Education, Bangkok (summarized in Dasen and Seagrim, 1970).

Boring, E. G. (1942), *Sensation and Perception in the History of Experimental Psychology*, Appleton-Century-Crofts.

Bowden, E. A. F. (1970), 'Accuracy of time estimation among rural and urban Baganda: a reinterpretation', *Percept. mot. Skills*, vol. 28, p. 54.

Brislin, R. W. (1970), 'Back translation for cross-cultural research', *J. cross-cult. Psychol.*, vol. 1, pp. 185–216.

Brown, R. (1965), *Social Psychology*, Free Press.

Brown, R. W., and Lenneberg, E. H. (1954), 'A study in language and cognition', *J. abnorm. soc. Psychol.*, vol. 49, pp. 454–62.

Bruner, J. S., Goodnow, J. J., and Austin, G. A. (1956), *A Study of Thinking*, Wiley.

Bruner, J. S., Olver, R. R., and Greenfield, P. M. (1966), *Studies in Cognitive Growth*, Wiley.

Brunswik, E. (1956), *Perception and the Representative Design of Psychological Experiments*, University of California Press.

Burt, H. E., and Dobell, E. M. (1955), 'The curve of forgetting for advertised material', *J. appl. Psychol.*, vol. 9, pp. 5–21.

Butcher, H. J. (1969), *Human Intelligence: Its Nature and Assessment*, Methuen.

Campbell, D. T. (1964), 'Distinguishing differences of perception from failures of communication in cross-cultural studies', in F. S. C. Northrop and H. H. Livingstone (eds.), *Cross-Cultural Understanding: Epistemology in Anthropology*, Harper & Row.

Campbell, D. T. (1967), 'Eliminating plausible rival hypotheses by supplementary variation'. Paper presented at the meeting of the American Psychological Association, Washington, D.C.

Carroll, J. B., and Casagrande, J. B. (1958), 'The function of language classifications in behavior', in E. E. Maccoby, T. M. Newcomb and E. L. Hartley (eds.), *Readings in Social Psychology*, Holt, Rinehart & Winston.

Carter, R. E. (1966), 'Some problems and distinctions in cross-cultural research', *Amer. behav. Sci.*, vol. 9, pp. 23–4.

CATTELL, R. B. (1963), 'Theory of fluid and crystallized intelligence: a critical experiment', *J. educ. Psychol.*, vol. 54, pp. 1–22.

CHIN, R., and CHIN, A. (1969), *Psychological Research in Communist China, 1949–1966*, MIT Press.

CLAUSEN, J. (1950), 'An evaluation of experimental methods of time judgment', *J. exp. Psychol.*, vol. 40, pp. 756–61.

CLOWES, M. (1971), 'On seeing things', *Artif. Intell.*, vol. 2, pp. 79–116.

COLE, M., and BRUNER, J. S. (1971), 'Cultural differences and inferences about psychological processes', *Amer. Psychol.*, vol. 26, pp. 867–76.

COLE, M., and GAY, J. (1972), 'Culture and memory', Amer. Anthrop., in press.

COLE, M., GAY, J., and GLICK, J. A. (1968), 'Reversal and non-reversal shifts among Liberian tribal people', *J. exp. Psychol.*, vol. 76, pp. 323–4.

COLE, M., GAY, J. A., GLICK, J., and SHARP, D. W. (1968), 'Linguistic structure and transposition', *Science*, vol. 164, pp. 90–91.

COLE, M., GAY, J., GLICK, J. A., and SHARP, D. W. (1971), *The Cultural Context of Learning and Thinking: An Exploration in Experimental Anthropology*, Basic Books.

CORAH, H. L. (1964), 'Color and form in children's perceptual behavior', *Percept. mot. Skills*, vol. 18, pp. 313–16.

COTTLE, T. J., and HOWARD, P. (1969), 'Temporal extension and time zone bracketing in Indian adolescents', *Percept. mot. Skills*, vol. 28, pp. 599–612.

COWLEY, J. J., and MURRAY, M. (1962), 'Some aspects of the development of spatial concepts in Zulu children', *J. soc. Res.* (Pretoria), vol. 13, pp. 1–18.

D'ANDRADE, R. G. (1961), 'Anthropological studies of dreams', in F. L. Hsu (ed.), *Psychological Anthropology: Approaches to Culture and Personality*, Dorsey Press.

DARWIN, C. (1872) *The Expression of the Emotions in Man and Animals*, John Murray.

DAS, R. S. (1963), 'Analysis of the components of reasoning in non-verbal tests and the structure of reasoning in a bilingual population', *Archiv für die gesamte Psychologie*, vol. 115, pp. 215–29.

DASEN, P. R. (1970), 'Cognitive development in Aborigines of central Australia', unpublished Ph.D. thesis, Australian National University, Canberra.

DASEN, P. R., and SEAGRIM, G. N. (1970), 'Inventory of cross-cultural Piagetian research', vol. 2, unpublished newsletter.

DAVID, K. H., and BOCHNER, S. (1967), 'Teacher ratings of IQ and Porteus Maze scores of Pitjandjara children, *Percept. mot. Skills*, vol. 25, pp. 639–40.

DAVIS, C. M., and CARLSON, J. A. (1970), 'A cross-cultural study of the strength of the Müller–Lyer illusion as a function of attentional factors', *J. Person. soc. Psychol.*, vol. 16, pp. 403–10.

DAWSON, J. L. M. (1963), 'Psychological effects of social change in a West African community', unpublished D.Phil. thesis, University of Oxford.

DAWSON, J. L. M. (1967a), 'Cultural and physiological influence upon spatial-perceptual processes in West Africa: Part I', *Int. J. Psychol*, vol. 2, pp. 115–28. Reprinted in D. R. Price-Williams (ed.), *Cross-Cultural Studies*, Penguin, 1969.

DAWSON, J. L. M. (1967b), 'Cultural and physiological influences upon spatial-perceptual processes in West Africa: Part II', *Int. J. Psychol.*, vol. 2, pp. 171–85.

DAWSON, J. L. M. (1970), 'Effects of sex hormones on cognitive style in rats and men', unpublished paper.

DE LEMOS, M. M. (1969), 'The development of conservation in Aboriginal children', *Int. J. Psychol.*, vol. 4, pp. 255–69.

DEREGOWSKI, J. B. (1967), 'The horizontal–vertical illusion and the ecological hypothesis', *Int. J. Psychol.*, vol. 2, pp. 269–73.
DEREGOWSKI, J. B. (1968a), 'On perception of depicted orientation', *Int. J. Psychol.*, vol. 3, pp. 149–56.
DEREGOWSKI, J. B. (1968b), 'Difficulties in pictorial depth perception in Africa', *Brit. J. Psychol.*, vol. 59, pp. 195–204.
DEREGOWSKI, J. B. (1968c), 'Pictorial recognition in subjects from a relatively pictureless environment', *Afric. soc. Res.*, vol. 5, pp. 356–64.
DEREGOWSKI, J. B. (1969), 'A pictorial perception paradox', *Acta Psychol.*, vol. 31, pp. 365–74.
DEREGOWSKI, J. B. (1970), 'Effect of cultural value of time upon recall', *Brit. J. soc. clin. Psychol.*, vol. 9, pp. 37–41.
DEREGOWSKI, J. B. (1971a), 'Responses mediating pictorial recognition', *J. soc. Psychol.*, vol. 84, pp. 27–33.
DEREGOWSKI, J. B. (1971b), 'Orientation and perception of pictorial depth', *Int. J. Psychol.*, vol. 6, pp. 111–14.
DEREGOWSKI, J. B., and SERPELL, R. (1971), 'Performance on a sorting task with various modes of representation: a cross-cultural experiment', *Human Development Research Unit Reports*, no. 18, University of Zambia.
DESCOEUDRES, A. (1914), 'Coleur, forme, ou nombre?', *Archives de psychologie*, vol. 14, pp. 305–41.
DOAN, F. (1967), 'The effect of response meaningfulness on verbal paired-associate learning in Anglo-American and Mexican-American fifth-grade children', *Dissert. Abstr.*, no. 67–3276.
DOGBEH, R. (1967), 'Intelligence and education', in E. R. Wickert (ed.), *Readings in African Psychology from French Language Sources*, Michigan State African Studies Center.
DOOB, L. W. (1960), *Becoming More Civilized: A Psychological Exploration*, Yale University Press.
DOOB, L. W. (1961), *Communication in Africa. A Search for Boundaries*, Yale University Press.
DOOB, L. W. (1965), 'Psychology', in R. A. Lystad (ed.), *The African World: A Survey of Social Research*, Praeger.
DORE, R. P. (1961), 'Function and cause', *Amer. soc. Rev.*, vol. 26, pp. 843–53.
DU TOIT, B. M. (1966), 'Pictorial depth perception and linguistic relativity', *Psychol. Afric.*, vol. 11, pp. 51–63.
EGGAN, D. (1961), 'Dream analysis', in B. Kaplan (ed.), *Studying Personality Cross Culturally*, Harper & Row.
EIBL-EIBESFELDT, I. (1970), *Ethology, the Biology of Behavior*, Holt, Rinehart & Winston.
EKMAN, P. (1972), 'Universals and cultural differences in facial expressions of emotions', *Nebraska Symposium on Motivation*, in press.
EKMAN, P., and FRIESEN, W. V, (1971), 'Constants across cultures in the face and emotion', *J. Person. soc. Psychol.*, vol. 17, pp. 124–9.
EKMAN, P., FRIESEN, W. V., and ELLSWORTH, P. (1971), *Emotion in the Human Face: Guidelines for Research and an Integration of Findings*, Pergamon Press.
EKMAN, P., FRIESEN, W. V., and TOMKINS, S. S. (1972), 'Facial Affect Scoring Technique (Fast): a first validity study', *Semiotica*, in press.
EKMAN, P., SORENSON, E. R., and FRIESEN, W. V. (1969), 'Pan-cultural elements in facial displays of emotions', *Science*, vol. 164, pp. 86–8.
ELKIND, D. (1961), 'Children's discovery of the conservation of mass, weight and volume: Piaget replication study II', *J. genet. Psychol.*, vol. 98, pp. 219–28.

ELKIND, D. (1967), 'Piaget's conservation problems', *Child Devel.*, vol. 38, pp. 15–27.

ERVIN, S. M. (1964), 'Language and TAT content in bilinguals', *J. abnorm. soc. Psychol.*, vol. 68, pp. 500–507. Reprinted in I-Al-Issa and W. Dennis (eds.), *Cross-Cultural Studies in Behavior*, Holt, Rinehart & Winston, 1970.

ETUK, E. E. S. (1967), 'The development of number concepts: an examination of Piaget's theory with Yoruba-speaking Nigerian children', *Dissert. Abstr.*, no. 67–12, 685.

EVANS, J. L., and SEGALL, M. H. (1969), 'Learning to classify by color and by function: a study of concept-discovery by Ganda children', *J. soc. Psychol.*, vol. 77, pp. 35–53.

EYSENCK, H. J. (1959), *Maudsley Personality Inventory*, University of London Press.

EYSENCK, H. J. (1971), *Race, Intelligence and Education. Towards a New Society*, Temple Smith.

FANTZ, R. L. (1961), 'The origin of form perception', *Sci. Amer.*, vol. 204, pp. 66–72.

FARBER, M. L. (1953), 'Time perspective and feeling tone: a study in the perception of the days', *J. Psychol.*, vol. 35, pp. 253–7.

FERGUSON, G. (1954), 'On learning and human ability', *Canad. J. Psychol.*, vol. 8, pp. 95–112.

FISHMAN, J. A. (1960), 'A systemization of the Whorfian Hypothesis', *Behav. Sci.*, vol. 5, pp. 323–39.

FLAVELL, J. H. (1963), *The Developmental Psychology of Jean Piaget*, Van Nostrand.

FONG, S. L. (1965), 'Cultural influences in the perception of people: the case of Chinese in America', *Brit. J. soc. clin. Psychol.*, vol. 4, pp. 110–13.

FONSECA, L., and KEARL, B. (1960), *Comprehension of Pictorial Symbols: An Experiment in Rural Brazil*, Bulletin no. 30, Department of Agricultural Journalism, College of Agriculture, University of Wisconsin.

FRAKE, C. O. (1962), 'The ethnographic study of cognitive systems', in T. Gladwin and W. C. Sturtevant (eds.), *Anthropology and Human Behavior*, Anthropological Society of Washington.

FRENCH, D. (1963), 'The relationship of anthropology to studies in perception and cognition', in S. Koch (ed.), *Psychology: A Study of a Science*, vol. 6, McGraw-Hill.

FRIJDA, N. H., and JAHODA, G. (1966), 'On the scope and methods of cross-cultural research', *Int. J. Psychol.*, vol. 1, pp. 109–27. Reprinted in D. R. Price-Williams (ed.), *Cross-Cultural Studies*, Penguin, 1969.

FRIJDA, N. H., and PHILIPSZOON, E. (1963), 'Dimensions of recognition of expression', *J. aborm. soc. Psychol.*, vol. 66, pp. 45–51.

FURBY, L. (1971), 'A theoretical analysis of cross-cultural research in cognitive development. Piaget's conservation task', *J. cross-cult. Psychol.*, vol. 2, pp. 241–55.

FURTH, H. G. (1966), *Thinking without Language: Psychological Implications of Deafness*, Free Press.

FURTH, H. G. (1969), *Piaget and Knowledge: Theoretical Foundations*, Prentice-Hall.

GARDNER, R. W. (1953), 'Cognitive styles in categorizing behavior', *J. Person.*, vol. 22, pp. 214–33.

GAY, J., and COLE, M. (1967), *The New Mathematics and an Old Culture: A Study of Learning among the Kpelle of Liberia*, Holt, Rinehart & Winston.

GAY, J., and WELMERS, W. (1971), *Mathematics and Logic in the Kpelle Language*, Institute of African Studies, University of Ibadan.
GEIGER, H. (1880), *Contributions to the History of the Human Race*, trans. D. Asher, Trubner.
GHENT, L. (1960), 'Recognition by children of realistic figures presented in various orientations', *Canad. J. Psychol.*, vol. 14, pp. 249–56.
GHENT, L. (1961), 'Form and its orientation: a child's eye view', *Amer. J. Psychol.*, vol. 74, pp. 177–90.
GHENT, L., and BERNSTEIN, L. (1961), 'Influence of the orientation of geometric forms on their recognition by children', *Percept. mot. Skills*, vol. 12, pp. 95–101.
GIBSON, E. J. (1969), *Principles of Perceptual Learning and Development*, Appleton-Century-Crofts.
GIBSON, J. J. (1966), *The Senses Considered as Perceptual Systems*, Houghton Mifflin.
GLADSTONE, W. E. (1858), *Studies on Homer and the Homeric Age*, vol. 3, Oxford University Press.
GLICK, J. A. (1969), 'Culture and cognition: some theoretical and methodological concerns', paper presented at the American Anthropological Association Meeting, 21 November.
GLUCKMAN, M. (1967), 'Psychological, sociological and anthropological explanation of witchcraft and gossip', *Man*, vol. 3, pp. 20–34.
GOODENOUGH, F. L. (1936), 'The measurement of mental functions in primitive groups', *Amer. Anthrop.*, vol. 38, pp. 1–11.
GOODENOUGH, W. H. (1957), *Cultural Anthropology and Linguistics*, Georgetown University.
GOODNOW, J. J. (1962), 'A test of milieu effects with some of Piaget's tasks', *Psychol. Monogr.*, vol. 76, no. 555.
GOODNOW, J. J. (1969), 'Problems in research on culture and thought', in D. Elkind and J. H. Flavell (eds.), *Studies in Cognitive Development*, Oxford University Press.
GOODNOW, J. J. (1970), 'Cultural variations in cognitive skills', *Cog. Stud.*, vol. 1, pp. 242–57. Reprinted in D. R. Price-Williams (ed.), *Cross-Cultural Studies*, Penguin, 1969.
GOODNOW, J. J., and BETHON, G. (1966), 'Piaget's tasks: the effects of schooling and intelligence', *Child Devel.*, vol. 37, pp. 573–82.
GOODY, E. N. (1970), 'Kinship fostering in Northern Ghana and the Kpembe study', unpublished manuscript.
GREEN, D. R., FORD, M. P., and FLAMER, G. B. (1971), *Measurement and Piaget*, McGraw-Hill.
GREENFIELD, P. M. (1966), 'On culture and conservation', in J. S. Bruner, R. R. Olver and P. M. Greenfield, *Studies in Cognitive Growth*, Wiley. Reprinted in D. R. Price-Williams (ed.), *Cross-Cultural Studies*, Penguin, 1969.
GREENFIELD, P. M., and BRUNER, J. S. (1966), 'Culture and cognitive growth', *Int. J. Psychol.*, vol. 1, pp. 89–107.
GREENFIELD, P. M., and BRUNER, J. S. (1971), 'Learning and language: work with the Wolof', *Psychol. Today*, July.
GREENFIELD, P. M., REICH, L. C., and OLVER, R. R. (1966), 'On culture and equivalence: II', in J. S. Bruner, R. R. Olver and P. M. Greenfield, *Studies in Cognitive Growth*, Wiley.
GREGOR, A. J., and MCPHERSON, D. A. (1965), 'A study of susceptibility of geometric illusion among cultural subgroups of Australian aborigines', *Psychol. Afric.*, vol. 11, pp. 1–13.

GREGORY, R. L. (1966), *Eye and Brain, the Psychology of Seeing*, World University Library.

GREGORY, R. L., and WALLACE, J. G. (1963), 'Recovery from early blindness: a case study', *Exp. Psychol. Soc. Monogr.*, no. 2.

GUILFORD, J. P. (1959), 'Three faces of intellect', *Amer. Psychol.*, vol. 14, pp. 469–79.

GUNN, J. A. (1929), *The Problem of Time*, Allen & Unwin.

GUTHRIE, M. (1963), 'Structure of abilities in a non-Western culture', *J. educ. Psychol.*, vol. 54, pp. 94–103.

GUTTMAN, R., and GUTTMAN, L. (1963), 'Cross-cultural stability of an intercorrelation pattern of abilities: a possible test for a biological basis', *Hum. Biol.*, vol. 35, pp. 53–60.

HARARI, H., and MCDAVID, J. (1966), 'Cultural influence on retention of logical and symbolic material', *J. educ. Psychol.*, vol. 57, pp. 18–22.

HEBB, D. O. (1949), *The Organization of Behavior*, Wiley.

HEIDER, E. R. (1972a), 'Universals in colour naming and memory', *J. exp. Psychol.*, in press.

HEIDER, E. R. (1972b), *Natural Categories*, American Psychological Association Convention Proceedings, in press.

HEIDER, E. R., and OLIVIER, D. C. (1972), 'The structure of the color space in naming and memory for two languages', *Cogn. Psychol.*, in press.

HERON, A. (1966), 'Experimental studies of mental development in conditions of rapid cultural change', *Proceedings of the XVIIIth International Congress of Psychology*, Symposium 36, Moscow.

HERON, A. (1968), 'Studies of perception and reasoning in Zambian children', *Int. J. Psychol.*, vol. 3, pp. 23–9.

HERON A., and SIMONSSON, (1969), 'Weight conservation in Zambian children – a non-verbal approach', *Int. J. Psychol.*, vol. 4, pp. 281–92.

HERSKOVITS, M. J. (1950), *Man and his Works*, Knopf.

HERSKOVITS, M. J., CAMBELL, D. T. and SEGALL, M. H. (1956), *A Cross-Cultural Study of Perception*, Northwestern University Press.

HESS, R. D., and SHIPMAN, V. C. (1965), 'Early experience and the socialization of cognitive modes in children', *Child Devel.*, vol. 36, pp. 869–86.

HEUSE, G. A. (1957), 'Etudes psychologiques sur les noirs Sudannais et Guinéens', *Revue psychologique des peuples*, vol. 12, pp. 35–68.

HIRSH, J. (1967), *Behavior – Genetic Analysis*, McGraw-Hill.

HOFSTAETTER, P. R. (1954), 'The changing composition of "intelligence": a study in T-technique', *J. genet. Psychol.*, vol. 85, pp. 159–64.

HOIJER, H. (1951), 'Cultural implications of some Navaho linguistic categories', *Language*, vol. 27, pp. 111–20.

HOLMES, A. C. (1963), *A Study of Understanding of Visual Symbols in Kenya*, Overseas Visual Aids Centre, London.

HONIGMANN, J. J. (1969), 'Psychological anthropology', *Annals*, vol. 383, pp. 145–58.

HORTON, R. (1967a), 'African traditional thought and Western science: I. From tradition to science', *Africa*, vol. 37, pp. 50–71.

HORTON, R. (1967b), 'African traditional thought and Western science: II. The "closed" and "open" predicaments', *Africa*, vol. 37, pp. 155–87.

HSU, F. L. (1961), *Psychological Anthropology: Approaches to Culture and Personality*, Dorsey Press.

HUBEL, D. H., and WIESEL, T. N. (1963), 'Receptive fields of cells in striate cortex of very young visually inexperienced kittens', *J. Neurophysiol.*, vol. 26, pp. 995–1002.

HUDSON, W. (1960), 'Pictorial depth perception in sub-cultural groups in Africa', *J. soc. Psychol.*, vol. 52, pp. 183–208. Reprinted in I. Al-Issa and W. Dennis (eds.), *Cross-Cultural Studies in Behavior*, Holt, Rinehart & Winston, 1970.

HUDSON, W. (1962a), 'Cultural problems in pictorial perception', *S. Afric. J. Sci.*, vol. 58, pp. 189–96.

HUDSON, W. (1962b), 'Pictorial perception and educational adaptation in Africa', *Psychol. Afric.*, vol. 9, pp. 226–39.

HUDSON, W. (1967), 'The study of the problem of pictorial perception among unacculturated groups', *Int. J. Psychol.*, vol. 2, pp. 89–107, Reprinted in D. R. Price-Williams (ed.), *Cross-Cultural Studies*, Penguin, 1969.

HUNT, J. MCV. (1961), *Intelligence and Experience*, Ronald Press.

HYDE, M. G. (1970), *Piaget and Conceptual Development*, Holt, Rinehart & Winston.

INGENKAMP, K. (1969), *Developments in Educational Testing: The Proceedings of an International Conference Held under the Aegis of the Pädagogisches Zentrum Berlin*, University of London Press.

INHELDER, B., and PIAGET, J. (1958), *The Growth of Logical Thinking from Childhood to Adolescence*, trans. A. Parsons and S. Milgram, Routledge & Kegan Paul.

INHELDER, B., and SINCLAIR, H. (1969), 'Learning cognitive structures', in P. H. Mussen, J. Lange and M. Covington (eds.), *Trends and Issues in Developmental Psychology*, Holt, Rinehart & Winston.

INTERNATIONAL UNION OF PSYCHOLOGICAL SCIENCE (1966), *International Directory of Psychologists*, 2nd edn.

IRVINE, S. H. (1964), 'Selection of Africans for post-primary education in Southern Rhodesia. Pilot survey June–July 1962', *Bull. Inter. Afric. Lab. Inst.*, vol. 11, pp. 69–93.

IRVINE, S. H. (1966), 'Towards a rationale for testing attainments and abilities in Africa', *Brit. J. educ. Psychol.*, vol. 35, pp. 24–32.

IRVINE, S. H. (1969a), 'Contributions of ability and attainment testing in Africa to a general theory of intellect', *J. biosoc. Sci.*, suppl. 1, pp. 91–102.

IRVINE, S. H. (1969b), 'Culture and mental ability', *New Sci.*, 1 May, pp. 230–31.

IRVINE, S. H. (1969c), 'Factor analysis of African abilities and attainments: constructs across cultures', *Psychol. Bull.*, vol. 71, pp. 20–32.

IRVINE, S. H. (1970), 'Affect and construct: a cross-cultural check of theories of intelligence', *J. soc. Psychol.*, vol. 80, pp. 23–30.

IRWIN, M. H., and MCLAUGHLIN, D. H. (1970), 'Ability and preference in category sorting by Mano schoolchildren and adults', *J. soc. Psychol.*, vol. 82, pp. 15–24.

JAHODA, G. (1956), 'Assessment of abstract behavior in a non-Western culture', *J. abnorm. soc. Psychol.*, vol. 53, pp. 237–43.

JAHODA, G. (1958), 'Child animism: I. A critical survey of cross-cultural research: II. A study in West Africa', *J. soc. Psychol.*, vol. 47, pp. 197–222.

JAHODA, G. (1966), 'Geometric illusions: a study of Ghana', *Brit. J. Psychol.*, vol. 57, pp. 193–200. Reprinted in D. R. Price-Williams (ed.), *Cross-Cultural Studies*, Penguin, 1969.

JAHODA, G. (1970), 'A cross-cultural perspective in psychology. Presidential address delivered to section J (Psychology) of the British Association', *Advance. Sci.*, vol. 27, pp. 1–14.

JAHODA, G. (1971), 'Retinal pigmentation, illusion susceptibility and space perception', *Int. J. Psychol.*, vol. 6, pp. 199–208.

JAHODA, G., and STACEY, B. (1970), 'Susceptibility to geometrical illusions according to culture and professional training', *Percept. Psychophys.*, vol. 7, pp. 179–84.

JEFFREY, W. E. (1966), 'Discrimination of oblique lines by children', *J. comp. physiol. Psychol.*, vol. 62, pp. 154–6.

JENSEN, A. R. (1969), 'How much can we boost IQ and scholastic achievement?', *Harv. educ. Rev.*, vol. 39, pp. 1–123.

KAPLAN, B. (1961), *Studying Personality Cross-Culturally*, Harper & Row.

KELLAGHAN, T. (1968), 'Abstraction and categorization in African children', *Int. J. Psychol.*, vol. 3, pp. 115–20.

KENDLER, H. H., and KENDLER, T. S. (1962), 'Vertical and horizontal processes in problem solving', *Psychol. Rev.*, vol. 69, pp. 1–16.

KENDLER, H. H., and MAYZNER, M. A. (1956), 'Reversal and non-reversal shifts in card-sorting tests with two or four categories', *J. exp. Psychol.*, vol. 51, pp. 244–8.

KENDLER, T. S., and KENDLER, H. H. (1959), 'Reversal and non-reversal shifts in kindergarten children', *J. exp. Psychol.*, vol. 58, pp. 56–60.

KENDLER, T. S., and KENDLER, H. H. (1970), 'An ontogeny of optional shift behaviour', *Child Devel.*, vol. 41, pp. 1–27.

KENDLER, T. S., KENDLER, H. H., and LEARNARD, B. (1962), 'Mediated responses to size and brightness as a function of age', *Amer. J. Psychol.*, vol. 75, pp. 571–86.

KIDD, A. H. (1962), 'The culture-fair aspects of Cattel's Test of *g*: culture free', *J. genet. Psychol.*, vol. 101, pp. 343–62.

KIDD, A. H., and RIVOIRE, J. L. (1965), 'The culture-fair aspects of the development of spatial perception', *J. genet. Psychol.*, vol. 106, pp. 101–11.

KILBRIDE, P. L., and ROBBINS, M. C. (1968), 'Linear perspective, pictorial depth perception and education among the Baganda', *Percept. mot. Skills*, vol. 27, pp. 601–2.

KILBRIDE, P. L., ROBBINS, M. C., and FREEMAN, R. B. (1968), 'Pictorial depth perception and education among Baganda school children', *Percept. mot. Skills*, vol. 26, pp. 116–18.

KLINEBERG, O. (1938), 184: 'Emotional expression in Chinese literature', *J. abnorm. soc. Psychol.*, vol. 33, pp. 517–10.

KNOWLES, D. W., and BOERSMA, F. J. (1968), 185: 'Optional shift performance of culturally different children to concrete and abstract stimuli', *Alberta J. educ. Res.*, vol. 14, pp. 165–77.

KROEBER, A. L., and KLUCKHOHN, C. (1952), *Culture: A Critical Review of Concepts and Definitions*, Peabody Museum, Cambridge, Mass.

KUNNAPAS, T. M. (1955), 'An analysis of the "vertical–horizontal illusion"', *J. exp. Psychol.*, vol. 49, pp. 371–4.

LAMBERT, W. W. (1971), 'Comparative studies of personality', in W. W. Lambert and R. Weisbrod (eds.), *Comparative Perspectives on Social Psychology*, Little, Brown.

LANDAUER, T. K., and WHITING, J. W. M. (1964), 'Infantile stimulation and adult stature of human males', *Amer. Anthrop.*, vol. 66, pp. 1007–28.

LANTZ, D. L., and LENNEBERG, E. H. (1966), 'Verbal communication and color memory in the deaf and hearing', *Child Devel.*, vol. 37, pp. 765–79.

LANTZ, D. L., and STEFFLRE, V. (1964), 'Language and cognition revisited', *J. abnorm. soc. Psychol.*, vol. 69, pp. 472–81.

LASHLEY, K. S. (1938), 'The mechanism of vision: XI. Preliminary studies of the rat's capacity for detail vision', *J. gen. Psychol.*, vol. 18, pp. 123–93.
LENNEBERG, E. H. (1953), 'Cognition and ethnolinguistics', *Language*, vol. 29, pp. 463–71.
LENNEBERG, E. H. (1967), *Biological Foundations of Language*, Wiley.
LENNEBERG, E. H., and ROBERTS, J. M. (1956), *The Language of Experience*, Indiana University Press.
LÉVI-STRAUSS, C. (1963), *Structural Anthropology*, trans. C. Jacobson and B. G. Schoepf, Basic Books.
LÉVI-STRAUSS, C. (1966), *The Savage Mind*, Weidenfeld & Nicolson.
LÉVY-BRUHL, L. (1922), *La mentalité primitive*, Presses Universitaires de France. Trans. *How Natives Think*, Allen & Unwin, 1926.
LINDZEY, G. (1954), *The Handbook of Social Psychology*, vol. 1, Addison-Wesley.
LINDZEY, G. (1961), *Projective Techniques and Cross-Cultural Research*, Appleton-Century-Crofts.
LINDZEY, G., and ARONSON, E. (1968), *The Handbook of Social Psychology*, vol. 2, Addison-Wesley, 2nd edn.
LINDZEY, G., and ARONSON, E. (1969), *The Handbook of Social Psychology*, vol. 3, Addison-Wesley, 2nd edn.
LITTLEJOHN, J. (1963), 'Temne space', *Anthrop. Q.*, vol. 36, p. 1–17.
LLOYD, B. B. (1971), 'Studies of conservation with Yoruba children of differing ages and experience', *Child Devel.*, vol. 42, pp. 415–28.
LLOYD, R., and PIDGEON, D. A. (1961), 'An investigation into the effects of coaching on non-verbal test material with European, Indian and African children', *Brit. J. educ. Psychol.*, vol. 31, pp. 145–51.
LOUTTIT, C. M. (1931), 'Racial comparisons of ability in immediate recall of logical and nonsense material', *J. soc. Psychol.*, vol. 2, pp. 205–15.
LOVELL, K. (1959), 'A follow-up study of some aspects of the work of Piaget and Inhelder on the child's conception of space', *Brit. J. educ. Psychol.*, vol. 29, pp. 104–17.
LOVELL, K. (1961), *The Growth of Basic Mathematical and Scientific Concepts in Children*, University of London Press.
LOVELL, K. (1969), 'Psychological aspects of research in education', in R. Jolly (ed.), *Education in Africa*, East African Publishing House.
LOVELL, K. (1971), 'Some problems associated with formal thought and its assessment', in D. R. Green, M. P. Ford and G. B. Flamer (eds.), *Measurement and Piaget*, McGraw-Hill.
LYONS, J. (1968), *Introduction to Theoretical Linguistics*, Cambridge University Press.
LYONS, J. (1970), *Chomsky*, Collins.
MACARTHUR, R. S. (1967), 'Sex differences in field dependence for the Eskimo: replication of Berry's findings', *Int. J. Psychol.*, vol. 2, pp. 139–40. Reprinted in D. R. Price-Williams (ed.), *Cross-Cultural Studies*, Penguin, 1969.
MACARTHUR, R. S. (1971), 'Mental abilities and psychosocial environments: Igloolik Eskimos', paper presented to Mid-Project Preview, International Biological Programme/Igloolik Project, Toronto, 13 March.
MACCOBY, E. E. (1971), 'Sex differences and their implications for sex roles', Address to LXXIXth Annual Convention of American Psychological Association.
MCFIE, J. (1961), 'The effect of education of African performance on a group of intellectual tests', *Brit. J. educ. Psychol.*, vol. 31, pp. 232–40.

MACKINTOSH, J., and SUTHERLAND, N. S. (1962), 'Visual discrimination by the goldfish: the orientation of rectangles', *Anim. Behav.*, vol. 11, pp. 135–41.
MACLAY, H. (1958), 'An experimental study of language and non-linguistic behavior', *S.W.J. Anthrop.*, vol. 14, pp. 220–29.
MACLEAN, U. (1960), 'Blood donors for Ibadan', *Comm. Devel. Bull.*, vol. 11, pp. 26–31.
MAGNUS, H. (1877), *Die geschichtliche Entwicklung des Farbensinnes*, Veit.
MAISTRIAUX, R. (1955), 'La sous-évolution des noirs d'Afrique. Sa nature – ses causes – ses remèdes', *Revue psychologique des peuples*, vol. 10, pp. 167–89, 397–456.
MALINOWSKI, B. (1927), *Sex and Repression in Savage Society*, Routledge & Kegan Paul.
MAYO, P. R., and BELL, J. M. (1972), 'A note on the taxonomy of Witkin's field-independence measures', *Brit. J. Psychol.*, in press.
MEAD, M. (1932), 'An investigation of the thought of primitive children with special reference to animism', *J. Roy. Anthrop. Inst.*, vol. 62, pp. 173–90.
MEADE, R. D. (1959), 'Time estimates as affected by motivational level, goal distance and rate of progress', *J. exp. Psychol.*, vol. 58, pp. 275–9.
MEADE, R. D. (1963), 'Effect of motivation and progress on the estimation of longer times', *J. exp. Psychol.*, vol. 65, pp. 564–7.
MEADE, R. D. (1968), 'Psychological time in India and America', *J. soc. Psychol.*, vol. 76, pp. 169–74.
MEADE, R. D., and SINGH, D. (1970), 'Motivation and progress effects on psychological time in subcultures of India', *J. soc. Psychol.*, vol. 80, pp. 3–10.
MELIKIAN, H. (1969), Acculturation, time perspective, and feeling tone: a cross-cultural study in the perception of the days', *J. soc. Psychol.*, vol. 79, pp. 273–5.
MERMELSTEIN, E., and SHULMAN, L. S. (1967), 'Lack of formal schooling and the acquisition of conservation', *Child Devel.*, vol. 38, pp. 39–52.
MILLER, G. A. (1956), 'The magical number seven, plus or minus two: some limits on our capacity for processing information', *Psychol. Rev.*, vol. 63, pp. 81–97.
MILLER, G. A., and MCNEILL, D. (1969), 'Psycholinguistics', in G. Lindzey and E. Aronson (eds.), *The Handbook of Social Psychology*, vol. 3, Addison-Wesley.
MOHSENI, N. (1966), 'La comparaison des réactions aux épreuves d'intelligence en Iran et en Europe', thèse d'université, Université de Paris.
MORF, A. (1962), 'Recherches sur l'origine de la connexité de la suite des premiers nombres', in P. Greco and A. Morf (eds.), *Etudes d'épistémologie génétique: XIII. Structures numériques élémentaires*, Presses Universitaires de France.
MORGAN, P. (1959), 'Observations and findings on the 7-squares test with literate and illiterate black groups in Southern Africa', *J. Nat. Inst. Personn. Res.*, vol. 8, pp. 44–7.
MUNDY-CASTLE, A. C. (1966), 'Pictorial depth perception in Ghanaian children', *Int. J. Psychol.*, vol. 1, pp. 289–300. Reprinted in D. R. Price-Williams (ed.), *Cross-Cultural Studies*, Penguin, 1969.
MUNDY-CASTLE, A. C., and NELSON, G. K. (1962), 'A neuropsychological study of the Knysna forest workers', *Psychol. Afric.*, vol. 9, pp. 240–72.
MURPHY, G., and MURPHY, L. B. (1968), *Asian Psychology*, Basic Books.
NADEL, S. F. (1937), 'Experiments on culture psychology', *Africa.*, vol. 10, pp. 421–35.

NANDA, P. C., DAS, J. P., and MISHRA, H. K. (1965), 'Discrimination of geometrical patterns in tribal, rural and urban children', *J. soc. Psychol.*, vol. 67, pp. 197–200.

NAROLL, R. (1970), 'What have we learned from cross-cultural surveys?', *Amer. Anthrop.*, vol. 72, pp. 1227–88.

NEISSER, U. (1967), *Cognitive Psychology*, Appleton-Century-Crofts.

NICHOLS, H. (1891), 'The psychology of time', *Amer. J. Psychol.*, vol. 3, pp. 453–529.

NISSEN, H. W., MACHOVER, S., and KINDER, E. F. (1935), 'A study of performance tests given to a group of native Negro children', *Brit. J. Psychol.*, vol. 25, pp. 308–55.

OKONJI, M. O. (1969), 'The differential effects of rural and urban upbringing on the development of cognitive styles', *Int. J. Psychol.*, vol. 4, pp. 193–305.

OKONJI, M. O. (1970), 'The effect of special training on the classificatory behaviour of some Nigerian Ibo children', *Brit. J. educ. Psychol.*, vol. 40, pp. 21–6.

OKONJI, M. O. (1971), 'A cross-cultural study of the effects of familiarity on classificatory behaviour', *J. cross-cult. Psychol.*, vol. 2, pp. 39–49.

OKONJI, M. O. (1972), 'Child rearing and the development of cognitive style in Uganda', prepublication draft, Human Development Research Unit University of Zambia, Lusaka.

ORNSTEIN, R. E. (1969), *On the Experience of Time*, Penguin.

OSGOOD, C. E. (1955), 'Fidelity and reliability', in H. Quastler (ed.), *Information Theory in Psychology*, Free Press.

OVER, R. (1968), 'Explanations of geometrical illusions', *Psychol. Bull.*, vol. 70, pp. 545–62.

PARSONS, C. (1960), 'Review of Inhelder and Piaget's *The Growth of Logical Thinking:* a logician's viewpoint', *Brit. J. Psychol.*, vol. 51, pp. 75–84.

PELUFFO, N. (1967), 'Culture and cognitive problems', *Int. J. Psychol.*, vol. 2, pp. 187–98. Reprinted in D. R. Price-Williams (ed.), *Cross-Cultural Studies*, Penguin, 1969.

PIAGET, J. (1928), *Judgement and Reasoning in the Child*, trans. M. Warden, Routledge & Kegan Paul, reprinted 1951.

PIAGET, J. (1950), *The Psychology of Intelligence*, Harcourt, Brace & World.

PIAGET, J. (1953), *The Origin of Intelligence in the Child*, trans. M. Cook, Routledge & Kegan Paul.

PIAGET, J. (1954), *The Construction of Reality in the Child*, trans. M. Cook, Basic Books.

PIAGET, J. (1962), *Play, Dreams and Imitation*, trans. C. Gattegno and F. M. Hodgson, Norton.

PIAGET, J. (1966), 'Nécessité et signification des recherches comparatives en psychologie génétique', *Int. J. Psychol.*, vol. 1, pp. 3–13.

PIAGET, J. (1969), *The Mechanisms of Perception*, trans. G. N. Seagrim, Routledge & Kegan Paul.

PIAGET, J., and INHELDER, B. (1956), *The Child's Conception of Space*, trans. F. J. Langdon and J. L. Lunzer, Norton.

PIKE, K. (1954), *Language in Relation to a Unified Theory of the Structure of Human Behavior*, vol. 1, Summer Institute of Linguistics, Glendale.

PIKE, K. (1956), *Language in Relation to a Unified Theory of the Structure of Human Behavior*, vol. 2, Summer Institute of Linguistics, Glendale.

PIKE, K. (1960), *Language in Relation to a Unified Theory of the Structure of Human Behavior*, vol. 3, Summer Institute of Linguistics, Glendale.

POLLACK, R. H. (1963), 'Contour detectability threshold as a function of chronological age', *Percept. mot. Skills*, vol. 17, pp. 411–17.
POLLACK, R. H. (1970), 'Müller–Lyer illusion: effect of age, lightness contrast and hue', *Science*, vol. 170, pp. 93–4.
POLLACK, R. H., and SILVAR, S. D. (1967a), 'Racial differences in the pigmentation of the *fundus oculi*', *Psychonom. Sci.*, vol. 7, pp. 159–60.
POLLACK, R. H., and SILVAR, S. D. (1967b), 'Magnitude of the Müller–Lyer illusion in children as a function of the pigmentation of the *fundus oculi*', *Psychonom. Sci.*, vol. 8, pp. 83–4.
POOLE, H. E. (1968), 'The effect of urbanization upon scientific concept attainment among Hausa children of Northern Nigeria', *Brit. J. educ. Psychol.*, vol. 38, pp. 57–63.
POORTINGA, Y. H. (1971), 'Cross-cultural comparison of maximum performance tests; some methodological aspects and some experiments with simple auditory and visual stimuli', *Psychol. Afric.*, monogr. suppl. 6.
PORTEUS, S. D. (1931), *The Psychology of Primitive People*, Arnold.
PRICE-WILLIAMS, D. R. (1961), 'A study concerning concepts of conservation of quantities among primitive children', *Acta Psychol.*, vol. 18, pp. 297–305. Reprinted in D. R. Price-Williams (ed.), *Cross-Cultural Studies*, Penguin, 1969.
PRICE-WILLIAMS, D. R. (1962), 'Abstract and concrete modes of classification in a primitive society', *Brit. J. educ. Psychol.*, vol. 32, pp. 50–61. Reprinted in I. Al-Issa and W. Dennis (eds.), *Cross-Cultural Studies in Behavior*, Holt, Rinehart & Winston, 1970.
PRICE-WILLIAMS, D. R. (ed.) (1969), *Cross-Cultural Studies*, Penguin.
PRICE-WILLIAMS, D. R., GORDON, W., and RAMIREZ, W. (1969), 'Skill and conservation: a study of pottery-making children', *Devel. Psychol.*, vol. 1, p. 769.
PRINCE, J. R. (1968), 'The effect of Western education on science conceptualization in New Guinea', *Brit. J. educ. Psychol.*, vol. 68, pp. 64–74.
PRINCE, R., and MOMBOUR, W. (1967), 'A technique for improving linguistic equivalence in cross-cultural surveys', *Int. J. soc. Psychiat.*, vol. 13, pp. 229–37.
PURDY, J. D. (1968), 'Associative learning rates of second, fourth and sixth grade Indian and white children using a paired-associate learning task', *Dissert. Abstr.*, 68–17, 486.
RAPIER, J. L. (1967), 'Effects of verbal mediation upon the learning of Mexican-American children', *Calif. J. educ. Res.*, vol. 18, pp. 40–48.
RAY, V. F. (1953), 'Human color perception and behavioral response', *Trans. N.Y. Acad. Sci.* vol. 16, pp. 98–104. Reprinted in I. Al-Issa and W. Dennis (eds.), *Cross-Cultural Studies in Behavior*, Holt, Rinehart & Winston, 1970.
RÉRAT, G. (1963a), 'La crise des cadres Africains: quelques faits concernant l'Afrique Noire Francophone', *Travail humaine*, vol. 26, pp. 219–28.
RÉRAT, G. (1963b), 'Problèmes de promotion Africaine', *Travail humaine*, vol. 26, pp. 229–41.
RIESEN, A. H. (1947), 'The development of visual perception in man and chimpanzee', *Science*, vol. 106, pp. 107–8.
RIESEN, A. H. (1958), 'Plasticity of behavior: psychological aspects', in H. F. Harlow and C. N. Woolsey (eds.), *Biological and Biochemical Bases of Behavior*, University of Wisconsin Press.
RIVERS, W. H. R. (1901), 'Primitive colour vision', *Pop. Sci. Month.*, vol. 59, pp. 44–58.

RIVERS, W. H. R. (1905), 'Observations on the senses of the Todas', *Brit. J. Psychol.*, vol. 1, pp. 321–96.

RIVOIRE, J. L. (1962), 'Development of reference systems in children', *Percept. mot. Skills*, vol. 15, p. 554.

ROBBINS, M. C., KILBRIDE, P. L., and BUKENYA, J. M. (1968), 'Time estimation and acculturation among the Baganda', *Percept. mot. Skills*, vol. 26, p. 1010.

ROSENHAM, D. L. (1967), 'Cultural deprivation and learning; an examination of method and theory', in H. L. Miller (ed.), *Education for the Disadvantaged*, Free Press.

ROSENTHAL, R. (1966), *Experimenter Effects in Behavioral Research*, Appleton-Century-Crofts.

ROSS, B. M., and MILLSOM, C. (1970), 'Repeated memory of oral prose in Ghana and New York', *Int. J. Psychol.*, vol. 5, pp. 175–81.

RUDEL, R. G., and TEUBER, H. L. (1963), 'Discrimination of direction of line in children', *J. comp. physiol. Psychol.*, vol. 56, pp. 892–8.

SALUS, P. H. (ed.) (1969), *On Language, Plato to von Humboldt*, Holt, Rinehart & Winston.

SAPIR, E. (1907-8), 'Herder's Ursprung der Sprache', *Mod. Philol.*, vol. 5, pp. 109–42.

SARBIN, T. R., and HARDYCK, C. (1955), 'Contributions of role-taking theory: VII. Conformance in role perception as a personality variable', *J. consult. Psychol.*, vol. 19, pp. 109–11.

SCHLOSBERG, H. (1954), 'Three dimensions of emotion', *Psychol. Rev.*, vol. 61, pp. 81–8.

SCHWITZGEBEL, R. (1962), 'The performance of Dutch and Zulu adults on selected perceptual tests', *J. soc. Psychol.*, vol. 57, pp. 73–7.

SEARS, R. R., and WISE, G. W. (1950), 'Relation of cup feeding in infancy to thumb-sucking and the oral drive', *Amer. J. Orthopsychiat.*, vol. 20, pp. 123–38.

SEGALL, M. H., CAMPBELL, D. T., and HERSKOVITS, M J. (1963), 'Cultural differences in the perception of geometric illusions', *Science*, vol. 139, pp. 769–71. Reprinted in D. R. Price-Williams (ed.), *Cross-Cultural Studies*, Penguin, 1969.

SEGALL, M. H., CAMPBELL, D. T., and HERSKOVITS, M. J. (1966), *The Influence of Culture on Visual Perception*, Bobbs-Merrill.

SERPELL, R. (1968a), '*Discrimination of orientation by Zambian children*', *Human Development Research Unit, Report no. 7*, University of Zambia, Lusaka.

SERPELL, R. (1968b), '*Cultural influence on attentional preference for colour over form*', *Human Development Research Unit, Report no. 8*, University of Zambia, Lusaka.

SERPELL, R. (1969a), 'Cultural differences in attentional preference for colour over form', *Int. J. Psychol.*, vol. 4, pp. 1–8.

SERPELL, R. (1969b), '*Cross-cultural differences in the difficulty of copying orientation: a response organization hypothesis*', *Human Development Research Unit, Report no. 11*, University of Zambia, Lusaka.

SERPELL, R. (1971a), 'Preference for specific orientations of abstract shapes among Zambian children', *J. cross-cult. Psychol.*, vol. 2, pp. 225–40.

SERPELL, R. (1971b), 'Discrimination of orientation by Zambian children', *J. comp. physiol. Psychol.*, vol. 75, pp. 312–16.

SERPELL, R., and DEREGOWSKI, J. B. (1971), '*Frames of preference for copying orientation: a cross-cultural study*', *Human Development Research Unit, Report no. 20*, University of Zambia, Lusaka.

SHAPIRO, M. B. (1960), 'The rotation of drawings by illiterate Africans', *J. soc. Psychol.*, vol. 52, pp. 17–30.

SHEPP, B. E., and TURRISI, F. D. (1966), 'Learning and transfer of mediating responses in discriminative learning', in N. R. Ellis (ed.), *International Review of Research in Mental Retardation*, vol. 2, Academic Press.

SHERMAN, J. A. (1967), 'Problems of sex differences in space perception and aspects of intellectual functioning', *Psychol. Rev.*, vol. 74, pp. 290–99.

SIGEL, I. E., and HOOPER, F. H. (1968), *Logical Thinking in Children*, Holt, Rinehart & Winston.

SLOANE, H. N., GORLOW, L., and JACKSON, D. N. (1963), 'Cognitive styles in equivalence range', *Percept. mot. Skills*, vol. 16, pp. 387–404.

SMEDSLUND, J. (1963), 'Development of concrete transitivity of length in children', *Child Devel.*, vol. 34, pp. 389–405.

SMITH, I. M. (1964), *Spatial Ability*, University of London Press.

SOMERSET, H. C. A. (1968), *Predicting Success in School Certificate: A Uganda Case Study*, East African Publishing House.

STEFFLRE, V., VALES, C. V., and MORLEY, L. (1966), 'Language and cognition in Yucatán: a cross-cultural replication', *J. Person. soc. Psychol.*, vol. 4, pp. 112–15.

STEPHAN, F. J., and MCCARTHY, P. J. (1958), *Sampling Opinions*, Wiley.

SUCHMAN, R. G. (1966), 'Cultural differences in children's color and form preferences', *J. soc. Psychol.*, vol. 70, pp. 3–10.

SUCHMAN, R. G., and TRABASSO, T. (1966), 'Color and form preference in young children', *J. exp. child Psychol.*, vol. 3, pp. 177–87.

SUTHERLAND, N. S. (1957), 'Visual discrimination of orientation by octopus', *Brit. J. Psychol.*, vol. 48, pp. 55–71.

TAGIURI, R. (1969), 'Person perception', in G. Lindzey and E. Aronson (eds.), *The Handbook of Social Psychology*, vol. 3, Addison-Wesley.

TAJFEL, H. (1969), 'Social and cultural factors in perception', in G. Lindzey, and E. Aronson (eds.), *The Handbook of Social Psychology*, vol. 3, Addison-Wesley.

TAUBER, E. S., and KOFFLER, S. (1966), 'Optomotor response in human infants to apparent motion: evidence of innateness', *Science*, vol. 152, pp. 382–3.

TAYLOR, A. (1962), *Educational and Occupational Selection in West Africa*, Oxford University Press.

THURSTONE, L. L. (1938), 'Primary mental abilities', *Psychomet. Monogr.*, vol. 1.

TRIANDIS, H. C. (1964), 'Cultural influences upon cognitive processes', in L. Berkowitz (ed.), *Advances in Experimental Social Psychology*, Academic Press.

TRIANDIS, H. C., MALPASS, R. S., and DAVIDSON, A. R. (1972), 'Cross-cultural psychology', in *The Annual Review of Anthropology*, Stanford University Press.

TRIANDIS, H. C., VASSILOU, V., and NASSIAKOU, M. (1968), 'Three cross-cultural studies of subjective culture', *J. Person. soc. Psychol.*, monogr. suppl., part 2, pp. 1–42.

TUCKER, L. R. (1959), *A Method for Synthesis of Factor Analytic Studies*, PRS Report, Dept. of the Army, Adjutant General's Office, Personnel Research Section, Washington, D.C.

TYLER, S. A. (1970), *Cognitive Anthropology*, Holt, Rinehart & Winston.

UKA, N. (1962), *The Development of Time Concepts in African Children of Primary School Age*, Institute of Education, Ibadan.

VANDENBERG, S. G. (1959), 'The primary mental abilities of Chinese students: a comparative study of the stability of a factor structure', *Ann, N.Y. Acad. Sci.*, vol. 79, pp. 257–304.

VANDENBERG, S. G. (1966), *The Primary Mental Abilities of South American Students*, Louisville Twin Study, University of Louisville.

VANDENBERG, S. G. (1967), 'The primary mental abilities of South American students: a second comparative study of the generality of a cognitive factor structure', *Multivar. behav. Res.*, vol. 2, pp. 175–89.

VERNON, P. E. (1955), '*The assessment of children*', *Stud. Educ.*, vol. 7, pp. 189–215, University of London Institute of Education.

VERNON, P. E. (1961), *The Structure of Human Abilities*, Methuen.

VERNON, P. E. (1965a), 'Environmental handicaps and intellectual development', *Brit. J. educ. Psychol.*, vol. 35, pp. 9–20 and 117–26.

VERNON, P. E. (1965b), 'Ability factors and environmental influences', *Amer. Psychol.*, vol. 20, pp. 723–33.

VERNON, P. E. (1966), 'Educational and intellectual development among Canadian Indians and Eskimos', *Educ. Rev.*, vol. 18, pp. 79–91 and 186–95.

VERNON, P. E. (1967a), 'Administration of group intelligence tests to East African pupils', *Brit. J. educ. Psychol.*, vol. 37, pp. 282–91.

VERNON, P. E. (1967b), 'Abilities and educational attainments in an East African environment', *J. spec. Educ.*, vol. 1, pp. 335–45. Reprinted in D. R. Price-Williams (ed.), *Cross-Cultural Studies*, Penguin, 1969.

VERNON, P. E. (1969), *Intelligence and Cultural Environment*, Methuen.

VINACKE, W. E. (1949), 'The judgment of facial expressions by three national-racial groups in Hawaii: I. Caucasian faces'. *J. Person.*, vol. 17, pp. 407–29.

VINACKE, W. E., and FONG, R. W. (1955), 'The judgment of facial expressions by three national-racial groups in Hawaii: II. Oriental faces', *J. soc. Psychol.*, vol. 41, pp. 185–95.

VYGOTSKY, L. S. (1962), *Thought and Language*, trans. E. Hanfmann and G. Vakar, MIT Press.

WALLACE, A. (1961), 'The psychic unity of human groups', in B. Kaplan (ed.), *Studying Personality Cross-Culturally*, Harper & Row.

WARR, P. B., and HAYCOCK, V. (1970), 'Scales for a British personality differential', *Brit. J. soc. clin. Psychol.*, vol. 9, pp. 328–37.

WATSON, J. B. (1924), *Behaviorism*, University of Chicago Press, reissued 1961.

WERNER, O., and CAMPBELL, D. T. (1970), 'Translating, working through interpreters and the problems of decentering', in R. Naroll and R. Cohen (eds.), *Handbook of Method in Cultural Anthropology*, Natural History Press.

WHITING, B. B. (ed.) (1963), *Six Cultures: Studies of Child Rearing*, Wiley.

WHITING, J. W. M. (1954), 'The cross-cultural method', in G. Lindzey (ed.), *The Handbook of Social Psychology*, vol. 1, Addison-Wesley.

WHITING, J. W. M. (1968), 'Methods and problems in cross-cultural research', in G. Lindzey and E. Aronson (eds.), *The Handbook of Social Psychology*, vol. 2, Addison-Wesley.

WHITING, J. W. M., and CHILD, I. L. (1953), *Child Training and Personality*, Yale University Press.

WHITING, J. W. M., LANDAUER, T. K., and JONES, T. M. (1968), 'Infantile immunization and adult stature', *Child Devel.*, vol. 39, pp. 59–67.

WHORF, B. L. (1956), 'The relation of habitual thought and behavior to language', in J. B. Caroll (ed.), *Language, Thought and Reality: Selected Writings of Benjamin Lee Whorf*, MIT Press and Wiley.

WICKERT, F. R. (1967), *Readings in African Psychology from French Language Sources*, African Studies Center, Michigan State University.
WITKIN, H. A. (1961), 'Cognitive development and the growth of personality', *Acta Psychol.*, vol. 18, pp. 245–57.
WITKIN, H. A. (1963), 'Witkin *et al.* on Zigler on Witkin *et al.* (letter), *Contemp. Psychol.*, vol. 8, p. 363.
WITKIN, H. A. (1967), 'A cognitive-style approach to cross-cultural research', *Int. J. Psychol.*, vol. 2, pp. 233–50.
WITKIN, H. A., DYK, R. B., FATERSON, H. F., GOODENOUGH, D. R., and KARP, S. A. (1962), *Psychological Differentiation*, Wiley.
WITKIN, H. A., LEWIS, H. B., HERTZMAN, M., MACHOVER, K., MEISSMER, P. B., and WAPNER, S. (1954), *Personality through Perception*, Harper & Row.
WOBER, M. (1966), 'Sensotypes', *J. soc. Psychol.*, vol. 70, pp. 181–9.
WOBER, M. (1967), 'Adapting Witkin's field independence theory to accommodate new information from Africa', *Brit. J. Psychol.*, vol. 58, pp. 29–38. Reprinted in D. R. Price-Williams (ed.), *Cross-Cultural Studies*, Penguin, 1969.
WOBER, M. (1969), 'Distinguishing centri-cultural from cross-cultural tests and research', *Percept. mot. Skills*, vol. 28, p. 488.
WOBER, M. (1970), 'Confrontation of the H–V illusion and a test of 3-dimensional pictorial perception in Nigeria', *Percept. mot. Skills*, vol. 31, pp. 105–106.
WOBER, M. (1972), *A Phenomenon Demonstrated in Africa*, Social Psychology Section, Department of Sociology, Makerere University, Occasional Paper no. 2.
WOODROW, H. (1951), 'Time perception', in S. Stevens (ed.), *Handbook of Experimental Psychology*, Wiley.
WOODWORTH, R. S. (1910a), 'The puzzle of color vocabularies', *Psychol. Bull.*, vol. 7, pp. 325–34. Reprinted in I. Al-Issa and W. Dennis (eds.), *Cross-Cultural Studies in Behavior*, Holt, Rinehart & Winston, 1970.
WOODWORTH, R. S. (1910b), 'Racial differences in mental traits', *Science*, vol. 31, pp. 171–86.
WOODWORTH, R. S. (1938), *Experimental Psychology*, Holt, Rinehart & Winston.
ZERN, D. (1967), 'The influence of certain developmental factors on fostering the ability to differentiate the passage of time', *J. soc. Psychol.*, vol. 72, pp. 9–17.
ZERN, D. (1970), 'The influence of certain child-rearing factors upon the development of a structured and salient sense of time', *Genet. Psychol. Monogr.*, vol. 81, pp. 197–254.
ZIGLER, E. (1963), 'A measure in search of a theory. Review of Witkin *et al.* *Psychological Differentiation: Studies of Development*', *Contemp. Psychol.*, vol. 8, pp. 133–5.

Author Index

Subject Index